"The true stories and reminders of what works and doesn't work in *SMART Man Hunting* will help you make the right choices to make your dreams come true."　—John Gray, Ph.D., best-selling author of *Men Are from Mars, Women Are from Venus*

"Liz's modern dating strategies will encourage you to have Chemistry, Compatibility and Communication with a life partner."
—Dr. Pat Allen, best-selling author of *Getting to I Do*

"Liz's book will make you laugh and the lessons learned are invaluable."　—Jan King, best-selling author of *It's a Girl Thing*

"This dating guide will help you boost your ego and increase your dating by 500 percent, using multiple dating options."
—Robert Allen, best-selling author of *Multiple Streams of Income*

"*SMART Man Hunting*'s light-hearted approach and romance tips can help you turn a relationship into an exciting love affair."
—Gregory J. P. Godek, best-selling author of *1001 Ways to Be Romantic*

"Kelly's codes are eye-opening and very much on target, such as ASF for All Sports Fanatic, RR for Relentless Renter, or GWO for Guy with Offspring. Not only does she describe these various types of men, but she gives extremely useful strategies on how to deal with them."　—Sabina Dana Plasse, editor, *Smart Woman* magazine

"Liz is very insightful; take her advice and you may be hearing wedding bells soon."　—Elizabeth Espinosa, KTTV's *FOX 11 News*, Los Angeles

"The ABC Man Codes are fun and a helpful way to look at the person you are dating to see if they are for you."
—Mike Gargiulo, WTTG *FOX 5 News*, Washington, D.C.

"Liz is on the fast track to becoming the next Candace Bushnell, who wrote *Sex and the City*."
—Marty Bass, WJZ-TV *CBS 13 News*, Baltimore

SMART
Man Hunting

The Fast Track Dating Guide
for Finding Mr. Right

LIZ H. KELLY

CITADEL PRESS
Kensington Publishing Corp.
www.kensingtonbooks.com

CITADEL PRESS BOOKS are published by

Kensington Publishing Corp.
850 Third Avenue
New York, NY 10022

Copyright © 2003, 2006 Liz H. Kelly

An earler edition was published with the ISBN 0-595-24639-7.

All Kensington titles, imprints, and distributed lines are available at special quantity
discounts for bulk purchases for sales promotions, premiums, fund-raising, educational,
or institutional use. Special book excerpts or customized printings can also be created
to fit specific needs. For details, write or phone the office of the Kensington special
sales manager: Kensington Publishing Corp., 850 Third Avenue, New York, NY
10022, attn: Special Sales Department; phone 1-800-221-2647.

AUTHOR'S NOTE
While the examples given in this book are based on true stories, some of the details
have been changed to protect the not-so-innocent.

CITADEL PRESS and the Citadel logo are Reg. U.S. Pat. & TM Off.

First printing: January 2006

10   9   8   7   6   5   4   3   2   1

Printed in the United States of America

Library of Congress Control Number: 2005934009

ISBN 0-8065-2734-X

THIS BOOK IS DEDICATED TO my parents, Anne and Phil, who met on a blind date and have been happily married for more than forty years. Their partnership inspired me to write this book and is a true model of unconditional love that lasts for anyone seeking a life mate. I thank them for giving me the courage to take chances, the confidence to build relationships, and the ability to have a sense of humor about it all.

And in memory of William Hupfeldt, who encouraged me to write this book. Billy was fortunate to find true love with his wife, Kathy, and their two sons, William and Tanner. He was diagnosed with ALS at the young age of 41 and fought the disease with grace. Billy's big grin, positive spirit, and zest for life live on in the hearts of many hometown fans.

Contents

Preface

WHEN A DIVORCE brought me back into the dating scene, I was amazed to discover how much everything had changed. Like most women, I wasn't sure how to meet the right men. But I was sincere in my desire to give love another chance. I moved to a new, much larger city and embarked on a Man Hunt determined to find the right partner versus someone to fill a void. I discovered that the dating scene had changed considerably since I was in my 20s, before I was married. I met many more divorced singles, and Internet dating had become an acceptable way to meet men. It was a New Era filled with new wireless connectors and icebreaker technology. I needed to learn how to navigate it.

I realized that I had to completely change how I thought about the dating process. I needed to expand my thinking about how, when, and where to meet people. Luckily, the dating scene had changed a lot for the better while I was out of it. Because more people than ever are single, all kinds of new options for meeting people had opened up. The only thing keeping me from turning to these options was my own old-fashioned ideas about the "right" way to meet someone. Whatever those ideas were, they weren't working. My dating was limited and I knew it was time for a new strategy.

I began to realize that Man Hunting is a numbers game. You have to try to encounter as many men as possible before one will "hit." I knew I had to get out of my own zone—my area of comfort, or what I call my Home Box. This meant I had to open myself up to all the New Era dating options: Internet dating, speed dating, professional matchmakers, and singles events, and learn how to position myself to meet more men through serendipity.

I also had to prepare myself emotionally and mentally for my Man Hunt. First, I expanded my network of friends and turned to them for support and advice through my dating journey. Then, I gave myself a Confidence Face Lift, Style Makeover and worked on bouncing back from rejection. Most important, I adopted my no fear attitude to dating to achieve my goal of boosting my numbers, ego, and odds of finding Mr. Right. Finally, one of my most important realizations came to me when, after working for three dot.com bombs, I found myself unemployed. Suddenly, I saw that finding a man is a lot like a finding a job and requires the same skill set. I started applying the same interview skills that I taught hiring managers in corporations for years to dating, so I could identify and hire a great man.

My strategy worked! I was inundated with dates with all kinds of men. During my Man Hunt, I had four to seven dates a week and boosted my dating by 500 percent! With all of these Mr. Right options, it took the edge off and my new job was to make choices. Were they all good fits? No. In fact, I dated so many men in order to bring some levity to the whole process I started to categorize them.

My man code categories became a dating shorthand for my girlfriends. Guys also started getting very curious about which codes applied to them. I'd call my girlfriends and announce that I'd gone out with yet another WD (Wounded Divorcé), wondering why I wasn't meeting more BAs (Bachelor Available). Finally, as a party amusement, I formalized my categories in the form of twenty-six codes.

To provide new hope to singles, I've taken my dating strategy a step further by providing more coaching through seminars, advice columns, profile makeovers and one-on-one consultations. I work with clients to set dating goals, enhance their presentation online and offline, and role-play scenarios to help them go after their desires. My greatest reward has been seeing my coaching clients succeed. I want you to succeed and sound like this client:

Liz is *awesome*!! I took her advice and read her book, *SMART Man Hunting*. Not only did I become a smart man hunter, I became a fiancée and will be married in a year! Liz, you're a Godsend!—Thanks a million, Gretchen

This guide will help you size up what you've got on your hands and how to handle him. I have found that there are good guys, bad guys, and mostly maybe guys, which are defined in the ABC Man Codes for you. By providing you with strategies, questions, and true-story examples, you can make better choices by knowing when to say, "You're fired" versus "You're hired!"

I went a step further with this revised book version by creating a fun compatibility quiz to help couples quickly determine whether their extremes complement or clash. I found that it wasn't about looking at one or two characteristics, but reviewing the total package when choosing your man. Word about these codes keeps spreading, and as I've used them, you'll find many new success stories and strategies in this updated version. Check out the new Love Match (LM) code for the guy who is good in bed. The LM is my new Go/No-Go code. I don't know how I missed him in the past. Honestly, it's probably because I never had out-of-this-world sex until after the last printing of this book. You have to find the emotionally ready guy who is also good in bed. It's all about the package!

My divorce was primarily due to the fact that I did not ask the right questions during the courting phase. Somehow I decided to overlook the clues regarding the potential for future conflict. I focused on our connections based on mutual interests in art and bike riding instead of the differences in our value systems. After I was married for only six months, we found several disconnects as we dug deeper into what really mattered to each of us. While we parted as friends, we may have avoided the "D" word if we had taken a closer look pre-wedding bells. He was a nice guy, just not the right guy for me. Next!

Dating is often twisted by hormones, age pressures, and the

desire for companionship. Avoid getting hooked on out-of-this-world sex if the total package is screaming "run." A lot of heartache can be avoided during dating by asking the right questions during the Dating Assessment Dance. As I dated, I learned how to say Next faster by identifying the red flags and observing their actions when meeting Man Candidates. Based on my interview training experience in the corporate world, I developed a series of questions and clues for first dates, second dates, third dates, and beyond to determine a Candidate's long-term chances. I also learned how to apply my marketing communications and sales presentation skills to achieve greater success in attracting the right men. In the end, though, you have to trust your own feelings. Finding Mr. Right is about positioning yourself for success, listening to your GUT instincts, and gauging your LIFE Match compatibility meter.

To research my dating strategy, I also interviewed hundreds of singles and happily married couples. You'll find their true confessions, success stories, turn-ons, turn-offs, and warning signs to assist you in your Man Hunt journey. I surveyed bachelors and bachelorettes on hot topics such as should a woman make the first move, how can a woman predict whether a guy will be good in bed, and what is the significance of a first kiss.

Whether you are looking for a good catch or advising single girlfriends, I hope *SMART Man Hunting* shows you how to prepare yourself to get out there, make the most of the New Era dating options available, and size up the man landscape faster in order to make the best choice for you. Remember, there are a lot of attractive, single men out there and you can find a Perfect Match. You have to believe he is out there, and then let me lead you toward him. The *SMART Man Hunting* winning formula includes ways to stay balanced in your approach, maintain your confidence, know when to say "Next," use the comic codes to keep your sense of humor, and keep dating until you find your Perfect Match.

Happy Hunting!

SMART Man Hunting

—⊚—

What Is SMART Man Hunting?

ARE YOU TIRED of trying to figure out where the single, attractive, and available men hang out? Have you ever spent too much time focusing on Mr. Wrong? Are you ready to have some fun and be SMART about your Man Hunt?

New Era Dating

If you are a single woman seeking Mr. Right, you may have already realized that it's a whole New Era in dating. Thanks to the divorce rate, more people than ever, of all ages, are dating. While it may seem difficult these days to know where to find your mate, we're actually living in the best possible time for dating. According to the 2000 U.S. census, 45 percent (100.7 million) of all Americans are single (non-married). Because of the sheer number of people looking, the 21st century has produced countless possibilities and new ways to meet a mate. And because of these new options a woman no longer needs to play the "gatherer" role, but can now proactively hunt for her man.

SMART Man Hunting is a dating guide that shows you how to position yourself for success by using New Era dating options, knowing your key selling points, and playing the LIFE Match Game. You can identify your Mr. Right faster, while saving yourself from spending weeks, months, and years with Mr. Wrong. Why is the divorce rate at 50 percent? It may be that women aren't making very smart choices about the men we pick (or allow to pick us!) or the way we go about it. For example, often women only look for boyfriends in very small ponds. By expanding our Home Box— our comfort zone—we automatically increase the number of available Man Candidates in our lives. Man hunting is about finding Mr. Goodenough. *SMART Man Hunting* is about finding Mr. Wonderful. I don't want you to settle for Mr. Goodenough. Your man definitely needs to be good in bed, along with being emotionally connected to you. The more candidates you have to choose among, the more likely it is that you'll find the right one for you, rather than accept an offer from the one who's there. Nearly all women have been burned at some point. We all promise ourselves that we will be smarter the next time. But are we? How can we be without something to guide us? *SMART Man Hunting* provides you with a step-by-step approach to dating that shows you when to say next versus when to take a closer look at the many candidates that the New Era Dating Options will provide you. Take the fear that you'll make another mistake out of dating and rest easy in knowing that *SMART Man Hunting* will show you the way.

SMART Man Hunting is based on interviews with hundreds of active daters (men and women), happily married couples, and my own experience gained from having hundreds of dates. It will help you find a man who thinks you are fantastic together with a long-lasting and meaningful relationship—everything most women desire.

What does SMART Man Hunting mean?

- SMART means boosting your dating numbers, ego, and odds of finding Mr. Right.
- SMART does not mean desperate.
- SMART does not mean aggressive.
- SMART means, as a friend said to me, "Stepping out that door, taking chances, and testing new waters to find what you want."

- SMART means not putting all your eggs in one basket.
- SMART means demanding that guys treat you with respect.
- SMART means taking care of yourself and being surrounded by positive people who make you feel good.
- SMART means identifying red flags early and listening for clues so you can find Mr. Right faster.
- SMART means positioning yourself for dating success by getting out of your Home Box.
- SMART means loving your life first so you naturally attract the dates that you desire.
- SMART means knowing your passions and key selling points so you make great first impressions.
- SMART means having a sense of style and sending out the right body language signals.
- SMART means finding a man with the right combination of characteristics that complement versus clash with yours.
- SMART means finding your Mr. Wonderful versus Mr. Goodenough.

The SMART Man Hunting Strategy

As a wise 40-something girlfriend said to me, "This is the age of working smarter, not harder. We all want to do everything efficiently. Man Hunting may not be politically correct, but we all know what it is."

So how are you going to get SMART about the hunt? Follow the guidance of this book. You'll find it is divided into four sections:

Part I: Get Ready for SMART Man Hunting

This section helps you prepare for your man hunt. The first thing to do is transform your thinking and open yourself to New Era Dating Options. You no longer need to rely on your Home Box of friends, family, and co-workers to bring you a man. Begin taking full advantage of New Era dating opportunities and acceptance shifts evolving in the new century. Chapter 1 shows you some new ways to think about yourself and the New Era, while Chapter 2 prepares you to get "out there" by helping you to give yourself a "Confidence Face Lift," "Style Makeover," and to develop a "No-Fear Attitude." You're encouraged to approach your Man Hunt like a Job Hunt by using the same skill set. It also provides you with a Winning Hunter's Toolkit and Office Romance Do's and Don'ts for your Man Hunt.

Part II: Explore the New Era of Man Hunting

Are you ready to boost your dating numbers? Many people are afraid to try Internet dating, speed dating, professional match-makers, or singles events because, as one wise man said, "It's like taking a fish out of water. People don't know what to do." This part of the book will tell you everything you need to know to survive out of the water, along with dating coaching examples, profile makeovers, new virtual love connectors, fun internet dating features, and success stories. In-depth discussions show you exactly how to handle all the New Era dating options and how to make the most of them. What you should be looking for and dating safety tips are included. You can find love using these 21st century dating strategies.

Part III: The Dating Assessment Dance

Once you start actively dating, Part III shows you how to assess, analyze, and review the total man. You'll find first date success strategies and "good in bed" indicators from bachelorettes. Don't make the same mistake for the second or third time by not using all available means to closely evaluate potential partnership candidates. One 50-year-old man commented to me, "I am finding through my divorce that I married someone whom I barely even knew." By using the right body language, the KISS Test, the Love Match Pre-Test, Emotional Readiness Pre-Test, and LIFE Match Compatibility Questions, you'll attract the dates you desire and make wiser Mr. Right choices. You'll also find out why trusting your GUT instincts is the most important factor when identifying the right man.

Part IV: SMART ABC Man Codes

This A-Z guide to New Era men saves you time and effort since it allows you to quickly size up and handle any candidate. From the ASF (All Sports Fanatic) to the ZZ (Zodiac Zealot), you can use these twenty-six comic codes to help you keep a sense of humor and quickly weed out the undesirables on your dating journey. The codes are based on true stories from women who have found great men, along with tales of being dumped, manipulated, and taken for granted. You'll also find the SMART ABC Man Codes Hollywood Quick-Reference Guide with celebrity examples from romantic comedies. Use this codebook as a compatibility guide to quickly identify the characteristics and extremes of your Mr. Right. He must be a BA (Bachelor Available) and LM (Love Match) as a starting point or I recommend throwing him out of the game. We have all made mistakes. The goal is to know how to identify any type of man, know when to say, "Next," and keep dating until you find someone who complements your ABC codes as a Perfect Match. To compare your man's extremes with your characteristics, there is an ABC Codes Compatibility Quiz in Appendix I of this book. Have fun with the codes and the quiz!

In short, *SMART Man Hunting* is a New Era dating guide that helps you get SMARTer by showing you how to:

Search proactively for Mr. Right with confidence and sex appeal using New Era dating options.

Meet more high-quality men, boost your ego and position yourself for dating success.

Assess potential candidates to identify your Mr. Wonderful.

Review the Total Man using the SMART ABC Codes as a Compatibility Guide.

Trust your GUT instincts and LIFE Match results to know when to say, "You're Hired!"

SMART Man Hunting can also provide you with tips for life skills. You can gain new man- and job-hunting strategies. Using the notes gathered during my research, you can learn better ways to approach life from the people whom I met on the journey. You will not only benefit from new SMART Man Hunting skills, you can live a "winner's life." And as a wise girlfriend told me, "Everyone wants to be with a winner."

Along with helping women on the hunt, men have found this guide to be a useful reminder for how to be SMART about hunting women. One male fan commented, "It's a book that puts all the best dating advice you ever heard but, sadly, forgot under one cover. I found the dating stories and particularly the codes to be a kind of useful shorthand for sizing up personality types—including my own."

Let me be your Dating Coach and strategist to help you navigate the 21st-century-dating playing field. You can't afford to be Bridget Jones, who wasted weeks, months and years chasing the wrong guy. If this scenario sounds familiar, or you know a good friend who could use an outsider's advice, consider a Dating Coach. We have coaches for everything else in life, so why not get a little help in the love department? One woman actually called me for advice and shared, "My friends gave me a Dating Coach as a birthday present." We were able to quickly identify her goals and old patterns that needed to be broken.

With the help of a Dating Coach, you can make great first impressions, avoid first date disasters, and find your true love faster. Why take the long road that Bridget Jones chose when you can gain more control over your dating destiny?

Follow the *SMART Man Hunting* plan and you'll quickly boost your dating numbers, ego, and odds of finding Mr. Right. Based on my dating coach successes and hundreds of interviews with singles and happily married couples, this plan can put you on the fast track toward finding and identifying your man.

PART I

Get Ready for SMART Man Hunting

1

~⊙~

Transform Your Thinking

ARE YOU READY to proactively search for Mr. Right? Are you open to trying new man-hunting strategies by thinking outside your Home Box? Are you prepared to make changes that can fill your life with more happiness?

Throw Out Your Old Approach to Dating

In order to find Mr. Right, you will need to give some serious thought to how you've always approached dating in the past and start thinking about new dating options outside your comfort zone or Home Box. Why? Because staying in your Home Box is why you are currently single. Finding the right mate is a numbers game. Once you define what you want, the more men you meet, the likelier it is that one will "hit."

Have you always thought that fate will bring you your mate? Do you go about your life thinking that "the one" will just cross your path? This strategy could be the reason why all your dates or relationships turn out to be with Mr. Wrong. This dating strategy is called "dating by serendipity" and is equivalent to having no strategy at all.

One 34-year-old marketing consultant who met his mate at a car wash asked me, "What's wrong with meeting someone through osmosis?" Nothing's wrong with it. It can happen—it just doesn't happen very often. Your mate may be at the car wash, but Mr. Wrong and a few lunatics might be there too. Men are likelier to meet women through serendipity because it's a riskier strategy for women. We're less likely to be open to meeting people in this manner since it's in our interest to keep our guard up. For all you readers out there who have met dates "on the street," congratulations. For everyone else still seeking a high-quality mate, there are alternative winning search strategies and tips for increasing your chances of serendipity for you here—so keep reading.

Get Out of Your Home Box

Your Home Box refers to all your regular activities and relationships, including your work, your friends, your family, and all your day-to-day activities. It's where you live your life and feel most comfortable. It's also where you're not meeting any new men. Why? That's just the way it is. It could be that you've already dated the available men in your Home Box. Or you may have exhausted the supply of people your friends and family know to set you up with—that is, if you've even let yourself be open to this. More on that later. We all love to stay within the comfort and security of the Home Box. But if you're going to be a SMART Man Hunter, you have to move out from your home territory into new hunting grounds.

What's Stopping You?

You know as well as anyone that this is a New Era in dating. Everyone is dating. People of all ages are getting together to go out. Dating shows draw huge audiences on television. The media has broadcast all the new dating options available, such as Internet dating and singles clubs. So why are you at home?

Overcome Your Old-Fashioned Ideas About Dating

Here are some of the things that may be stopping you, together with a few counterarguments.

You think if you "put yourself out there" you'll seem desperate.

Nothing is further from the truth. It's *not* actively dating that gives you that oh-so-slightly-desperate aura.

You've been out of the dating scene for a while and you don't know how to handle what might come up.

Keep reading. This book is for you. It shows you exactly what to do on different types of dates.

Your judgment hasn't been so great in the past and you're a little afraid of your ability to make a sound choice in a man.

Relax and let the experiences of hundreds of active daters and happily married couples guide you. Arm yourself with Part IV's SMART ABC Man Codes and the Dating Assessment Dance steps in Section III and you'll rebuild your confidence in your ability to choose. And anyway, your past choices may have been influenced by the fact that you didn't have a choice. Get it? You took whatever came along. It's a New Era. This time around, you get to choose.

You're still recovering from your last relationship.

Fair enough. You don't want to make the mistake of going out there before you're ready. Your heart won't be in it and you'll come off as needy or depressed or both. But if you're reading this book it means you're heading in the right direction. You can either put the book down and take a complete timeout, or keep reading to help rebuild your confidence and get ready to get out there again.

Your life or work is too demanding to allow the time and energy that a SMART Man Hunt requires.

It's time to take a good hard look at your priorities. What's important to you? Career or love? You can have both but love requires effort too. Read on. You're an ideal candidate for the section "Approach Your Man Hunt Like a Job Hunt." If career is truly your top priority right now—you go, girl. But maybe this inclination is an excuse for something else. One of my 40-something acquaintances keeps intermingling time management statements with dating. One night she said, "I told my friends that I'll have time to date next month if they want to set me up." She makes it sound too mechanical for my taste. Who doesn't have time to find love? You may be in denial about whether you're ready for a relationship or not. Consider consulting a counselor or at least spend some time thinking about yourself—provided you're willing to make the time to do that.

You don't think women should be proactive about dating. You consider yourself a "Rules" girl.

But how can you be a "Rules" girl when there's no man to allow you to practice? You can still be a "Rules" girl and let the man take the lead if that's what you want. That still begs the question of how you're going to meet and assess men. Women who like the more passive role in relationships still need to open up the door for men to enter.

You're comfortable in your Home Box.

That means you're comfortable being single too. You know the saying "no pain, no gain?" Well, it applies here. Sometimes you need to make yourself a little uncomfortable to move forward in life. I met a very attractive woman in Beverly Hills who told me, "I haven't had a date in two years." When I asked her what she did to meet new people, she replied, "I just hang out with my friends." If she had made any effort to venture outside her home box, I am certain she would have had a ton of dates and options. Get out of your home box fast.

What Have You Got to Lose?

Besides what's stopping you, you might want to ask yourself what you think you have to lose by SMART Man Hunting. In other words, why are you afraid? Assessing your fears and addressing them is very important if you're going to truly be proactive about dating. You have to adopt a No Fear attitude if you're going to put yourself out there to keep your confidence sex appeal.

Putting yourself out there is a necessary part of dating. Most men learned to put themselves out there at an early age since they have been traditionally trained to take the lead in dating. Aside from other reasons such as the differences in male and female psychology, this active dating strategy could be the reason why your exes always seem to "bounce back" and find someone again so quickly after your breakup. They just seem to know what to do to meet women. Well, it's time women learned what to do to meet men as well.

Adopt a No-Fear Attitude

Do not be afraid to get out in the New Era dating playing field. Adopt a No-Fear Attitude and be prepared to deal with rejection. Yes, rejection is part of the game. But rejection is a fact of life. Give yourself a pep talk about it. How many times have you been rejected and survived only to discover that the rejection was the best possible thing for you?

Remind yourself that you have no control over what makes someone attractive to someone else. Usually it's a combination of chemistry and psychology. Just because you don't have that chemical/psychological hook that makes someone want you doesn't mean there's something wrong with you. In any case, different people are looking for different things in relationships.

This time around be SMART and keep the focus on what you want and are looking for in a partner. And stop worrying about what someone else wants. A 30-something male actor told me, "Women shouldn't worry about rejection. They should worry about finding out if the other person is interesting, or what they're about." I've met men who never called me back after our first meeting despite the fact that I felt a connection. I learned very quickly not to take the rejection too seriously and to just keep saying, "Next!" If the guy was not wild about me, then why torture myself trying to make it work? I was tired of torture.

With *SMART Man Hunting*, you'll learn to let rejection roll off your back and to not take things too personally. This No-Fear Attitude is actually an important skill in love and work. Overly sensitive people who fear rejection are a pain to have to tiptoe around. If you can eliminate this unflattering quality from your repertoire, your bosses and boyfriends will be grateful for it. An upside to SMART Man Hunting is that it gives you an opportunity to practice. In SMART Man Hunting, you'll be able to deal with rejection because the rewards will be much greater than the losses.

You will gain more confidence with every encounter. One woman told me, "You got me to practice dating by using *SMART Man Hunting*'s advice and it made me feel so much more confident." The more you just do it, the better results you will see. Don't let hesitation or fear show on your face. Approach every situation with confidence. Be bold, be brave, and use these smart moves.

Play the REAL Numbers Game

By getting out there and taking chances, you will boost your numbers, ego, and odds of finding your Mr. Wonderful. However, you want to play the REAL Bachelor or Bachelorette Dating Game versus trying out for a reality TV show. Consider this advice from Keith Kormanik, a hot Baltimore bachelor who was recently on ABC's *The Bachelorette*. He was part of a pool of 25 bachelors, and shared his experience with me. Keith explained, "It was fun and a great experience, but it's definitely a process falling in love with someone." Remember that the whole idea behind SMART Man Hunting is to broaden your choices in men by working a numbers game. Men have done it for years, so why shouldn't women use this approach? The more men you date, the better your options and ability to make a sound choice for yourself will be. But this numbers game has another upside. Not only will you be meeting more men, you may be making friends and business contacts along the way. Not everyone will be a "keeper," but some of the people you meet may work for you on other levels. As a result, your Home Box keeps getting bigger and bigger. At this point, serendipity may even work for you.

For my book research, I interviewed hundreds of winners who found their soul mate by playing the REAL dating numbers game. By using multiple dating options (Internet dating, match-making, speed dating, singles events, blind dates, and being in tune with your body language clues during your daily travels), singles can increase their numbers by 500 percent. (I had four to seven dates a week using this approach before finding my man. You can do it too.)

A 40-year-old casting director in Los Angeles had 200 replies to her profile through a matchmaker. Out of these 200 bachelors, she ended up going out with five and then married one of the five (read more about her success story in Part III). These odds are even better than those on *The Bachelorette*. She commented, "One out of a hundred is about the same odds of finding someone when I'm casting a show."

When Does Serendipity Work?

Serendipity works when you are dating actively and are not desperate. In the movie *Serendipity*, both John Cusack ("Jonathan") and Kate Beckinsale ("Sara") were dating other people when they accidentally met while holiday shopping in New York City. This osmosis plan may work when your Home Box has grown to include new people and activities. However, relying solely on serendipity gives you that needy attitude that makes men avoid you. Stepping outside of your home dating box of friends, family, and work makes you more open-minded and boosts your ego. When you are being proactive about dating, you might just find your man when you least expect it. While I was out there actively dating, I ended up meeting an attractive guy in a local drug store. I was rushing to catch a plane back to the east coast for Thanks-giving. The last thing on my mind was meeting a man. He was reading a book while waiting for his prescription and made small talk with me. After the holidays, we ended up dating for a few months and it was magical. Osmosis, yes, but it shouldn't be your one and only strategy.

Transform Your Thinking Wrap-up

Hopefully, by now you're convinced and ready to begin SMART Man Hunting. You're willing to leave your Home Box and adopt a No Fear attitude. You're prepared to learn how to bounce back from rejection and to not take things personally. Using this out-of-your-comfort-zone approach to dating, I have found more high-quality men and made great business contacts along the way. By mining for gold and bouncing back from rejection, I have felt much happier and enriched as a person.

An important part of SMART Man Hunting is to adopt a positive attitude and be confident. Chapter 2 shows you how. When you're confident, you'll be amazed at the good things that come your way. By using this SMART Man Hunting technique, you will be beaming with confidence and become a magnet for men simply by the way you approach life. On your Man Hunt journey, you might discover that Mr. Right is someone you already know. He may just enter into your life through serendipity. Alternatively, this guide is about getting out there, taking chances, boosting your ego by actively dating, and being SMART about your selection process. In the end, you might find natural synergies bring you and your life partner together. But by then, you'll have a wealth of dating experience and man analysis to draw upon. You can do it! Remember, No Fear!

2

~~⊘~~

Boost Your Confidence Inside and Out

SO YOU'VE DECIDED to take the plunge and start to Man Hunt the SMART way. Hopefully, Chapter 1 convinced you to get out there and be proactive about dating by taking advantage of all the New Era dating options available. Chapter 2 is about making sure that your dating journey starts off on the right foot in order for success to be assured. If you are not finding high-quality mates, recognize that it may be time to make some changes inside and out. Take a timeout, give yourself a Confidence Face Lift and a Style Makeover, and then go find your man!

Before you go out there cold, let's do some preparation. Like the beginning of any endeavor, it's always a good idea to do some self-assessment and review. The number one thing that guys tell me they want in a woman is someone who "loves their life." This preparation step will help you enrich your life and more naturally attract the dates that you desire. And because men are so visual, it's also worth taking a look at your sense of style.

The first step is to take a look inside yourself and be open to making adjustments. Be honest, and ask yourself some tough questions:

Personal Assessment Questions

- Am I really happy with my life?
- Do I have a good support network of friends and associates?

- What are my personal interests and hobbies?
- Do I set aside enough non-work or play time for myself?
- Am I taking care of myself mentally and physically?
- What's my approach to life? Am I generally positive or do I project a negative attitude?
- Do I feel secure about the way I look? Do I need to update my style?
- How do people tend to respond to me? Are they genuinely happy to see me or hear from me?
- Do I make sure that I'm given respect by everyone in my life, including my dates?

Answering "no" to even one of the above questions could mean it's time to make a few changes in your life. If you're not sure about the answers to these personal assessment questions, start asking your close friends for some honest advice. While one of the biggest things you can do is decide to open yourself up to all the New Era Dating Options and to begin Man Hunting the SMART way, you may also need to make a few other changes in yourself.

Give Yourself a Confidence Face Lift

A 30-something girlfriend commented to me, "It's all in your approach. Project a positive attitude in your dating journey and you will find success." Have your dating experiences been more in the nature of disasters than dreams? Building or rebuilding your confidence can solve a lot of your current dating troubles. A wise 37-year-old girlfriend once told me, "Confidence is the greatest sex appeal." If you are truly happy with your life, the world will line up to meet you.

Confidence is everything in the dating game. Here's why. Confidence

- Is sexy!
- Lets men know you like yourself and won't put up with nonsense

- Means you know there are many men who are anxious to go out with you—which only makes you more attractive
- Is when you take rejection lightly and not personally
- Allows you to relax and enjoy the dating process
- Makes it clear that you are not desperate—the date killer
- Makes dating fun
- Means you're happy with yourself, your looks, and your life

So how do you paint a smile on your face? Why is it so important? Another friend gave me excellent advice. She said, "Guys have basic requirements. They want someone who is happy and confident." If your confidence has taken some pummeling lately, try my recruiter girlfriend's advice. She told me, "Fake it until you make it because nobody wants to be near someone who is not confident." You want everyone to say, "I want to have what she's got." People will naturally want to meet you if you are glowing with positive energy. And if your confidence has suffered a blow, think back on the good times in your life. Ask yourself, how did you get there? What were you doing that boosted your self-esteem? What changes can you make now to rebuild your confidence?

Try These Confidence Boosters

When I started gathering these confidence-building tips from friends—both male and female—I was inundated with good ideas. That just goes to show you how important it is to present self-assurance and a positive attitude. If you try some of these tips, you should have more confidence and be more comfortable with yourself. Here are some confidence boosters and reminders.

- Recognize that you are a hot ticket item with unique qualities who deserves only the best. If you need to be reminded of your positive attributes, ask your friends to help you. While you may not have everything on someone else's checklist, you do have great key selling points that make you special.

- Consider updating your looks to boost your self-esteem and attract your desired dates. Get a new haircut or makeover, buy some new clothes, join a gym and get back into shape, or get serious about losing a few pounds. Do whatever it take to maintain your body's best image. One 40-year-old girlfriend told me, "Love your body just the way it is today." You don't need to have plastic surgery to find a man, but you need to maintain an appealing presentation.

- If you are not sure what needs to be done, ask your close friends. What might be a painful conversation at first can bring you ultimate success in the dating arena. By making a commitment to be at the top of your game physically, you'll feel more confident and men will come your way. For example, my closest confidant and neighbor told me, "Your hair is too bleached blonde. We have to tone it down." She sent me to her hair stylist one hour away and, wow, it was worth the drive! In addition to fixing my color, the stylist also recommended new makeup and lipstick.

- Eliminate the friends or associates who don't give you the appreciation you deserve. Who needs people around who are tearing you down when you are trying to build yourself up?

- Try something new. Go out on a limb and try something you've always wanted to do. Sign up for a Tai Kwon Do class, go horseback riding, or take a ski lesson. Don't do these things to meet a man—yet. Do it for you to show yourself you can learn some new tricks.

- Pamper yourself. Have a facial, get a massage or manicure, take in an art exhibit. The idea here is to do something nice for yourself, something that makes you feel good.

- Treat yourself better. Make sure you take your vitamins, drink enough water, and eat right. Get out in the fresh air once in a while. These things are basic but you'd never believe how many people ignore this stuff.

- Finally, the best confidence booster is to have a dating plan and to stick with it. The more you date, the better you'll feel. Handling all the different situations that arise in your dating journey will also reinforce all your new positive feelings about yourself. Remember, No Fear.

Consider a few examples of women with powerful confidence and sex appeal in romantic comedies. You won't find these images in *Playboy*, but wow, those actresses have what guys want. In all of these movies, the female roles naturally drew an audience with their No Fear attitude and command performance. You want to come across to guys with the same sense of presence. Close your eyes and place yourself in their shoes if it helps. Think movie star. Think hot ticket. You are a hot commodity and need to give off confidence versus a boastful vibe to attract the dates that you desire.

Beaming Confidence In	Movie
Diane Keaton	*Something's Gotta Give*
Halle Berry	*Swordfish*
Frances McDormand	*Laurel Canyon*
Eva Mendes	*Hitch*
Sandra Bullock	*Speed*
Julia Roberts	*Pretty Woman*
Salma Hayek	*Frida*

Confidence is the greatest sex appeal out there without a doubt, but before you go too far, we need to be prepared to pass a guy's pre-screening visual test. Are you ready for a style makeover?

Boost Your Sex Appeal with a Style Makeover

Because men are much more focused on visuals, you really need to take an honest look at the way you present yourself before you get out there. Are you ready to boost your sex appeal on the outside? This section offers tips on how to update your style and know what guys are watching so you get past the bachelor's prescreening tests. When I first moved to Los Angeles, a casting director told me, "We have to lose your button-down sweaters. They make you look like a grandmother." Boost your ego by taking the time for a Style Makeover and listen to your friends' advice. I have thrown out all of my grandmother sweaters. What do you need to give to the Salvation Army?

Color Charts

Have you ever seen someone wearing the latest style and the color and shape are all wrong for that person? You cannot just go buy what is hot—you need a sense of style. I met with a style consultant who gave me a tablet with my colors. She said, "I'm placing on X on the colors that you are never to wear. I don't care if they are all the rage in the stores—do not wear them." She told me to avoid pastels and buy clothes with more vivid blues, greens, reds, and purples. She added, "You are naturally drawn to your colors." You probably already know which colors make you look best, but it can get confusing when colors become popular so why not get your chart done by a pro?

Fashion Checks

My mother actually sent me to this style consultant as a birthday present after my divorce, and what a great gift! I got too relaxed when I was married and needed to update my style. After we went through my colors, the style consultant showed me photos in a magazine to point out which styles complemented my face and body type. This style consultant advised me to wear V-neck tops versus a scooped neckline because I have a narrow face. She also told me to wear clothes with a shine to accent the highlights in my hair. I was told to avoid patterns and wear solid colors. Her final piece of advice was very important. "You don't have to change your entire look overnight." She added, "I've had very upset husbands call me because their wife threw out everything in the closets and then went wild with the credit cards buying new clothes." I don't want you to go broke, but rather start the process of updating your style. You'll need to find out what colors and styles work best for you. Give anything that receives an X from your consultant or friends to the Goodwill.

Facial Essentials

Another Style Makeover step is to take care of your face and evaluate your makeup. Before you even apply makeup to your most important feature, you need to make sure you are taking care of your skin. Daily cleansing and monthly facials will enhance your skine tone and reduce wrinkles.

What's involved in a facial? My hair stylist sent me to a pro at a Long Beach spa for a full facial. The experience was very powerful and now I am hooked on this beauty step. While my expert shared, "Every facial is different depending on the person," here are the five basic steps that he followed:

1. *Cleanse*—My cleanse involved a steaming first, then professional skin care. My expert explained, "The cleanse is skin care's most important regimen. In cities, we have smog sitting on our face. You also touch your face all day long and need to remove the dirt." He advised me to cleanse every morning and evening as part of my daily routine.

2. *Exfoliate*—This step will dissolve dead skin cells. A pineapple and papaya exfoliate was applied to my skin. You need to ask your expert what works best for you. Our expert explained, "Pineapple growers no longer have fingerprints because it naturally removes them." He added, "You should exfoliate bi-weekly or as needed."

3. *Massage*—In order to improve your blood circulation and relieve facial tension, a massage is a standard step in this beauty treatment. In my case, it was an "acupuncture" pressurized massage for my face and feet that was very uplifting. Our expert explained, "The massage defines lines and wrinkles." I was ready for this release in pressure and could see the change in my face afterwards.

4. *Mask*—In the next step, a mask is applied to your face. This mask, our expert explains, "is a cocktail for the skin." It's

like taking a multi-vitamin. To remove the mask, he wrapped a warm towel around my face, which added to my relaxing escape.

5. *Moisturizer*—Finally, a moisturizer was applied to my skin. You definitely want a moisturizer with sun protection, which is now offered by most major brands. I never go out of the house now without a base moisturizer to protect my skin from the sun. It's just not worth exposing myself to dangerous rays.

After this very empowering facial, the beauty expert sold me a daily cleanser for $30.00 that will last a few months. He shared, "You don't have to spend a fortune on these products. However, the movie star skin you see is not using a cleanser from a drug store. You may want to pay a premium to get nicer results." It's your choice, but no matter which route you take, using a daily cleanser and monthly facials will give you beautiful skin. Your skin will be more vibrant when you wake up in the morning next to your man.

Makeup Art

If you want to learn about beauty tips, Los Angeles and New York are probably the two best places to observe style, other than Europe. While recently watching the Oscars, a beauty consultant shared makeup basics on the red carpet for the biggest night in town. He emphasized, "It's simple to be glamorous," and proceeded with his must-have checklist for special occasions:

Makeup Must-Haves from Hollywood

1. Accent beautiful skin with a nice base color.
2. Rub blush on the cheeks for a feminine and romantic look.
3. Wear gloss on the lips.
4. Add shimmering eyeshadow.
5. Apply black mascara to accent your eyes

I remember my mother taking me for a beauty makeover in New York City at 16 years old. I was thinking it was way over the top and can only now appreciate her efforts to teach me a sense of style at a very early age. I did not really wear makeup on a daily basis until I moved to Los Angeles, where Hollywood's billboard images dominate the scene. I was way too comfortable in my skin when I was married and needed to fast forward my makeup skills in this fast-track town. Through a few good girlfriends and makeup consultants, I found out what a base, concealer, and black mascara could do to lighten up my face. I rarely go out now without these basics.

To gather more makeup insights, my girlfriend and I went to see two beauty consultants in a Beverly Hills department store. You need to constantly be updating your style, and I wanted to gather the latest tips for you. Our first advisor was a very attractive 62-year-old woman who had been happily married for 31 years and did not look a day over 45 to me. She told me, "Less is more. A guy doesn't want to wake up in the morning and get a big surprise when you take your makeup off." When I asked her to elaborate, she explained, "Cleanliness is really important. You want to have the right base color for your skin tone, nice clean hair, and not-too-heavy perfumes." This Beverly Hills beauty consultant was working with a 30-something male partner, who told me, "There are five basic facial features that you need to pay attention to." Together, these beauty experts went through these beauty tips with us:

BEAUTY TIPS FROM BEVERLY HILLS

Feature	Makeup Strategies
Inviting Eyes	"Use eye shadow and liner sparingly and only when needed. Use a concealer that matches your skin tone to reduce bags under your eyes."

Lengthy Eyelashes	"Use sculpting mascara to sculpt upward and separate lashes. This mascara will not clump. Volumizing mascara makes your eye lashes thicker and builds fine lashes."
Glossy Lips	"Use lip gloss versus heavy lipstick so a guy will want to kiss you. At night and for parties, you can go heavier, but keep in mind, less is more."
Colorful Cheeks	"You can use a bronzer in summer so you get a fresh color. At night, use a blush with a little shimmer on the cheekbones."
Shapely Eyebrows	"You want to have clean and manicured eyebrows. Remove facial hair and wax your mustache so it looks clean."

Our male beauty consultant's final advice was, "Go get a men's magazine and read the cover. Read the articles to find out what guys are thinking." And if you think this makeup and style stuff doesn't matter, think again. Men are much more visual than women so you have to pay a lot more attention to your look. Guys are lucky because we often overlook male mistakes in the style department. When I interviewed bachelors, the number-one thing that they wanted in a woman was a chemistry connection.

Bachelor Survey Says . . . Your Style Matters

Along with a smile, check out what men are watching in these Bachelor Style Survey observations and fashion advice tips:

- "My advice, try to look good even at times when you don't necessarily have to. You don't have to kill yourself looking great all the time, but sometimes the simplest things can transform you into a more desirable-looking creature. Like wearing your hair out, or wearing eyeliner, or just more attractive shoes."

- "You can take the most plain girl in the world, clean her up, fix her hair up all nice, put her in a killer outfit, and you can't even recognize the plain-Jane girl who was wearing sweats at the grocery store an hour ago."
- "The first two minutes is a screener for most guys. I think it depends on the guy. I definitely notice their figure, which you don't always get to see."
- "As long as the outfit is coordinated, it's fine with me."
- "My turn-ons are good calves and high heels. I get turned off by labels showing at the back of the neck of a dress, blouse, or T-shirt and inappropriate clothes for the occasion."
- "If she is wearing open-toed shoes, she needs to have manicured toes."
- "When I was walking through Zurich, Switzerland, the women were very creative with their styles. They would create their own look by combining a bunch of different accessories. The whole outfit had a different look. You knew they weren't being bought by a store image."
- "Wearing baggy pants or sweats isn't always the most attractive look for a woman."
- "This one is personal for me. I think those extremely long pointed shoes look ridiculous. They look like Wicked Witch of the West shoes."
- "Anything original or unique is a turn-on. As long as it's clothing versus a costume and represents their personality."
- "Women who dress in cookie-cutter stuff that everyone's got is a turn-off. It almost seems like they're all trying to be Paris Hilton."
- "If a woman wears capri pants, she needs to be thin or they will make her look fat."
- "If your underwear is sticking out of the top of your pants, it's only cute if you want to get laid."

- "I'm not impressed by women who wear expensive clothes just because it's expensive."
- "When they look like they're trying to dress like someone on TV, it turns me off."
- "Low-rise jeans or sweats low is good if you don't have any fat hanging over the sides. It's so unappealing to see fat hanging out that I have to ask—does the girl own a mirror?"
- "Some of the furry boots make women look like they should be in Antarctica. If it's eighty degrees outside and they're wearing furry boots, there is something about it that I don't buy into."
- "I seriously wish American women would take a page out of a European womens' book because European women generally dress better, and sexier. Don't get me wrong, I'm all for feminism and everything that comes along with it, but American women have gotten so complacent and comfortable that they're starting to look like us men, which is a shame, because they are the more attractive sex. My advice: Lose the shapeless sweatpants and sneakers. I mean, torch them. Just like our bad college beer posters, this stuff has gotta go."

A Hot Parisian Bachelor's Style Insights

After hearing many American bachelors comment that European women have the best sense of style, I decided to go to the source to gather more insights for you. I met an attractive lawyer from Paris, France, in Los Angeles during his summer study program at UCLA, who was the perfect candidate to ask for helpful style observations. You know when you meet a man that has that special combination of charisma, sex appeal, and style—that was this guy. He was confident versus boastful, and naturally drew women to him.

I emailed this hot 30-something Parisian bachelor to gather his visual turn-ons and turn-offs from a European's perspective. His detailed response pleasantly surprised me, and I recommend that every woman read his style observations. If you have any doubts about whether guys really care about looks, these insights will make you think again before you walk out the door.

Turn-Ons

"Of course dress is important. As we have many changes of weather in France for instance, the look of women in fall really differs from her look in the summer. Therefore, the designers have to find new styles from one season to another, because the effect of time on the design and clothes is real. In any event, regardless of the clothes, the first thing that I notice is the general silhouette of the lady. The way she walks, her legs, her hands. I do not have a foot fetish but of course, high heels plus nice legs, everybody loves.

"Actually what turns you on is the feeling that the woman is perfectly in control of herself, which implies that she controls her body and the way she wants to be looked at. This is something I like, because that means that this woman will always be willing to look nice and will always be careful of the way you look at her. Of course, I am not saying that she must go to the grocery store dressed as a movie star at the Oscars. Most of all, this implies to reciprocate: The man should not just rely on the fact that, as a man, he is supposed to be more laid back than the woman. He must pay attention to all these details as well."

Turn-Offs

"I am turned off if they do not have nice 'extremities.' By that I mean that if some aspects of the woman seem too neglected, you are disappointed. For instance, in our firm there is a woman who is very pretty . . . if you look at her very fast. But when you get closer, you realize that, for example, she has eaten her nails, that her feet are very dry (with a kind of layer of 'stone' on her heel). There, you realize that she is not sexy anymore and that she neglects herself. In France we have a saying, '*Le diable est dans les details*' (the devil is in the details). Details are essential to me."

Guys have told me that they have a 30-second first glance test, but can you pass their more detailed two-minute pre-screening? Once you get past a guy's visual checklist, your confidence sex appeal is what really matters and then you have more power to choose. Your sense of style is your ticket through the front door.

Think of your Man Hunt as an adventure, and this Style Makeover is just part of enhancing your total package. Find the look that works best for you. Boost your sense of style before and after you get out there for better dating results. Consider setting up appointments with style and beauty consultants to identify your colors, fashions, facial essentials, and makeup. Wear colors that complement your skin tone and hair. You can make subtle and inexpensive changes to your wardrobe that can make lasting impressions. You might start by adding a new belt, necklace, or scarf to your wardrobe. When my friend visited Los Angeles from New York City, we spent hours at discount department stores hunting beauty bargains. She has a great eye for fashion and graciously offered to help me find a new pair of jeans. I listened carefully to her advice and walked out with hip new pants, a sexy top, and hot new belt.

To stay on top of your style sense, be open to making updates every year so you have a fresh look. As another wise friend told me, "Life is about updates." You need to be continually updating your look and listening to friends' advice. I cannot close this section without bringing up one more area to update. If you wear eyeglasses, you really need to buy a new pair every few years so your look is current. When I was reviewing internet dating profiles, I critiqued photos from a man who had really outdated glasses. I could barely see his eyes through the lenses and advised him immediately to invest in a new pair of glasses. You wear glasses over one of your most important facial features, the eyes, so please keep them updated.

Remember, you want to increase your odds of passing the right guy's KISS Test so you can engage him in the LIFE Match Game. The better you feel about your presentation, the better you will feel about yourself. You want your confidence sex appeal to shine inside and out, so don't skip this important dating preparation step.

Make Dating Positive

Now that you've given yourself a Confidence Face Lift and Style Makeover, it's time to talk about your SMART Man Hunting dating approach. It's always best to know what your approach is going to be and to arm yourself with what you expect or hope to achieve before you try on some of the New Era dating options or even go out with someone you met by osmosis. The key is to be positive.

1. *Be comfortable with you.* This comfort level isn't just about your renewed confidence; it's about not trying to twist yourself into shapes because you think that's what your date wants. One 30-something girlfriend told me, "Relax and be yourself around potential soul mates." She added, "Don't dress up to fill the part that you think he wants you to be." By being yourself, your smile will be more natural and pronounced. By wearing what makes you feel good or doing what you enjoy, you will be more attractive. Don't try to fit anyone's mold because you will always lose in the end.

2. *Know that you can take it or leave it.* At the earlier stages of dating, there isn't a whole lot invested emotionally. If someone isn't what you're looking for, don't continue dating him even if he is a nice guy. Cut your losses early. Remember that you can leave it. Don't have a scarcity consciousness and fear that no one else will want to go out with you. If you try to close a deal too fast, he might run. If you don't sense any interest walk away with a smile. There's always more men where that one came from.

3. *Follow a no bull policy.* Set boundaries, respect yourself, and do not put up with any more bull. You deserve the best and should not tolerate anything less. One 50-something woman commented to me, "Think about the people who make you feel really good about yourself. Surround yourself with people that give you the same feeling and respect. You will be much happier." If the guy is constantly late picking you up,

talking on the cell phone during dinner, and making excuses, you know where to run. Imagine saying, "You're fired!" and then politely tell him you've decided to take a pass.

4. *Take advantage of the New Era dating ratios.* Believe it or not, women have the numbers advantage in the New Era dating scene. This advantage has evolved with demographic shifts and the fact that more men are willing to try these modern options and wait until later years to find a mate. One 30-year-old male friend told me, "I decided to stop Internet dating because the odds are in the favor of women." He added, "I think the ratio is 10 men for every 6 women on some Internet sites, which makes it tough for men to win."

5. *Don't let go in the bedroom too fast.* Another 40-year-old male entrepreneur said to me at the coffee shop one day, "Women have the power to control the world because they are the ones that determine when to have sex. You need to tell all your girlfriends to go slowly with sex and they will always win." Remember, you want him to think you are the hottest ticket in town. Let him get to know you and show his appreciation before you let go in the bedroom. If asked when a woman should have sex with a guy, most men will say "As soon as possible" (see bachelor survey results in Part III), but the reality is that you are probably better off establishing some respect before jumping into bed.

   A 45-year-old actress told me, "I told my fiancé that I needed to sleep on the couch the first night that I slept at his house because after only three dates it was too early for me to stay in the same room. He completely understood and it made it more special when we did decide to be with each other." By taking a slow approach to intimacy, she actually made their bond stronger and now is planning her wedding to this 50-something executive. And if you must let go early, just make sure your gut is really good with a guy.

6. *Approach Man Hunting as an opportunity to have some fun.* Above all, try to have some fun on your journey to find Mr.

Right. Do not take every initial meeting so seriously. Learn to laugh at yourself, and share funny moments with potential mates. If you are nervous or anxious during a date, no one will want to come back for more. Remember, if something does not work out, there is another opportunity waiting for you around the corner. One girlfriend pointed out to me, "Men are like buses. A new one comes along every ten minutes."

7. *Hit the reset button if you need to get back on the right track.* SMART Man Hunting is about finding the right guy, but also about realizing when you might be dating Mr. Wrong. You want dating to be positive, and if you are in a bad relationship, it is never too late to give yourself a Confidence Face Lift. Be prepared to hit the reset button and make major changes to improve your sense of self-worth. If you know anyone who is in a bad relationship, give them this book immediately. Gently advise them that because you care about them, you wish they would walk away, rebuild their self-esteem, and then decide if they want to give the relationship another try. You will most likely see different results.

Confidence Face Lifts Are Never Too Late

Confidence Renewal #1—A New Lease on Life

Do you know anyone dating the wrong guy? It is probably due to the need for more confidence. I coached a 40-something woman to leave her boyfriend after 13 years because he did not treat her with respect. He was taking advantage of her generous nature and she could not see it. When she had back surgery, her self-absorbed boyfriend simply dropped her off at the hospital, and later complained that she was interrupting his schedule by being at home recovering. After pointing out that this behavior was totally unacceptable for months, I finally convinced her to walk away.

Not only did this freeloader boyfriend leave her on the operating table alone, she told me that he never thanked her for paying for his vacations, new clothes, and living expenses over the years. He was not even smooth enough to thank her for the little things such as being taken out to dinner. Hello. Next. When she kicked him out of her apartment, we quickly worked on ways to re-build her confidence and self-esteem. Here are some of the goals that we set for her successful comeback:

1. She moved into a new apartment, which put her in a new space without memories of this loser.

2. She gave her ex-boyfriend's Ralph Lauren polo shirts and Armani suits that she bought to a homeless person in down-town Los Angeles. Her ex expected her to pack up his clothes and ship them to him because he only traveled with carry-on luggage. Breaking her old patterns, she felt great satisfaction by giving his clothes to someone who was grateful and sincerely looking for a job. With a big grin, she told me, "I bet he's the best-dressed bum in the States."

3. On the work front, she set a goal to find a new job because her boss was not keeping promises to process her visa and it was time for change.

4. She spent time with girlfriends doing things that made her feel happy such as museum visits, a trip to Barcelona, golf, and dinners.

5. To update her look, she met with a style consultant, bought new jewelry, and had professional photos taken for her Internet dating profile.

6. Within six months, she moved back to London from Los Angeles to work for the direct competitor of her company in the States. She had zero loyalty to her Los Angeles employer after working 70-hour weeks with few rewards. The new job was a win-win because they fast-tracked her visa, moved her back to Europe, and gave the new company the competitive edge.

7. Once she arrived in London, we set goals for her to meet new and attractive men in wine tasting classes, Shakespeare Globe Theater group lectures, and graduate school classes.

When her ex-boyfriend called to ask for his clothes a year after the break-up, she told him, "You've got to be kidding. I was not about to pack up your clothes and send them to you." When he begged for her to come back to him, she told him with renewed confidence, "It's way too late for that now." He apologized for his rudeness over the years with his tears evident in his voice, but there was no turning back in this case. Next!

Confidence Renewal #2—
Man Running Back with a Ring

In the second case, I coached a beautiful woman to leave her man after a four-year relationship because she wanted to get married and the guy was a Relentless Renter (RR) (read more about this guy in the SMART Man Codes). When we first met on the set of the TV show *The Other Half*, I told her, "He will rent forever and never buy. You deserve better and need to leave this guy." The show's producer, Dick Clark, did not agree because it took him seven years to propose to his girlfriend. However, this 34-year-old actress was tired of waiting. She took my advice over Dick Clark's, and the confidence renewal process began.

After the show, we had lunch and continually met for coaching sessions over a one-and-a-half-year period to help her rebuild her life and self-esteem. She had great positive energy, and told me, "When I had heard it from enough people that it was time to leave, I finally decided to kick him out of my place." The challenge was that the guy did not believe her and would not leave. Because he traveled almost 50 percent of the year for his job, it made it difficult to get him out, so she just decided to take back her life and start dating again. She told me, "I had to get back into me. I was so focused on making him happy and the relationship work, and now it was time to do things that interested me." So what did she do?

1. She enrolled in nursing school so she could start building a life with her own income.

2. She also got more into acting and made some money working with an agent.

3. She ventured out again socially instead of sitting home alone crying when she did not get her ring. She went to jazz clubs, happy hours, and Monday Night Football events. Suddenly, the men started lining up to meet her and she realized that her Relentless Renter was not the only deal in town.

4. Travel was another passion that she took time to do for herself

versus waiting for this guy to schedule weekend getaways. She went to visit her sister often in Las Vegas and had a blast checking out the casinos.

When she called me in July about one and a half years later to tell me she just received an engagement ring, I was ironically driving to meet Confidence Renewal #1 to see her new apartment. Confidence Renewal # 2 told me with a big smile, "As soon as he started seeing that I wasn't waiting for him and that he might lose me, he started changing his tune." She added, "He now makes an effort to make the relationship fresh and exciting. He incorporates me into his day-to-day activities and calls me often to check in and see if I need anything. We are going to get married next summer and you must be there."

Boost Your Confidence Wrap-up

With your renewed confidence and new approach to dating, continually remind yourself that you are a unique and special person who deserves a top-gun partner. Don't be nervous on your Man Hunt. Wear a big smile, dress for success, be patient, and relax because the right one will eventually come to you. And once you find a man, if something does not feel right, don't be afraid to walk away immediately. You are smart, sexy, and confident and only deserve the best!

You will find that the Man Hunt process is similar to a job search. Hopefully, you have a few job hunting skills that can help you navigate the New Era dating playing field. Compare your Man Hunt to a Job Hunt in the next chapter.

3

～⊙～

Approach Your Man Hunt Like a Job Hunt

MAN HUNTS are very similar to job hunts. You may not like this idea since it doesn't satisfy your more romantic notions of love, but the sooner you accept this concept as a simple fact, the sooner you'll be dating. If your feminist instincts clash with the idea that you're looking to hire a husband, don't think of it that way. Look at it as though you're simply making sure that the broadest number of opportunities (dates) are placed in your life for evaluation. You want to be sure to find a job that is the best fit for you, right? It's the same with dating.

When I found myself unemployed, I decided to conduct parallel searches for a man and new job. The unemployment rate was at the highest level since 1994 and I had left a vice president's position. I prepared mentally for the "over-qualified" stamp, assessed my savings, and started creating my search strategies. Instead of waiting for the job and then finding a man, I decided that life is too short and it was time to seek both. One 40-year-old dot.com founder told me, "Your approach is perfect for finding a man and a job."

When looking for a man or a job, you're using the same set of skills and strategies. Just like finding the right place to work, you want to find the right match where you feel great about your selection. How can you use your job hunting skills to find and identify your Mr. Wonderful?

The Winning Hunter's Strategic Plan

In order to win in your Man Hunt as well as your life journey, here is some advice from happy and confident people who steered me down a path to success. These winning strategies form a coherent plan of action and can help you find a man and/or job.

1. Define Your Requirements

Whether you are seeking a man or job, you need to at least start out with a few parameters concerning what you are seeking. It helps to define your ideal situation. A woman I know who met her husband on the Internet, gave me this advice: "Target market." Her point was that by defining what you want, you can find him faster. (More on this can be found in Chapter 9, What You Should Know Before You Go.) By being clear about what you want, you'll avoid wasting time with Mr. Wrong. Later, I remind you to stay open, but if you're looking for someone with the same education level as you and that's a Masters degree, there's probably no point spending too much time with a fitness trainer with a degree from massage school. Even though your Man Hunt may take you down surprising paths where you meet guys who are different from your original vision, it is helpful to know what you truly want in a man up front. In other words, what are the deal breakers for you?

Try to be realistic about your requirements. An older and wiser 50-something girlfriend who is about to get married emailed me the following: "I look at a relationship in a very different light than I did ten or fifteen years ago. I don't need someone to complete me, save me, or be me. Getting to that place gave me a whole new world of possible candidates."

2. Be Patient and Persistent, Not Desperate

I met with a 30-something male executive coach who told me that my best Job Hunt strategy was "Patience, persistence, and don't take things too personally." There are many parallels to my Man Hunt strategy that apply to this job search advice. Just getting out there once or twice is not enough, you have to keep trying. Eventually something is going to click. Be prepared for rejection (see previous section) and persistently knock on doors. Do not give up until you meet your goals. Another friend pointed out to me, "It is important not to be desperate when looking for a job or a man."

3. Check Your Needs at the Door

I approached each first date interview or job networking event in a very light-hearted fashion to avoid giving off needy vibes. Neediness implies desperation. If the shoe were on the other foot, would that be attractive to you? Try to figure out what's making you feel needy or desperate. Then remind yourself that you have plenty of time and that lots of opportunities are waiting for you. (Review the Confidence Boosters in Chapter 2.)

One morning I walked into a major healthcare firm for a breakfast networking meeting. The host kicked off the session by sharing, "We decided to hold these smaller meetings because the organization's members found the larger events exhausting since they got bombarded with requests for jobs and consulting work." When we went around the table to share names and interests, I decided to try a new strategy. I stated with a smile, "I am here to learn from you and promise not to harass you for a job. I am unemployed, but really came to learn new buzz words to help me prepare for future interviews."

You know what happened after the meeting? I received three potential job leads. Not acting desperate and letting people get to know me without pressure achieved a much better result. By lightening up and using a sense of humor, I had much greater success. The same holds true for dating. If you respond to your Mr. Right candidates with a light approach, they will want you more. One 40-something woman said to me, "Just play nonchalant. Just say, 'Okay, fine, no problem' when they say they are busy." With this non-desperado style, your man is much more likely to come running after you.

When I date, instead of giving off needy and negative vibes, I keep myself busy with positive activities and friendships that make me feel good about myself. The perfect positive project for me was writing this dating book. I also continued taking my piano lessons with a "no pressure to be Beethoven" approach, participated in a book club, and frequently got outside for walks on the beach and hikes in the mountains. I learned to laugh at my mistakes, made mental notes to avoid repeating the same patterns that did not work, and just kept getting up in the morning and plunging forward with the Man and Job hunts.

4. Don't Try to Force Things

Pressure to close a deal too fast is related to being needy. When we are over-anxious, we might take too much of a lead in the dating process. In other words, don't be pushy. Let things unfold naturally and you'll be much happier with the result. One wise 50-year-old male CEO told me, "If it's a real deal, you don't need to direct your romance because it will build naturally."

Dating is a delicate dance. A 40-year-old male friend said to me, "It's important to let the guy lead." By taking a non-needy and patient approach, you can easily let the guy lead. However, when I polled other men about whether a woman should make the first move, I found bachelors very open to women making advances (see more about this bachelor survey in Part III). No matter who makes the moves, if you are not interested, no feeling obligated just because someone likes you! And if he is not interested, just keeping saying, "Next." Remember, the trick is to be SMART, not desperate.

While it may feel frustrating to give up control over how a date or relationship is progressing, you'll win in the long run. Every time you want to exert control, try turning instead to something that is truly within your control. Do you dishes, pay your bills, work out, or visit a friend. Your dates would thank you for it.

5. Bounce Back from Rejection

Yes, I got rejected every day on both the Job and Man Hunt fronts. I had to learn how to bounce back quickly when countless recruiters told me, "You're over-qualified." Even though I reached out to my network of friends and contacts, many times they did not call me back right away. I decided that my best approach was to maintain a positive attitude, use my sense of humor to add levity when I did talk to people in my network, and just keep trying. People are busy, and my Job Hunt was not everyone's top priority.

Paralleling these Job Hunt rejections, I met many Mr. Wrong candidates on my Man Hunt. I set up coffee with men who seemed to be Mr. Right candidates, only to discover that they had lied about their age or that the photograph of themselves they'd posted on the Internet had been misleading. I was also stood up once because I was not SMART enough to catch some red flags. As I started making changes in my expectations and assumptions by learning from these mistakes rather than being disheartened by them, men lined up to meet me and the job offers started coming my way. Remember, mistakes are valuable lessons and will only make you SMARTer.

You will probably receive a few hot and cold messages from bachelors. I received the following responses to first encounters during the same week. If you receive a voicemail that sounds like the first one, hit the delete key immediately. You want your guy to sound like Bachelor # 2.

BACHELOR #1's Voicemail

- "Hi Liz, this is Joe from that whole evil online thing. I just wanted to call you back and say hi. I had a great time chatting the other evening . . . um . . . I'm not exactly sure it's exactly what they call a match . . . um . . . I enjoyed it . . . um . . . I just wonder if perhaps . . . I don't know . . . I'm not as initially beefed as maybe I should be and um . . . I don't know if that would be an issue or not . . . but I definitely enjoyed chatting and think the things you do are fascinating and quiet wonderful. . . . Having given that caveat, if you would like to call me back . . . um . . . I hope we can talk soon. Otherwise, it was a lot of fun. Thank you. Bye."

BACHELOR #2's Voicemail

Okay, wait three days, and the next one comes along:

- "Hey Liz, it's Tom. How are you? I had a great time last night. The conversation was awesome. Really enjoyed it . . . that was fun. It's very refreshing to be around a very beautiful, intelligent, and fun girl. Enjoyed it—look forward to the next time. Tag, you're it. Call me. I'll be around tonight. If you get a chance, call me."

6. Let People Know You're Looking—Ask for Help

Although I received many rejections, I also got lucky many times— usually when I asked for help. As you broaden your horizons, you'll be meeting many new people. Just like in a Job Hunt, you shouldn't be afraid to ask people to help you. Often you don't even need to ask, people will offer it to you. But this won't happen if you don't tell people you are looking for a man or a job. It pays to be open.

For example, I met a woman at a party who had a guy in New York City whom she wanted me to meet. When I went to the Big Apple for business the next week, I called the guy for a lunch date. While I was a little nervous making the initial call, I thought to myself, what have you got to lose? If nothing else, you will probably gain a friend. When he answered the phone, he was extremely receptive and willing to meet me for a 2:00 p.m. lunch. My gut was really good during this first encounter and I fell for him pretty quickly by surprise. After several months of dating, he confessed that long distance romance was not going to work for him. Despite the separation, he remains a good friend, cheerleader, and advisor.

In a similar scenario where I reached out for help, I had a lunch meeting with an Internet industry contact to brainstorm job search ideas. We shared Job Hunt strategies, but I also mentioned that I was writing this book. Then she told me, "By the way, I am a published author and can talk to you about how to get your book published." If I hadn't stepped out and asked this woman to lunch, or opened up and talked about my book, I might not have ended up with a great book coach.

I also sent out a group email to my friends announcing my Man Hunt. You would be surprised how many people replied with Mr. Right candidates. The opportunities are out there, but you might need to ask to find them.

7. Use a Give-and-Take Approach

Job and Man Hunts are also give-and-take situations. There is a lot of truth to the statement "What goes around, comes around." You need to offer your contacts and ideas to people. When you share what you know, you will be surprised how much more willing people are to help you in return.

While seeking a job or man, I also look for opportunities for my friends and business contacts along the journey. If I hear about a job lead that might not be for me, but can help someone else, I try to connect the parties. When I was working I took unemployed people out to lunch almost weekly to help them brainstorm job ideas. Guess whom I called when I lost my job? Similarly, if I meet a man that I like, but don't feel a love connection, I often offer to set him up with a girlfriend who may be a better match or invite him to a singles event.

8. Keep an Open Mind

Be open-minded in your travels and while networking because you never know who will introduce you to whom. You are bound to have something in common with most of the people you meet and there is some value in almost every connection. For example, my 30-something girlfriend met a 65-year-old man on a plane. He later introduced her to his best friend's son. At the very least, all the characters you encounter will further help you define what you want. Everyone can show you a new side to yourself and teach you something new.

9. Avoid the Perfectionism Ferris Wheel

During the course of your Man Hunt journey, it is important to remember that people are not perfect. If you are searching for a

100 percent match, you will quickly fall into a "Perfectionist Paradox" and never make a decision. This state ensures an endless ride on a Ferris wheel with no results. A 50-something marketing executive who is happy in his second marriage told me, "Marriage is about finding the person you love so much that you can live *with* their faults."

No matter what ABC Man Code (see Part IV) or other category your date might fit into, you must learn to accept people for who they are and determine whether or not their character meets your needs. In the Virtual Lover (VL) code example, you can read why a woman fell for a guy who only had 50 percent of her original Mr. Right checklist. The LIFE Match Game described in Chapter 12 will help you determine what's really important and make a final decision.

10. Evaluate the Candidates

Finding a life partner should be taken at least as seriously as seeking a new job. Early in the dating process, observe his actions and prepare your interview questions in advance to determine if it's worthwhile to proceed to the next step with someone. If the candidate makes it to the third date, you can start using the LIFE Match Questions found in Chapter 12 to further evaluate your compatibility and chances of success. In order to narrow the field, use Part III, The Dating Assessment Dance, as your guide. Pay close attention to red flags and heed their warnings. If you see major hurdles that would have to be overcome, be willing to move on fast to the next candidate. A 35-year-old male colleague told me, "One of the biggest mistakes that I see women make is they fixate on fixing a guy versus moving on." Make "people don't change" your mantra.

11. Make Friends and Don't Burn Bridges

At this point, I have dated many men and can attest to the fact that the majority of those relationships settled into friendships and nothing more. This outcome is not surprising given that we are all looking for a specific combination of elements in a potential life partner. The challenge of finding the right match is all the more reason to get out there and increase the number of men you meet. You might date any number of men more than once, getting to know them in a deeper way, but not proceed to the next level. It's always best to strive to maintain an ongoing friendship even if a romance doesn't work out.

I met two men through Internet dating who both ended up being great business connections. One candidate offered to share my resume with his top-gun friends at a major telecommunications company. The second potential candidate asked me to partner with him on a consulting deal for a wireless company. While I did not want to continue dating either of these men, I initially contacted them because we had similar interests. As a result, I ended up with two job leads.

Remember, it is a small world. Keeping your associations positive is even more important in the New Era. You might find that a candidate-turned-friend will one day help you find a job or a mate. One 30-something girlfriend commented to me, "I always try to end things on good terms. We originally came together for a reason and that connection is what's important." You never know when your paths will cross again so try to part on a good note. Remember Bachelor #2's awesome voicemail on page 42. He works for a major advertising company that was hosting a party for FOX Entertainment in Los Angeles. After this party, he took me to dinner in Beverly Hills with his boss, and guess who they knew? Suddenly, my ex-husband became the dinner conversation because he previously worked in their New York City office. It's a very small world once you get out there.

12. Pace Yourself

Similar to a job hunt, you shouldn't rush around frantically in your search for a man. While you will be surprised by all of your dating activity once you approach dating the SMART Man Hunting way and use the New Era dating options, remember to pace yourself.

You don't want to show up on your dates exhausted. You want to be at the top of your game for every interview. I made the mistake of trying every type of option at once. This climaxed during one week when I went on seven dates. Afterward, I retreated to my support network of friends and told them, "I cannot keep going out with strangers. I need to see you for dinner and take a time out." Once I pulled back from my Man Hunt efforts and resumed a better balance, my smile returned to my face.

13. Know Your Key Selling Points

If you were asked in a job interview to list your key strengths, you would know what to say, but would you know how to respond to the same question on a date? Guys want to know what you bring to the table in a relationship. What makes you unique? The first few dates are about marketing, so be prepared with a confident pitch. Similar to a job interview, you want to highlight your best attributes with a date.

Be ready to share your key selling points in a subtle way so you can make great first impressions and entice your dates to want more of you. Remember, you want to sound confident versus boastful. You don't want to go overboard with exaggerations either, or you might find yourself in divorce court down the road. Talk about your passions with enthusiasm so you paint a positive spin. Why would someone be enticed to go the distance with you?

- Are you a good cook?
- Do you like to hike or bike?
- Can you take great photographs?
- Do you have a fun and supportive circle of friends?
- Can you play piano?

These attributes are all key selling points that most men will find very attractive. A guy wants someone who can help him become greater as a couple. What makes you a hot ticket?

And what does the "wife" job description look like to a man? One recently married man proudly shared the "Bachelor Rules" that he developed over the years with college buddies. His friends use these guidelines for qualifying a Ms. Right candidate.

A Bachelor's Requirements for "Ms. Right"

I don't necessarily agree with this guy's Ms. Right requirements, but it is interesting to see what some men are using as guidelines. Here are the five must-haves that a group of guys in college dreamed up for their Ms. Right.

- "She must be physically attractive."
- "She must have the same beliefs, ideas, and athletic interests."
- "She must be eager to please." (read between the lines on this requirement)
- "She must be intellectually stimulating."
- "She must be mentally sound."

Most of the men who defined this Ms. Right job description are happily married now. What do you think of these bachelor requirements?

Once you define your key selling points, think about how you would write your Mr. Right job description. What are your must-haves in a guy?

14. Be Smart About Office Dating

While you've built great Man Hunting skills at work, it's better to use your interview and communications experience to date outside of the office. As a Human Resources professional, I've seen many people place their livelihood on the line by mixing romance with work. If you must go there, I have success strategies to help you protect your privacy, minimize office gossip, and test the waters before you go public. You can make office romance work if you date discreetly.

Before you fall for the hottie at your office, I must share a few words of caution. The sexual harassment laws are gray, and with the endless 21st century dating options out there now, you are no longer limited to friends, family, and work. As a Human Resources professional who has trained sexual harrassment classes, I advise singles to avoid office dating if possible. There are too many blurred lines in the law and these misunderstandings can destroy your reputation and put your livelihood at risk. For example, repeated advances (asking someone out or just saying you look nice) that are not well received are considered sexual harassment.

Okay, I admit that I have gone down the office romance path a few times over the years. While I've seen people get married who met at work, it always made me feel uneasy. I was very focused on my career and preferred having a private life outside of work. When I worked at an investment company, I dated a guy who had moved to my hometown of Baltimore whose entire social life revolved around friends from work. I felt very claustrophobic spending seven days a week with the same faces. I needed to get out fast. While working for a major telecommunications company, my boss, who was the HR director, advised me to be more discreet about dating a co-worker. She shared that the rumor mill was running wild about me at the VP level about events at an office happy hour the night before—ouch, oops!

Unfortunately, the woman usually loses when entering the gray area caused by dating a male boss. I've seen two extreme cases at Internet start-ups where a woman got involved with the CEO and was forced to leave the company by the board of directors. There was another case where two married VPs were having an affair at work. Not only did the woman get busted by a voicemail the guy left at her home, the secretary walked in on the two of them in the act in his office. The female VP was asked to stay with the company, but work from home. I've also seen peers get caught having sex in the elevator who got suspended from work as a result. Mixing sex and work is just risky business.

Keeping an open mind to your opinions, I sent out an Office Romance Survey. The responses show that while most people don't think it is a great idea to mix sex and work, the majority (80 percent) have dated someone at the office. Since most singles seem to have gone down the office romance road, I've added success tips to help you make it happen without risking your job.

Office Romance Survey Results

1. Do you think the office is a great place to date?
   Yes (29%)
   No (71%)

2. How many people have you dated at work?
   0 (20%)
   1–5 (71%)
   5–10 (9%)

3. Whom have you dated at work?
   Co-Worker (22%)
   Employee who works for me (3%)
   Someone in another department (43%)
   A client (15%)
   CEO (2%)

4. What influence does office romance have?
   Distracting (39%)
   Entertaining (23%)
   Tempting (20%)

5. Have you had sex at work?
   Yes (23%)
   No (77%)

Found Love at the Office?

"Yes, I got married to him. We've had a fabulous marriage for twelve years plus three kids."

"I had a great love at the office. We dated and lived together for two years. It didn't distract us from either of our jobs, but then we were twenty-three and twenty-five and working in different departments."

"I've never found love at the office, but there have been a lot of attractive prospects."

"No. Impossible. Girls at our work don't look at guys."

"Some of the greatest relationships I've ever had developed at the office."

"Yes, I dated two clients. One is still a friend and I lost the other as a friend and client when things broke up."

Bad Experience with Office Romance?

"My boss got upset when I started dating a co-worker in another department. It was very awkward."

"Would not recommend dating someone in your same office. Subject to a lot of gossip. Awkward when you break up."

"I dated the assistant of a CEO that we were building a business alliance with. He got pretty upset, fired her, and threatened my career."

"Not personally, but I have seen it wreak havoc with others. If it does not work out, it can cause a lot of problems."

"Efforts to keep the romance quiet to avoid gossip backfired. Another woman in the office became extremely interested in the same man to the degree of making open sexual advances."

"Not really, I made it a point to stay friends. Once there was some tension and we got over that and are still friends though 500 miles away."

Found Love at the Office?	**Bad Experience with Office Romance?**
"I met someone at work and later on we fell in love. Dated for over a year."	"Awkward situation with a vendor who was walking a political tightrope."

If your hormones go wild at work, here are some tips to help you keep your career intact while building the relationship. Because employees move around more and there is less loyalty to go the distance with a company, you might want to go for it if you have a really good gut feeling about a guy. If you are in the entertainment business, it will also be easier to mix love and work because you are usually on short-term assignments. If your romance doesn't work out, you're probably going to be off the set within weeks versus a corporate job that can last years.

Office Romance Success Strategies

1. *Be discreet*—If you must mix your career with love, keep a low profile about your feelings at the office. This means no sex in the elevator, garage, or in your office, even if it is after hours and you think no one is around. Instead of sharing your excitement about great sex the night before with a co-worker, call your friend who lives across the country—or out of the country. Whatever you do outside of the office is your business so keep it out there. Avoid telling your boss about your romance until you are close to walking down the aisle. Many companies have policies where one person has to leave or both people cannot report to the same boss if you get married. Once you get engaged, by letting your boss know before the wedding, your announcement might actually save your job.

2. *Set boundaries*—To build trust and protect your privacy, set a few boundaries at the beginning about how you are going to manage your relationship at work. Are you going

to tell anyone? Are you going to spend time together at lunch? Are you going to spend weekends with friends from work?

3. *Find other interests*—You will want to find interests outside of work to share as a couple. Do you both like to hike? Do you have any mutual friends outside of work? Without this foundation, your relationship will be built on talking shop, and that will get boring very fast.

4. *Avoid email*—Email and office romance can be a dangerous combination. You want to avoid leaving a documentation trail for your company. Even if you have a consensual relationship, you never know when something might go south and emails can be very incriminating.

5. *Use Instant Messenger*—Your best bet for office romance communications is instant messenger. Because it is managed by a different server such as AOL or Yahoo!, it cannot be traced. When you close the window, the messages are gone and no one can go back to them later. As long as you are careful, and remember to close the window when you walk away, instant messenger will let you flirt at work discreetly.

6. *Date your peers*—Date co-workers at your level or someone in another department to minimize legal twists. Even if you are both into each other, you want to avoid a quid pro quo (this for that) case at all costs. If you date your boss or a direct report, you are asking for potential trouble. For example, if you promote one of your employees whom you are also dating, another employee may file a case against you for discriminating against them if they think they are more qualified.

7. *Trust your gut*—The most important question to ask is what is your gut telling you about the guy? Is he really into you? Do you trust him? Is he talking future with you? If you are going to risk your reputation and livelihood, he better be worth it in my book.

You can make office romance work using the right approach. While I worked for a telecommunications start-up, my vice president actually dated and eventually married the CEO. This couple kept their love life out of the office, respected each other's role at work, and the gossip was minimized as a result. In a similar case, I interviewed a 30-something woman in Minneapolis who told me, "My boss dated a co-worker when I worked in the marketing department for a medical company. No one knew about their romance until they announced their engagement." She added, "Everyone was shocked and pleased." This couple had been so discreet and professional that their mutual boss let them continue working in the same department after they got married. What were their success strategies for office romance? The Minneapolis observer told me, "I'm sure it took a lot of work to make it work. They talked a lot on the phone even though they were two doors away from each other. No one ever knew that they were talking to each other." Both of these office romance couples continue to be happily married.

Instead of making love connections at the office, venture outside your Home Box of friends, family, and work. While many people find love at work, a break-up cannot only result in heartache, but may put you back in the unemployment line if you are not careful. It's your choice, but honestly, there are so many other options out there now for singles that my recommendation is resist whenever possible.

If you decide to mix love and work, be discreet, set boundaries, and trust your gut to increase your chances of office romance success.

Approach Your Man Hunt Like a Job Hunt Wrap-up

This chapter demonstrated that you *can* achieve success and meet Mr. Right by choosing to date proactively and approach your Man Hunt like a Job Hunt. You can be a better Man Hunter by using your professional skills outside the office to find romance. Leave your Home Box and be ready, willing, and able to meet new people by opening yourself to New Era dating options. You've learned how to bounce back from rejection, maintain your smile, exchange ideas, and not give up. I shared this thought about the journey with my friends: "I feel like I am playing the lottery. You just have to keep playing and eventually something will hit."

Get Ready for SMART Man Hunting— You're Armed and Ready

So how do you put all this information together in one hunter's winning package? Here is a simple tool kit for the next phase of your journey—getting out there. And don't just get out there. As one 39-year-old male musician told me, "You have to play to win."

The Winning Hunter's Tool Kit

- Change your ideas about dating and be willing to leave your Home Box.
- Prepare for the hunt by building your confidence inside and out.
- Define your Mr. Right requirements and keep them realistic.
- Be patient, not desperate, and keep your sense of humor.
- Bounce back from rejection and don't give up.
- Ask for help and use a give-and-take approach.
- Keep an open-mind and get off the Perfectionism Ferris Wheel.
- Pace yourself and don't burn bridges.
- Know your key selling points. What makes you unique and a hot commodity?
- Use your professional skills to Man Hunt outside of the office.
- If you start mixing office dating with your career, be discreet and set boundaries.

You are now a confident, sexy, and SMART Man Hunter, so it's time to get out there and explore the Man Hunting Landscape.

PART II

Explore the New Era of Man Hunting

4

⟿⟍

The Man Hunting Landscape—Expanding Your Home Box

WITH YOUR NEW Man Hunting approach, winning strategies, style sense, and confidence beaming across your face, you can now start benefiting from the substantial number of New Era dating options currently available. With the preparation of the previous section in place, you are ready to venture out and find a soul mate.

Don't be afraid to try new dating avenues. Your Man Hunt journey can easily be fast-tracked by modern technology and demand-driven dating providers. There are millions of wonderful people out there using the New Era dating options, and you might just find your man using new search engines. While I definitely hesitated before trying Internet dating, speed dating, professional matchmakers, and singles events, once I jumped in the game, I met many intelligent and interesting people out there. I also met many happy couples who shared their New Era dating success stories, which helped me fine-tune this winning strategy for you.

You can also find lawyers, TV producers, management consultants, commercial real estate brokers, marketing managers, national account managers, writers, teachers, and doctors. The majority of these candidates had the same objective—to find a special someone. So I encourage you to try one or several of these options if you are still seeking Mr. Right. Simply by getting out there and boosting your dating numbers, you will significantly increase your odds of finding your man.

What New Era Dating Options Are Available?

The main advantage of New Era dating options is that they allow you to broaden your dating spectrum. Remember, finding Mr. Right is a numbers game. You can find thousands of Mr. Right candidates via Internet dating sites, quickly meet available men through speed dating, and conduct more thorough searches using professional matchmakers.

In addition to enabling the proliferation of New Era dating options, technology has transformed the world of dating by making it a smaller place. It's easier and more pain-free than ever to not just *search for* but to *connect with* someone. Today, it's quite effortless for friends to set you up via email introductions and then for you to flirt via text messages or instant messenger. It's possible to become reacquainted with old boyfriends with whom there's still a spark. Through email correspondence and wireless flirtations, you can maintain long-distance romances or meet a diverse group of international business travelers. I met a 70-year-old woman who told me, "I've re-connected with an 85-year-old man. We email each other coast-to-coast on a regular basis and I am so in love that I may need to move back east." She was beaming from ear to ear.

Survey the Land—Expand Your Home Box Beyond Friends, Family, and Work

A wise 45-year-old male executive told me, "Life is about updates. You need to constantly update your approach to work, friends, family and dating." If you look beyond traditional dating approaches, you will find endless opportunities to expand your options.

Remember that the first order of business is to get out of your Home Box. Even if you may not be ready to start using the New Era dating options, it's good to get out and survey the territory.

You might want to start your Man Hunt by easing into it. Comfortably expand the boundaries of your home turf by changing your regular routines and associating with some new people. Try something new or learn something different—anything that shakes up your world a bit. You could take a yoga class or sign up for a photography class at a local college. This kind of "sticking your toe in the water" action will also engender confidence. Even if you are ready to plunge ahead and turn to the next two chapters that describe all the New Era dating options in further detail and how to best use them, it's never a bad idea to simultaneously work on Home Box expansion, so read on.

Jump into Your Passions

Think about your favorite hobbies and get more engaged in some of those passions. Sign up for activities and associations that you enjoy so that you can easily meet people who share the same enthusiasm for your interests. If you like golf, go to the driving range to expand your network of friends. Join a ski club if you like exploring the slopes. Not only will you meet new people, but you'll build the confidence that powers your sex appeal by doing the things that make you happy. As a result, you might just meet Mr. Right on your travels.

My 37-year-old piano teacher actually met her husband at tango dance lessons. She had not dated anyone seriously for three years, loved to dance, and told me, "I was horrifically lonely, so I decided to take classes as a way to meet people." After their second class together, she had a date with her 49-year-old entrepreneur dance partner. The couple went salsa dancing on their first date and never looked back. They were engaged ten days later, moved in together at three months, and then she became pregnant at seven months. During her first contractions, she decided that it was time to formally tie the knot before the baby arrived. The couple ran to the courthouse for a fast wedding and then to the hospital for delivery the same day. Simply by stepping out and exploring her passions, she was fortunate to find "the one."

If you notice that your favorite activities tend to be populated by mainly women, try an entirely different approach. While a book club might give you joy, you probably won't meet Mr. Right there either. A very wise 30-something woman who was recently married gave me some great advice regarding activities for meeting men. She started with this observation:

"A lot of women do stupid things recommended by women's magazines to meet men—things like taking a pottery class or trying to run into divorced dads' grocery carts at the supermarket. This is ridiculous. The men-to-women ratios for fun outdoor sporting activities are really far more favorable for single women."

She continued with these tips for activities where the odds favor females:

"When I was doing a lot of climbing, I signed up for a weekend ice-climbing course. There were two women and about thirty men. I got a lot of attention. Of course, it is not a good idea to sign up for something like this just to meet men. You should like the idea of learning about ice climbing. Kayaking is another good sport. Typically, ratios on rivers hover around seven men to one woman. If you are more of an indoors person, rock gyms are also good. Most of the guys you meet at these places are great. They are outdoorsy, adventurous, well traveled, fit, and they want to talk to you because they are sick of being around other guys all the time. A word of warning: These types of guys definitely do not fall for the 'helpless me' routine, so don't be too 'prissy.'"

Build Your Foundation of Friends and Community

Another move outside your Home Box is to consistently work on expanding and diversifying your foundation of friends. Diversifying your associates exposes you to many new outlets and people. But never neglect your core group of intimates and supporters. They are the ones who will see you through the Man Hunting process and will strengthen your backbone.

In addition to this foundation, be ready to expand more socially into your community to meet new people. You never know who might connect you to "the one." While I have a great core group of friends, I have also made countless contacts at the neighborhood coffee shop and through hobbies and business. By being open-minded to people's suggestions, you might be surprised what this approach can do. If your alumnae office invites you to an event, go. If your friend invites you to a networking event, go at least once to check it out. Simply by listening to a 40-something lawyer's advice in the coffee shop, I ended up testing Speed Dating for this book and as part of my Man Hunt. Not only did I meet a Mr. Right candidate at this event, I got a lucky break by being interviewed by Los Angeles's KNBC-4 News about my experience.

Another way to become more involved in your community is to engage in community activism or service work. You'll be doing something good for someone else or promoting a cause in which you believe. It stands to reason you might meet someone with similar interests and concerns as you. I volunteered for my neighborhood community association, and as a result, ended up swapping notes with a fellow board member who hosts a cable talk show on relationships. Friends and community are success keys for your Man Hunt journey.

Technology Expands Your Home Box

You can immediately start benefiting from the use of email, cell phones, video greeting, calling cards, personal organizers, pagers, the Internet, and text messaging technology. These advancements have created a new wireless world of courtship connections that can expand your search.

Flirt with your Man Candidates using new technologies. For

example, one of my top Man Candidates sent me a text message on my cell phone right after my first piano recital. The message was cute and simple: "Hi Liz, How was the recital?" How many points do you think he gained with this move? I sent him a warm reply.

Lastly, frequent flyer miles and modern communications have made international partners and long-distance relationships more feasible in the new millennium. Don't discount a long-distance man. If it is meant to be, you can make it happen—with a lot of help from wireless connections.

Use Email as a Dating Enabler

What did daters do before email? Essentially, email enables all New Era dating. You no longer need to wait for a party and hope to meet someone face-to-face there. Nor do you need to hope that there's enough time at a party for you to get to know someone who introduces himself to you. Today, friends can set you up via email with contacts all over the globe.

Because my parents were set up on a blind date by college friends and are still together more than forty years later, I welcome email introductions by friends.

While the old-fashioned blind date rarely included communication between the couple before the fact, email enhances the New Era dating process by providing a means to share information before you even lay eyes on each other. You can now compare interests, values, and even photos prior to a live encounter. I was set up through a mutual friend on a blind date via email that was a big success. My friend emailed both of us positive notes about each other and recommended that we meet. Since we both shared similar interests in the relationship business (he works for an Internet dating site), it was easy to strike up a dialogue with this guy. After our first date, I discovered that this male candidate spends a few weeks a month in Munich, Germany, for business. Despite this schedule, I was willing to give it a shot because there was clearly chemistry, similar value systems, and a mutual desire to explore a committed relationship. This communication medium allows you to easily broaden your search without geographic limitations.

As part of your SMART Man Hunting Strategy, a phone conversation can complement email communication before your first date. Sometimes it can be difficult to determine the tone if you rely solely on email or instant messenger. While both options are timesavers, nothing can completely replace live contact.

A word of caution about email blind dates: You don't want to wait too long for an in-person meeting. For example, my 40-year-old girlfriend was introduced via email to a 37-year-old candidate through a mutual friend. Even though she lives in Los Angeles and he resides in Baltimore, Maryland, the two exchanged emails several times a day for about three months before their first in-person meeting. While my girlfriend felt that she knew this candidate fairly well after months of email exchanges and a few phone calls, there was no Chemistry Connection when they finally met. In the end, she commented, "It was a total waste of time because I waited too long to meet him and then there was no physical attraction." The two parties were not even interested in maintaining a friendship.

Men also like email flirting because it takes the pressure off cold-calling women for dates. I met a man from Italy who recently moved to the United States. This 33-year-old film editor told me, "Email is the greatest way to test a woman's interest." Several of his test messages turned into exciting dates, he said, and one resulted in a long-term relationship.

Email introductions by friends can open many doors and increase your search bandwidth. However, it is important to have live contact sooner rather than later, and keep your expectations in perspective so you avoid time wasters.

Make Virtual Love

In order to help you take advantage of wireless technology, I decided to research the latest virtual love connectors to share creative ways to spark romance. As a former corporate training manager for Sprint PCS, I always have a cell phone connected to my hip and wanted to find out how wireless can help singles make virtual love. Once you have established a connection via email introductions, Internet dating, professional matchmakers, speed dating, singles events, or even the grocery store, wireless technology can offer fun ways to flirt in our fast-track world. Email, text messaging, instant messaging, voice and video greetings are the new substitutes for written correspondence. The majority of individuals now have at least one email address and cell phone that can be used for personal communications.

These virtual love connectors have made it so easy to communicate that there is no reason for a lack of regular contact anymore. What wireless technology is making communication easier for singles in the states? What is popular now in Europe and Asia that singles will see in the U.S. in the near future?

Email Text Messages

You can now flirt with someone virtually by emailing a cute text message to their cell phone. In many cases, you simply send the email to the number@(insert their wireless carrier).com, but check with your carrier for instructions.

Instant Messenger

Many dating sites now allow you to IM a member so you can get immediate feedback from a potential match. This new service can be a blast and help you make quick decisions. Check out the IM features on Yahoo! Personals, Perfectmatch.com, and Lavalife.com.

Mobile Dating Site Messages

Singles can now sign up for mobile services on Internet dating sites that let you flirt with other members by sending text messages directly to their cell phone. Check out the new mobile features on Lavalife.com and have fun using this new wireless connector.

Instant Cell Phone Messages

Similar to an online Instant Messenger, singles are signing up for services that allow you to carry on a continuous conversation using your cell phone. Instead of just sending text messages back and forth, you can have an uninterrupted text conversation via your cell phone. AOL offers this service, and many other Internet service providers will soon.

Photos from Your Phone

If you want to check out someone immediately, ask them to email you a picture using their photo cell phone. You no longer need to wait to have access to a PC. You can get instant photo access using a camera phone.

Video Greetings

You can now post video greetings on many Internet dating sites. (I had fun watching the videos on Lavalife.com.) Soon, you will also be able to send and receive video greetings via cell phone technology. I saw ads for videophones recently all over London and Barcelona. This new technology combines a visual with the voice so you can better screen the matches you meet online before a first date.

Multi-media Messages

Photos with embedded messages are being sent all over Europe. Fraternities are actually advertising parties by sending out an invitation to cell phones that include photos from the last party with funny descriptions. You can now combine a photo with a personal caption to capture someone's attention. In the U.S., you can send the photo as an attachment to an email with a text message. In the near future, daters in the States will also be able to combine the two into one image.

Dating Services WAP Sites

You will soon be able to access the Internet dating sites via your cell phone using WAP (Wireless Application Protocol). For example, your Match.com screen will be adjusted to fit the size of your cell phone or Blackberry screen so you will no longer need to wait until you reach a PC to view someone's online profile. You can currently access the Yahoo! and AOL sites on your cell phone through some wireless carriers in the U.S.

SMS Chat

SMS (Short Messages or Text Messages) Chat is the hot new way for singles to connect in Europe and Asia. Singles enter a chat room via a cable TV channel. The chat session has a VJ (Video Disc Jockey) who acts as a filter for what gets posted on the screen. Your cell phone number is hidden and an id name appears instead to protect your privacy. If you see someone whom you want to chat with outside the group, you can send a SMS to the VJ using the main number on the screen. The VJ then passes along your request to the id name with your number. If your cell phone has a keyboard, it clearly makes it easier to communicate and make virtual love via SMS Chat.

Virtual Singles Event

You can organize a virtual singles event where everyone competes in a scavenger hunt using cell phone cameras and GPS technologies. Why not have teams compete for who can take the most photos of items off a checklist that are located at specific coordinates? You can time-stamp your photos to ensure the photos are taken during this Virtual Singles Event. Your event coordinator can set up everything using wireless technologies.

Instant Matchmaking

In Asia, singles are now being connected instantly in bars via cell phone matchmaking services. You sign up for the service by filling out a questionnaire with your favorite hobbies and interests. When you are within 50 feet of someone with the same interests, you instantly receive a text message and photo that lets you know that a possible match is nearby. In the U.S., there is a similar service called

Dodgeball that was just purchased by Google.com. Stay tuned to see how this Instant Matchmaking service catches on in the States.

To help you succeed with virtual love connections, check out these Dating Dos and Don'ts. Avoid dating bloopers and increase your odds with wireless technologies by following these advice tips.

Virtual Love Dating Do's and Don'ts

Wireless Connector	Dating Do's	Dating Don'ts
Voicemail	Smile and leave fun, upbeat, and short voicemails with a specific plan of action. You want to smile so they hear a positive tone in your voice.	Don't leave rejection or breakup voicemails—unless the guy has just pushed you to the limit.
Text Messages	Send fun, short, and timely messages to spark romance using flirty SMS abbreviations (example: G8 = great).	Avoid long messages with way too much information.
Instant Messaging	Keep it simple and accent the positive. Let your sense of humor shine for the best results. Invite a phone conversation sooner versus later if the IM exchange goes well.	Steer clear of conversations about exes, finance, and your weaknesses. End IM sessions within minutes so you don't waste time online with someone who isn't a match.
Photo Phones	Share fun images when you look marvelous and happy. What are your best colors? What is your favorite outfit that makes you feel really good inside?	Don't send a photo with your ex or other men in the photo. You want the guy to focus on you. There is no need to bring others into the dating equation.
Video Phones	Act like you are being interviewed by CNN. Combine the visual with the voice by using a positive and upbeat tone. Wear something that makes you feel great, use makeup basics, and wear your colors for the best results.	Avoid sounding flat in your tone of voice. Don't record videos when you've just gotten out of bed or had a bad day.

While wireless technologies can fast-forward virtual love connections, watch out for misinterpretations and substituting other
forms of communications too soon. The tone of a text message is
often hard to judge, especially if sarcasm comes into play. The
videos and photos still have room to improve before we receive a
high-quality image, which may give you the wrong impression.
Consequently, I recommend virtual love as a complementary part
of the courtship equation. Regular phone contact and face-to-
face communication need to be a high priority early in the virtual
love game. Use wireless technologies to create unexpected pleasures and stir up romance.

Expanding Your Home Box Wrap-up

As you open yourself up to New Era dating options, remember
that the success key is to continually expand your Home Box.
Engage in new interests, focus on diversifying your foundation of
friends, take advantage of romantic wireless connections, and
expand your community.

Above all else, start to use the vast array of technology out
there to broaden your bandwidth. Now that you're engaged
proactively in your Man Hunt and you're armed with the necessary tools in the form of confidence, a dating toolkit, and virtual
love connectors, are you open to entering the New Era of dating?
Are you ready to enter the Web?

5

―――☙―――

Enter the Widest Web

HAVE YOU EVER sat home and wondered, Where are all the good men? Wonder no more. Because everyone works longer hours with limited amounts of free time today, singles are continually adopting new dating entry vehicles. New Era daters are accepting these new ways to meet candidates because they greatly expand their search options for Ms. or Mr. Right. Have you ever considered trying Internet matchmaking to find a man?

With over 50 million singles in the U.S. signing up for online dating services, you just can't afford to overlook this virtual love option. This avenue is now a widely accepted way to meet your mate. By taking advantage of the New Era dating trends and tools and meeting dates on the Internet, you can create a SMARTer approach to the Man Hunt. If you have any hesitation, think about this comment from a wise woman who met her husband online. "I'm more amazed by people that don't do Internet dating. What wouldn't you do to find happiness?" (You can read more about her success story at the end of this chapter.)

Stepping into Internet Dating

I, too, was initially hesitant about taking the plunge and using Internet matchmaking sites to date, but a close 40-something male friend encouraged me by saying, "It is like walking into a room with thousands of strangers and instantly finding people with whom you share common interests and goals." I decided to go for it, and discovered that women definitely have the demographic advantage here. Even though many people are not willing to publicly admit they have tried it, more fish are jumping in this wide ocean than you'd think. And because there are so many more men online, you really cannot pass up this opportunity as a woman.

A happily married couple who met on the Internet shared their encouraging story with me. She is a 40-year-old accountant who married a 42-year-old financial manager in Washington, D.C. While she was in the process of moving to Washington, D.C., from Arizona, she met her soul mate online. When I asked about what initially drew her to him, she said, "I liked the conversational tone of his emails. He wrote about Al King and it made me laugh." Both of them had been Internet dating for months without finding a mate.

The couple discovered many similarities and hit it off immediately. For example, they both had grown up in Phoenix and attended Arizona State. After three emails and two phone calls, they decided to set up a date. After the first date for drinks in Arlington, Virginia, they became almost inseparable outside of the office and agreed to date exclusively. She explained their relationship progression to me: "We shared our likes and dislikes and life experiences with each other." Within five months, they were engaged, and married at the end of eleven months. The accountant's advice to you:

"It's a numbers game. The more you put yourself in situations where you can meet people, the better your odds of finding the one." And with 50 million singles in this pond, internet dating provides the best odds.

Another woman I know, a 33-year-old single mother, met someone special through Internet dating. Not only did they share similar professions and an interest in sports, he was intelligent, adventurous, considerate, and very attractive. On their first dinner date she commented, "I knew that he was high quality when he offered to pay for the babysitter." The couple dated for approximately two years, and now maintains a friendship.

A girlfriend commented to me, "I think the Internet is the number one way for the 45-to-60-year-olds to find someone today." She expanded by telling me about two couples in their 50s and 60s who met over the Internet. She explained, "The first couple is a fifty-six-year-old nurse who married a fifty-six-year-old broker. The second couple is a sixty-year-old widow who is in a long-term relationship with a sixty-four-year-old retired doctor."

No matter what your age, the Internet provides dating results. But you have to be patient to find Mr. Right. You may not meet him right off the bat, so don't be discouraged. Eventually, you will find some very viable high-quality candidates. Take the experience of this 35-year-old woman who told me, "I went out on forty-eight Internet dates before I found my man, but now we have been happily married for three years."

The Ego Boost Benefit

While initially you may not want to step into the Internet dating scene, there are many rewards to trying this approach, provided you use the Net SMART Safety Tips (more on this later in this chapter). One 38-year-old business development manager finally convinced me to take the plunge by saying, "It's flattering to receive so many emails from men. The experience is a big ego boost."

How can you benefit from the Internet Dating Ego Boost? Well, first of all, the Internet will show you that there are plenty of men out there interested in meeting you. This attention is especially helpful if you've been suffering from a loss of hope or feelings of frustration over how to meet men. And if you are not receiving emails, update your profile or try a different dating site.

By successfully meeting and dating a variety of men, many of whom will be interested in you, you'll experience this Internet Dating Ego Boost. Online dating increased one girlfriend's confidence so much that she attracted a soul mate whom she met at a car wash! By setting low initial expectations, she avoided being disappointed and found the ego strokes to be invaluable. When she signed up with an Internet dating service and posted a personal ad online she received approximately fifteen emails per day in the first week, which eventually slowed to three emails per day at the six-week mark. She never had to initiate contact because her inbox was flooded with solicitations from inquiring male minds.

Another one of my girlfriends who is actively Internet dating told me, "I taped a sticky note on my phone that says 'The Ego Boost Benefit' after reading your book to encourage me to keep dating." Are you ready for an ego boost? This numbers game strategy takes the edge off your dating encounters because you now have options. When you have choices, you will feel more empowered and confident in your decisions. You are more likely to walk away from the nice guy and keep moving until you find Mr. Wonderful because you have the power to choose.

The Internet Dating Process

So how does Internet dating work? The best way to start is to sign up with an Internet matchmaking service. These websites allow you to scan personal ads posted by men or to post your own ad for a fee. You can either write to someone whose ad you like or you can wait to see who writes to you. The benefit of the site is that it keeps all correspondence between you confidential. Neither one of you has to know anything about the other that you don't want to reveal. So, if you correspond with someone and choose not to continue the correspondence, he'll never know how to reach you again. There are many sites out there; you just need to find the one for you. Simply run an Internet search for "Internet Dating Services," and quite a few will come up. There are all kinds of sites, matchmaking sites specific to certain religions (Christian, Jewish, etc.), special interests (skiing or writing), politics (red, blue, and green parties), and even sites for pet lovers. Each one has unique characteristics, so investigate a bit and ask your friends which ones they like.

Sites and Strategies—My Experience

After two years of resisting Internet dating, I finally decided to step into the arena and eventually tried many different Internet dating sites (as research, of course). Each site had a different personality and approach. I share my experiences with each service, but I'm not you, so I recommend that you try several yourself to discover which one provides the best results for you.

- Slow Start: I decided to start out safe and slow. The first site, The Right Stuff, was aimed at Ivy League graduates. I felt more comfortable using this venue as a starting point because the service's screening process was more extensive. You needed to mail written proof of your graduation from an Ivy League school prior to being placed on the site. Unfortunately, I only received a few responses and went on two dates in six months. The mechanics of the site did not make for easy online matchmaking and I needed to find more action. So long, Ivy League.

- Join the Crowds: I decided to venture into a more broad-based site, Match.com, and was overwhelmed by the response. I received more than two hundred emails in the first month alone. I also learned quickly about the female demographic advantage in the Internet dating arena. In comparison, a male friend of mine who is a 34-year-old actor told me, "I haven't received any inquiries from women in two months."

- Test Drives: After interviewing a 52-year-old friend for this book about his online dating experience, I decided to try a one-week trial subscription with another more popular site, Matchmaker.com. I received forty responses during the first week on this third site. Based on my previous experience, I was more prepared to handle the selection process for all the emails I received.

- In addition, I tried a two-week free trial on a fourth Internet dating site, Blinddatetv.com. This site allowed me to block emails from bad guys. I felt safer with this feature and used it when I came across IPs (Internet Psychos). You can read more about these online thrill seekers in Part IV's SMART ABC Man Codes.

- Personally Test Route: After interviewing an active female dater for this book, I also checked out a site called eHarmony.com that sets up singles based on a series of personality test questions. It took me a few hours to set up the profile, but it was a great exercise. While the photo check is the first step toward identifying a Love Match(LM), the personality plays just as important a role when finding a long-term partner, so I was willing to give it a try. After you complete the tests, the service sends you a few good matches and advises you to "treat them like gold." If you like the brief description of the guy, you can start engaging in several stages of correspondence that includes additional multiple-choice and short-essay questions regarding your likes and dislikes. If you make it to the final stages, you can then start sharing free-form emails and phone calls. While I had to drop out of the game due to the fact that I had too many Mr. Right candidates at the time, my girlfriend met with three men using this personality test route and felt a connection with all three. Because of her 100 percent success rate, you might want to take the time to try this site out.

- Feature Rich: You will also find many fun features on different dating sites now. I had a blast testing the Yahoo!Personals and Lavalife.com features. Both sites are offering video greetings that will make you laugh out loud. You can read more about these features later in this chapter.

- Expand Your Virtual Network: Friendster.com and My-space.com are hot new sites that allow you to expand your network and make love connections online. You create your own community, invite people to join your network, or you might get invited to join someone else's. Each member must provide a profile and his or her interests. You also need to supply your reason for joining. You might want to join for friendship, dates, a serious relationship, or "activity partners." Friendster is like going to a bar to meet people through friends, while Match.com is more like a blind date.

  It's your choice which way to go online. My advice is to try several options and see what you like best. Let the fun features fast track your experience so you can quickly know when to say, "Next," or take a closer look.

The Net Steps Process

After you've found a site you like, follow these 13 steps to find and identify your Mr. Right candidates:

Internet Dating Process

1. Enter by Registering for an Internet Dating Service
2. Write an Enticing Personal Profile
3. Add at Least Two Recent Photos
4. Receive a Flood of Emails from Men
5. Screen the Emails and Profile Resumes
6. Flirt Online with a Few Good Men
7. Move Toward Phone Contact or Move On
8. Pick Up the Phone for a Pre-screening Call
9. Set Up Coffee Talk or a Casual First Date
10. Take the KISS Test
11. Accept a Second Date If He Passes Go
12. Third Encounters and Beyond
13. Identify Mr. Right Candidates

1. Enter by Registering for an Internet Dating Service

You can easily sign up as a member or just test out an Internet dating site. Most Internet sites have a similar process. You will be given a username and password to protect access to your information. You will be asked to enter a credit card for payment or sign up for a free trial. Most dating sites have free trial periods so you can take a test drive for one to two weeks and determine whether this vehicle works for you before paying anything. If you want to start communicating with other members, you are usually asked to start paying for the service, but you can first see who responds to your profile.

2. Write an Enticing Personal Profile

While you will be asked to complete a series of multiple-choice questions about your vital statistics (age, age range that you want to date, interests) for your personal profile, use the profile headline and essays as marketing tools to entice suitors. The headline should be short and catchy. For example, I coached a 40-year-old woman in New York City to change her headline from "City Girl" to "French Dinner at 3:00 a.m.?" to attract younger men. The essays usually include a brief description of you and what you are seeking in a mate. Make your descriptions light-hearted, short, and include at least one marketing hook to encourage responses. Remember, you want to maximize your selection by boosting your numbers, so make every word count in a personal profile! I recommend five to seven sentence paragraphs versus the six-inch-long novels that can put your potential date to sleep online (see sample profiles in the Internet Dating Coaching Tips section). Before you post your profile, you might want to run it past a girlfriend or, even better, a male friend for an objective view as to how it comes across. Ask them to be honest—Does your profile create an attractive presentation and bring out the best in you?

3. Add at Least Two Recent Photos

Ask a girlfriend to take some current photos of you. Either use a digital camera or have the photo scanned onto a disk so you can upload it onto your computer. Upload a photo that makes you look good, but it should also be realistic and look like you. It's horrible to meet someone for the first time who looks nothing like their online photo. A 39-year-old executive who met her husband online shared, "I used a photo that was okay versus great because I didn't want anyone to be surprised." You will have much more success dating online with a photo and it's even better to add several pictures with different viewpoints. Photos of you engaged in your hobbies can also help build bridges. Outdoor hobby photos that include sailing, hiking, and biking will especially attract more men to your profile. Don't worry about adding a photo because no one will know your name unless you decide to tell them. (You can read more photo tips in the Internet Dating Coaching Tips section.)

4. Receive a Flood of Emails from Men

Once you set up the profile, you will probably find yourself singing, "It's Raining Men." There are so many more men than women trying Internet dating that the odds are in your favor. If you do not receive a big response initially, go back to your girl-friends or close male confidants and ask for more feedback on your profile. Sites actively promote new members so you should be overwhelmed in the first month. Eventually, the flood will recede and the stream of emails becomes more manageable. Updating your profile periodically will also stir up more activity if you find yourself in a lull. Change the headline and revise your essays at least once a month to attract new candidates.

5. Screen the Emails and Profile Resumes

Similar to hiring an employee, your next step is to screen the emails you receive. When email introductions spark your interest, consider the resumes by reviewing their profiles to search for top-notch candidates. Determine your selection criteria and then scan their profiles to determine who should be eliminated from contention immediately. (See a more in-depth discussion on "Weeding Through Email" later in this chapter.) You are now ready to write back to anyone who makes the first cut.

6. Flirt Online with a Few Good Men

Once you find a few good men, flirt online with short, sincere, and light-hearted email responses. Try making a comment about something in their profile. For example, you might write, "I saw that you like to travel. What is your favorite place to visit?" You will find that a short series of emails follows if there is sincere interest on the part of the candidate. Limit emails to a few sentences because let's face it, guys have a short attention span. Weave in your sense of humor in emails, but don't go overboard or you might be misunderstood. If you get into too much information in these initial emails, you may share something very personal only to never hear from the other party again. If his responses are sporadic and inconsistent, eliminate him. This passive approach is a sign of lack of interest.

Start the Sparks Online

Many dating coaching clients have asked me for email examples. Here are a few short examples that may give you some ideas for how to start the sparks online:

- "Your profile caught my attention for several reasons—I love NYC, love Europe, and have been part of the Internet entrepreneur world. So where did you live in Europe? I love the carpe diem lifestyle and enjoy being spontaneous."
- "Thank you for returning my wink. I like what you wrote about trusting your gut—I think it is really the most important indicator of many things in life and relationships. I will also try almost anything once. What do you like to do for fun?"
- "It's great to hear from you—and you stumped me with your question about where to find tapas—I had them while visiting Barcelona and really need to find them in Los Angeles. Do you have any suggestions?"

---

7. Move Toward Phone Contact or Move On

If your gut is not good, move on after a few emails or Instant Messenger exchanges. You don't want to spend too much time online because you really can't gauge the chemistry until the first date. After three exchanges, if a guy is not talking about a first date, just say, "Next!"

If your gut is good, immediately move toward a pre-screening call. I would often write to guys after one or two emails, "I'm not a big fan of too many email exchanges, would you like to talk on the phone?" If he asks for your phone number, ask for his number or give him your cell to protect your privacy.

8. Pick Up the Phone for a Pre-screening Call

Don't be afraid to call the guy. He wants you to call if he gave you his number. However, be SMART and safe when you place the call. Use Caller ID blocking (*67) to protect your privacy so your phone number won't be revealed on the first call. Then go for it. But remember, SMART women are not aggressive or desperate, so keep the call casual and light. You are simply pre-screening the candidates, similar to pre-screening employees. Don't spend hours on the phone telling him your whole life story. I made the mistake of talking for two hours to a guy one night only to find no chemistry connection on the first date. What a waste of energy! Simply listen to his tone of voice and test whether the conversation is easy or a struggle before deciding whether you want to accept an invitation for a first date from a guy.

9. Set Up Coffee Talk or Casual First Date

After you have weeded out undesirable candidates via email and the phone, you may be ready for face-to-face contact with someone. If you click on the phone with the Man Candidate, the next step is to set up Coffee Talk. (See more in Chapter 10.) You can let him make the call to action (where he suggests that you meet in person) and then agree only to meet in a safe neutral place. I like to talk for about 15–20 minutes and then say I have to go. If a guy does not jump in and ask me out, then I just say, "It was nice to talk to you," and get off the phone fast. If you do meet, I recommend picking a coffee shop because it is safe and alcohol-free. (Alcohol will blur your ability to assess the candidate. Employers don't interview job seekers while drinking, do they?) Don't recommend the shop on your block either. You are not ready to give out your address at this stage. Suggest a public meeting place close by, but not where you will bump into the neighbors or could be followed home.

10. Take the KISS Test

When you meet for the first time, relax. You don't have to prove anything to anyone. However, it's in your best interest to be dressed for success since he could be Mr. Right. Be courteous and interested in what he has to say, and focus on *your* evaluation. If you are not drawn to his personality and physically attracted to him, the deal is over. He will be doing the same thing, so don't feel guilty. The bottom line is that your primary concern should be to ask yourself, "Would I ever want to kiss this guy?" You can read more about First Date Tests in Chapter 10.

11. Accept a Second Date if He Passes Go

If he passes Go and you realize that you might want to kiss him, let him schedule a second date. Most men like to take the lead in the early stages of their Woman Hunt, so let him make the suggestions and figure out the details for the second date. If he asks you to call him, give it one shot before you close the books. If you do not hear back from him, it is okay. Move on to your next candidate and don't take it too personally. Remember, you do not want to be with someone unless he thinks you are the hottest thing out there.

12. Third Encounters and Beyond

Once you agree to meet him for a third encounter, expect a more proper date. Meet for a walk in the park, drinks, dinner, or any other plan he suggests. Just keep it safe by not having him pick you up at your house and not letting him take you home. Continue to keep your home and work addresses confidential. If subsequent dates aren't well planned in the sense that he calls you at the last minute, suggests something tacky, or is too quick to get you into his house or into yours, eliminate him. Remember, many guys use a third date rule as a goal to get you into the bedroom. You probably want to at least pass this milestone before you let your guard down.

If he continues to pass Go on subsequent dates, start asking more questions, take your time getting to know him, observe his actions, and get the facts. See more on this topic in Quick Qualifiers and Showstoppers in Chapter 11. Also, start to look at him closer by using the Love Match Pre-Test and LIFE Match questions in Chapter 12 and the SMART ABC Man Codes in Part IV.

13. Identify Mr. Right Candidates

If he makes it past the third date, then you are dealing with a Mr. Right candidate. You do not necessarily need to drop all other offers or grant more access to yourself or your life, but it is time to start asking tougher questions to uncover any true partnership potential using the LIFE Match Game. You are about to engage in the Dating Assessment Dance and should consider this discovery period an exciting part of the Man Hunt journey. Refer to Part III for more resources to help you to identify Mr. Right.

Weeding Through Email— The Net Selection Process

Once I was up and running in the Internet dating world, friends wondered how I sorted through all those emails to find the potential deals. It wasn't that difficult. Based on my experiences and interviews with female friends, here are some tips on narrowing the Internet dating field.

Here's what I found effective when sorting through Internet dating emails from male candidates:

- *Eliminate Impersonal Men* My first step was to eliminate anyone who seemed obviously insincere. Usually these men only looked at the photo and clearly had never read my profile. That included the many men who sent me poems and sales pitches without my name in the introduction. These guys are engaging in mass email campaigns and their cast-a-wide-net-and-see-what-gets-hauled-in strategy is beneath consideration. These electronic form letters deserve to go the way of all junk mail. One girlfriend commented to me: "If all they write me is, 'Hi Sally, you are cute, check out my profile and let me know what you think,' then I delete their inquiry."

An email introduction from a man should indicate that some thought went into its composition. It should demonstrate that the author actually read your profile and considered it by expressing interest in a mutual hobby or belief.

EMAILS DECODED

If you receive this email . . .

What's a girl to do?

"New England is a great place. Just went to a Mets / Yankees game. Great game. Anyway, my profile is attached. Let me know if you are interested."

This guy read your profile. The email is short and to the point. If his photos and vitals look good to you, take a closer look at his profile.

"I'm single and have a great life. I hope to marry again when I find the right gal. A couple of my favorite activities are dancing West Coast Swing and taking long rides in my stock Model T. I seek a fun lady who hasn't forgotten what it means to be a woman. If you're looking for only a friend, pass me by. If you're looking for a lot more with a good guy who has a lot to offer, drop me a line."

This guy is sending out a mass email campaign. There is nothing personalized in the email. It's all about him and his marketing pitch–NEXT!

"The Huntington Library is a great place. I grew up close to it. We used to sneak in after hours and mess around. It's actually in San Marino. Where do you get good tapas around here?"

This response shows a sense of adventure, an appreciation of art, and ends with an inviting question—take a closer look at this guy.

"Just a quick note to say Hi and let you know I'm very interested. I hore things are going good. Would like to talk to you. Love ya"

This email is short, but has typos and is way too casual for my taste. "Love ya"? NEXT!

"Thanks for writing. So what other exciting things do you enjoy? I love to surf, that's my main sports passion for the last decade, also rock climbing and cycling and hiking. Tell me more! BTW, I think your pics are lovely and your profile smart."

This guy is interested. He's taken the time to write a personal email—take a closer look.

"I enjoyed your profile and was wondering if you might enjoy mine . . . let me know if it piques your interest."

This guy did not read your profile. Unless he looks really cute to you—NEXT!

If a candidate makes a sincere effort in emails, then you can proceed to check out his photo for a chemistry test.

Look for a Chemistry Connection

The next step is to check out someone's photo. The best photo profiles include multiple pictures with headshots, hobby shots, and full body views. A word of caution should be added here because I discovered that many dates lie about their age and use misleading old photos. You might want to ask him about the age of the photo if you are suspicious. Look for hobby or vacation shots and ask them to tell you more about when they participated in the hobby, or visited the remote location depicted to gauge the age of the photo. Style of hair and dress are also giveaways for dated shots.

If your Internet suitor is wearing a hat in his photo, chances are that there's nothing growing under it. While baldness was not a deal breaker for me, others might feel differently. In addition to the hat trick, several men may provide pictures of themselves with dark hair. However, when you meet, you may find them to be completely gray.

If someone only posts a head shot photo, he may be hiding something about his body. Double check the height and weight listed in his profile to see if the numbers add up. If someone states that he is 5'10" and weighs 250 pounds, you may want to ask for more photos before meeting in person.

Don't overlook the importance of the photo as the first step in testing the Chemistry Connection. One 37-year-old marketing executive told me, "I first focused on reading the profile and then looked at the pictures later." While she found men with similar interests, they often failed her KISS Test. As a result of these failures, she shifted her selection process to checking out the photos first.

While everyone tries to put his best image forward in Internet dating profiles, nothing can completely replace the in-person meeting for a more reliable KISS Test.

Beyond the Checklist

Once you have established some mental and physical connections based on his email and photo, the next step is to further evaluate whether your interests, priorities, and personality match via email. I created a few key questions that I would ask several men and then compare their responses. For example, I often asked about their favorite country, because international travel is important to me.

I also asked Man Candidates to describe their ideal day to see how they might want to spend it with me. If the candidate liked getting up at 6:30 A.M., I knew this man did not have a chance because I am not a morning person. If the candidate responded that his ideal day consisted of having sex five times with me, I realized he was pretty much looking for one thing and that this was a bit forward for my taste. However, I connected well with the active types who enjoyed hikes, museums, movies, and cuddling by the fireplace in the evening.

End Communications with Perpetual Emailers

Beware of the Internet dating candidate who is a perpetual emailer. These men will email back and forth with you until your eyes cross, but somehow never find the opportunity to call or meet for coffee. Set a limit for this first phase of Internet courtship. If it seems that your candidate would rather be a pen pal than a suitor, move on fast. This behavior could be a sign that a man is only in it for the entertainment value, is a Married but Available (MBA) (read more about these men in Part IV, or otherwise emotionally unavailable.

One 39-year-old executive girlfriend told me, "I was often frustrated by men who never wanted to make the first move to ask for a phone number or suggest coffee." She exchanged emails with one candidate at least five times and there was no effort on his part to connect on the phone or meet for coffee. While he wrote eloquently and they seemed to share many similar interests, she just had to stop writing when it was clear their interaction wasn't going anywhere. He never followed up, and it left her with an empty feeling when the correspondence ended.

Beware of These Other Red Flags

In addition to the Net Selection Tips above, there can be any number of red flags in those first early emails. It pays to look for them. Here are a few warning signals:

- Spelling errors and poor grammar. This guy lacks education or is too lazy to be sure his writing is correct. Next.
- Brings up sex. That's what this guy is looking for. Next.
- Writes a long heartfelt letter. This guy is needy. Next.
- Too much information. You do not need to know his whole life story when you haven't even met in person to test the chemistry. Next.
- Talks about his ex. Avoid men who share details about their exes in your initial email exchanges. If he is bringing it up, he is probably not over her. Next.
- Asks you about your ex. Men don't need to know about your ex in the early email stages. Everyone has a past and you are obviously over it or you would not be Man Hunting. Next.
- Recites the resume. Is he trying too hard to prove himself to you by listing his life achievements in emails before a first date? You don't even know if you want to kiss him. Next.

Watch out for these email red flags that can save you from spending hours and valuable energy focusing on the wrong guy. If you see these warning signs, don't be afraid to just say, "Next." And once you start dating, remind yourself that if you are not "star struck" by the third date, you need to forget about them fast!

The Male Perspective on Internet Dating

During my research, I received hundreds of comments from men about the Internet dating selection process. Here are two representative samples of male thinking on the topic.

Bachelor #1's Internet Dating Story

This 36-year-old consultant found his wife through Internet dating. After using advanced search features, this man found five most likely to succeed candidates and ended up with a life partner.

The couple found an immediate connection. After two weeks of dating, he knew she was "the one." He described his mate as "thirty-four years old, never been married, and an excellent communicator." He likes the give-and-take dialogue in their relationship and says their discussions are "balanced versus competitive."

Bachelor #1's Internet Dating Advice

- Avoid long and demanding descriptions of what you are seeking in a partner.
- Avoid too much detail about yourself in your profile because it can be overwhelming.
- Provide a general description of yourself with enough information to spark an interest.
- Keep emails short when corresponding with potential Man Candidates.
- Be open-minded and approach your search as an adventure. Do not use a sexy picture unless you are only seeking sex.

Bachelor #2's Internet Dating Story

I also interviewed a 47-year-old fundraiser who has been dating using the Internet for some time. While he hasn't found a long-term commitment yet, he has found several relationships by Internet dating.

Bachelor #2's Internet Dating Advice

- Use more than one photo of yourself. It's easy to find one good shot, but multiple photos can present a better all-around image. More photos put men at ease because they sense that they know what they are getting.
- Don't feel intimidated or embarrassed about your age. There are plenty of men looking for peer-aged partners.
- Try to match education levels. Because this candidate is well educated and worldly, he seeks an intellectual partner who can share his interests.
- Be truthful about your statistics. You want to hook up with

someone in person eventually and the truth about your height, weight, or age will come out. What's worse, being rejected by a stranger because of who you really are, or being rejected after someone's expressed interest in you because you turned out to be dishonest?

- Try to put some thought into the essay in your web profile. The idea is to give someone a sense of who you are without getting too personal. Bachelor #2 told me, "I reviewed the essay answers for signs of someone who was curious about the world, had a sense of humor, and was naturally centered." While these qualities are not always easy to detect, he said, "You can eliminate the obvious opposites."

Internet Dating Coaching Tips

After testing more than seven dating sites and developing a "five Must Haves" strategy for creating successful Internet dating profiles, I started offering my services as a Dating Coach to help singles set goals, update profiles, and post great photos online based on my background in management, marketing, and photography. The results were very positive, and I wanted to share a few examples with you.

As a Dating Coach, I offer Profile Reviews, Profile Makeovers, and Photo Makeovers. To view my dating coaching service and receive free confidence boosters, visit www.smartmanhunting.com. If you have a profile created already, you might want to consider making a few updates based on these tips.

Profile Review

In order to help men and women find love online, I review the five Must Haves for their Internet dating profile and send them some very honest feedback. These profile tips are based on interviews with hundreds of active daters and happily married couples.

5 Must-Haves for a Great Online Profile

1. Write a Fun Headline
2. Post Attractive Photos
3. Keep It Light
4. Add a Marketing Pitch
5. Encourage Responses

1. Write a Fun Headline

You are trying to grab someone's attention so you use a catchy headline. You might try "Moonlight and Margaritas?" or "Pizza and Pinot?" to make it interactive and stand out in the crowd.

2. Post Attractive Photos

Many people don't realize how important the online photo can be in making a great first impression. Ask a friend to take a close-up photo and then one of you doing a favorite hobby. You can read more about photo tips in the Photo Makeover section on page 93.

3. Keep It Light

Keep your essays light and save your life story until after candidates pass the KISS Test on the first date. You want to find out whether you would ever want to kiss the person before you get too personal.

4. Add a Marketing Pitch

What makes you unique? Do you like to play guitar? Sail? Or have a big family? By sharing something unique about you, you're much more likely to attract the right dates.

5. Encourage Responses

You want to encourage a response from your profile and show an interest in the other person. Try asking, "What do you like to do for fun?" or "What is your dream vacation?" so that your profile invites a response. Remember you are playing a numbers game so the more responses you receive, the better your odds of finding a match.

Profile Makeovers

For Profile Makeovers, I send out a 10-question survey to gather the facts, and then schedule a follow-up phone interview to get more information if necessary. Using my Internet dating profile tips, I've worked with singles from Seattle to Detroit to New York to Washington, D.C., to Napa and in between to fine-tune and write their profiles.

Avoid being a Hallmark greeting card online. When I read many profiles, I find them empty and way too general. If your profile looks like this one that I found online, I must ask, where's the beef? What are we going to talk about?

Avoid Writing a Hallmark Greeting Card Profile

"ABOUT ME: Open, receptive, feminine, charming, casual, energetic, affectionate, fun-loving, sophisticated, humorous, problem-solver, healthy, team player, communicative, multi-talented, high integrity and morals. Beauty is in the eye of the beholder!

ABOUT YOU: A true gentleman. An achiever. Someone who knows who he is, yet is open to learning and growing. You can fill in the blanks if it's a Match, natch! I am interested in someone who is joyous about their life, someone who is kind, giving, and wants a committed relationship-marriage."

The dating introduction on any Internet dating profile is the most important essay. The topics are usually "About Me and Who I'd Like to Date." When I work with singles to enhance their profile, we spend the most time updating this introduction to make them sound unique and sexy. I work with both women and men across the country. Below are two before and after examples to show you how you can go from a Hallmark greeting card message to a unique marketing message.

Profile Makeovers—Before and After

Makeover #1—Chicago, IL, Creative Babe

Before—Not Your Typical Girl

My friends would describe me as fun to be around, with a great sense of humor. I love having friends over to BBQ in the summer or host get-togethers at my house. I love working in my garden, puttering around my house, shopping, trying new restaurants. On Sundays, I enjoy checking out a matinee, or watching an old movie on Turner, drinking coffee and reading the paper, maybe visit a local craft fair or flea market. If I could go anywhere, I would be lying on a beach or by a pool somewhere tropical, drinking a frosty cocktail. I like action and war pictures, being obsessed with my yard. I'm not your typical girl.

After—The Last Fling?

Are you ready for crème brulee with a twist? Because I love to learn new things, I recently decided to be adventurous and take a cooking class. For the final exam, my girlfriend and I had to pre-pare a gourmet meal. We made Cornish hens, a cheese soufflé (which fell when we brought it to the table) and crème brulee (have you ever used a blow torch?). Besides food fables, I love checking out live music at Ravinia or the Navy Pier. I also get a kick out of the end-of-the-summer festival called "The Last Fling." And have you ever seen a house with 400 tulips? I got a little car-ried away with my gardening last year and my house ended up looking like the horticulture building. I just had to laugh out loud.

My guy has a positive outlook on life, a quick wit, and enjoys my animated conversations. He gets a kick out of my brilliant new ideas and can be a cheerleader. He's game to check out new restaurants with me or just kick back, order a pizza, and watch a few classics on Turner (The *Thin Man* series is one of my favorites). We might plan a trip to St. Lucia and sit on a beach drinking frosty tropical cocktails. So tell me about you. What are your turn-ons? What do you like to do for fun?

Makeover #2—Long Beach, CA, Classic Rock Man

Before—Down by the Sea

I know they say never to talk politics, but I'm afraid that would be virtually impossible. I love to speak passionately about politics, religion, sex, and everything else that matters. Fortunately, after living in Southern California for most of my life, I've got a firm grasp on what's important. My friends and family, they are great. Through my involvement in a non-profit health care organization, I've been able to meet some amazing people who also care about the health care problem in the inner city. Back before my days of blue suits and sixty-hour weeks, I was a former elementary school spelling bee champ, a soccer player, and an SDSU graduate. Because I'm the youngest of four sons, I was raised on classic rock (Led Zeppelin, Pink Floyd, The Beatles), so forgive me if I'm not quite the urban hipster. I can, however, play guitar and can cover pretty much any popular song prior to 1990. And yes, I do take requests.

After—Beach Art

Are you looking for a surfer with a great family, friends, career, and interest in the arts? I've lived in Southern CA most of my life, but one of my favorite memories is of a summer day in NYC when I walked from 54th Street to the Guggenheim to the Met to the Whitney and back through Central Park. It was exhilarating to see so much art, history, and architecture in one day. Because I'm the youngest of four sons, I was raised on classic rock (Led Zeppelin, Pink Floyd, The Beatles). I play guitar and cook a mean spaghetti. And yes, I do take requests.

I'm looking for a committed relationship with a special someone who can also be a best friend. We enjoy just being together and click in many ways. I have dreams of watching the fall leaves change in my Maine cabin with you. We could sit on the porch staring at the stunning mountain view with a blanket wrapped around us and make wishes on the shooting stars. Enough about me. What do you like to do for fun?

Which profile makes you want to email them? Which one sounds like a more interesting date?

Photo Makeovers

Just like dating is a numbers game, taking great photos involves a lot of film. Most dating sites will tell you that a good photo can mean ten times more hits, so go wild with the camera to get a few amazing shots. As a corporate photographer, I was trained to take 100 photos to get five good ones. Ok, you probably don't need to take 100 photos, but take enough to get a few good shots (ask a friend to take at least one roll of 24 pictures of you) and wear a few different outfits so they don't look like they were all taken on the same day.

Your picture is your first impression online so make it count using these five fun photo tips.

1. Focus on You
2. Dress for a First Date
3. Accent Your Style
4. Find the Right Lighting
5. Select a Complementary Background

If you prefer to go to the pros, there are many photography services out there who are ready to make you look marvelous online. They can take casual shots that make great first impressions! No matter who takes the photos, you can use these tips to attract more dates online.

1. Focus on You

For the primary photo especially, post photos that include you and only you. Because singles want to see you first versus your whole package (the dog, family, softball team, etc.), this photo should be all about you. You can include others in secondary shots, but photos are really about attracting dates versus introducing family and friends. A 35-year-old lawyer asked me for advice on his profile photo. He actually cropped the picture, but you could still see a woman's arm around his shoulder and her long hair. Even though he told me she was his sister, how many women are going to say, "Next," to this guy because they never asked? You will get the best results if the photos focus on you.

2. Dress for a First Date

You want to post a casual shot where you are dressed for a first date. Avoid the corporate mug shots where you might look too serious. I coached a guy to remove his corporate coat and tie photo and replace it with a photo he liked from a family birthday party. In this much more appealing photo, he was wearing a black button-down shirt and had a fun and inviting smile. After this cool casual photo was posted, he received 35 emails the next day from women.

3. Accent Your Style

You want to pick out colors that are good for your skin tone. You've now had a Style Makeover so you know your colors. If you skipped this step, hire a style consultant or contact an Internet dating photography service and see if they offer advice on colors as part of their packages. For example, a 40-something woman was told by a style consultant, from Lookbetteronline.com "I want you to wear blues and greens versus busy patterns." This advice has been extremely helpful as she selects styles and colors. Wear your colors and styles only in profile photos.

4. Find the Right Lighting

Because lighting can greatly impact the quality of a photo, take your pictures in different settings so you have options. I coached a guy who just started Internet dating. He told me, "Wow, I got so many emails, but I can't see the faces of many women in their photos. I wish that I could see them." If you have a point and shoot camera, you might not be able to adjust the lighting, so you need to use trial and error to find the right light. If you have a more professional camera, there is usually an option for you to set the lighting or set it on automatic. For the best results, try taking shots inside with a red-eye reduction flash, and then outside when the sun is setting to get the best light. Lighting can mean everything in a photo.

5. Select a Complementary Background

The background in a photo can also make a huge difference. Try different backgrounds and make sure nothing is sticking out of someone's head by accident. When a woman recently asked me for photo advice, I immediately saw that her blonde hair was blended into a tan wallpaper background. She was so much more attractive than this photo presented her online. I recommended that she get her photos taken by the pros, and wow, what a difference the professional shots made! Try including a mix of colors by taking photos outside where you can get blues and greens in the background.

Your profile photo is the best way to attract the dates that you desire. When singles are scanning through hundreds of profiles, if not thousands, you want to have a great photo online to catch their attention. If you get a friend to take better profile photos or hire the professionals, I can guarantee that you will get many more dates online.

After using these Profile Makeover and Photo Makeover advice tips, one woman wrote to me about her success story:

Liz, I made most of the profile changes you suggested, thinking, "Okay, I'll do it but I just don't see how it could make a difference. Well, I am happy to report that I was receiving one to two responses per day and since implementing the profile changes, the responses have increased to six to eight per day! It is not the quantity that has impressed me the most, but the quality of the profiles. I am truly amazed and grateful for your helpful suggestions. Thank you!!!!!

You can also entice love online with the right marketing hook and by placing your best image online. To view more profile and online photo tips, visit www.smartmanhunting.com.

Fast Track Online with Fun Features

Once you have set up your Internet Dating Profile, and have posted some hot photographs, you want to take full advantage of the site features that can fast-track your selection process. Every site is different so check out the descriptions. Yahoo! Personals has icebreakers, Match.com lets you send "Winks," and Lavalife.com has "Smiles."

Yahoo! Personals Is Feature-Rich

After researching at least ten internet dating sites, I've found Yahoo! Personals to be the most feature-rich. This service gives you more fun ways to connect in today's fast-track dating world than the others that I researched.

Personalized Voice Greetings—You can now record a short voice greeting that can be posted on your Yahoo! Personals profile. The site encourages you to write a few notes in preparation, and then gives you several opportunities to record the message. After posting my voice greeting, I had a guy email me the next day, "I really like your voice and wanted to meet you." You will get the best response by using a positive and upbeat tone, and highlighting your key selling points. Focus on three unique qualities to keep it short so you invite conversations.

Webcam Views—Yahoo! Personals also provides a Webcam view through their Instant Messenger (IM) feature. During an IM exchange, a guy can send you a link to his Webcam. If you accept, voila, he is now on your screen live. If you have a Webcam, you can also let him have a live view of you. While I do not have a Webcam, I really enjoyed being able to see the guy on my screen while communicating online. It was a blast to see him smile when I cracked a joke in IM or blush if I gave him a compliment. You can also see whether his photos are a good representation of reality. Webcams are opening many new windows for online daters.

Personality Matching—You can also take a fun and interactive personality test on Yahoo! Personals. This quick assessment includes multiple choice, flash animations, and instant results. Once you receive your results, the site immediately tells you whether a potential match is compatible. Based on your *Personality Type* and *Love Style* codes, the system helps you quickly identify desirable dates and potential mates.

Lavalife.com Is Fun

You can check out the fun interactive features on Lavalife.com. My "research" on Lavalife.com made me laugh out loud and drew instant feedback from men. Here are some of my favorite features that you should check out.

Instant Messenger—This site tells you who is online so you can immediately start an IM session versus waiting for an email response. While you are doing the IM thing, you can click on their name and immediately see their profile and decide how far you want to take it. The first night that I tested IM there were "7 waiting" to talk to me. It was important to go through them quickly and spend time sending messages to the guys who met my Mr. Wonderful criteria. All you have to do is send a polite good-bye (easier said than done) and then click "Close" to move on to the next guy. You'll also find that singles can be very bold and flirty in these IM sessions. It's important to keep it light and don't let it go too long before you decide the next move. Try saying, "Sorry, I need to run tonight. Let's talk again" and see how a guy responds. And always follow my smart safety tips in the next section when meeting virtual strangers online.

Backstage Pass—Lavalife.com allows you to have hidden photos on your profile. You always want to post a public photograph, but this site allows you to have a "For your eyes only" photo album. Once you connect with another member online, then you get to decide whether they get a backstage pass to your photos. You can also ask for a pass to their behind the scenes photos. It's easy and adds sparks to the process immediately. And if you are hesitant to post your photos online, this feature is a great option to protect your privacy. I love this backstage pass concept.

Video Greetings—You will also find video greetings on Yahoo! Personals and Lavalife.com sites as we watch this feature start to gain popularity. I had a blast clicking on the "public videos" on Lavalife.com, and then asking members for access to their "private videos." It was very exciting to see and hear someone online so I could make an immediate decision about whether to say, "Next" or take a closer look. However, I must admit most of the videos were poor quality and the guys did not know what to say. Many video greetings sounded too much like a Hallmark Greeting card script, which makes me go to sleep. I hope the content and technology starts improving fast. I did have fun exchanges with guys in Berkeley, California, and Canada, who both made me laugh when I watched their videos.

The Internet dating site feature possibilities are endless online as we continue to make more virtual love connections.

Net SMART Safety Tips

Now that you have some insight into the Internet dating selection process, you should also review these SMART safety guidelines. While the worldwide web can introduce you to all kinds of new men, it can also expose you to men whose intentions may not be honorable or, worse, who are mentally unbalanced. Remember not everyone has the same value system as you. Be cautious when dealing with strangers and take pains to shield your privacy at all costs.

As a Dating Coach, I also answer questions from singles via email. One day I received a very scary question from a woman. She told me, "I met this guy online who lives in a different city. We talk on the phone several hours a day. I'm going to take a bus to see him and get a hotel room." I wrote back immediately and cautioned the woman not to make this trip. He should come to you, and you should not be paying the bill for the first long-distance encounter with a stranger.

While Internet dating requires the most security, these safety guidelines can also apply if you met the man through chat rooms, singles events, speed dating, professional matchmakers, or even serendipity. You need to proceed with caution and protect yourself when dealing with strangers. While you enjoy all the benefits that the New Era dating options offer, let these safety tips guide you through email, phone, and live contacts.

1. Be Anonymous When Connecting Online

First of all, any matchmaking website will give you an account that allows you to stay anonymous. You don't want to give out any information that could identify you when you share your email address either. I recommend that you set up an email account that uses an anonymous name. For example, if you have an email account you use to talk to friends, family, and business associates with your name in it, such as "lizsmith," then do not use this account. I created a separate email account to handle my Man Hunting correspondence under a totally different name that couldn't be used to identify me. Just figure out any kind of fictitious name or "handle." If you'd like, you can use an address that reveals something about yourself such as a hobby or personal attribute. For example, my email address was tied to my interest in sailing. One of my male candidates used "greeneyes" as his email address, which helped him stand out in the crowd.

2. Be Anonymous When Checking Email

If you are dealing with an experienced computer whiz, you may also run into privacy issues when using the Internet. One 34-year-old programmer showed me how he adds a link to his personal website with a tracking ID within his Internet dating solicitation emails. He was not receiving many Internet dating responses from women and wanted to see whether anyone was checking out his website.

Using this tracking ID, he obtains all kinds of information if you click on the link to his website and check out his photographs. He can actually look up the registered name and address for the IP address that you use to access his website. If women click this link from work, he told me, "I can actually see the name and address of their server." He has the information coded so that he can tell who, when, where and how often someone checks out his website photos.

How can you protect your privacy from this type of tracking guru? By clicking on a link to a personal website from a dial-up or cable line that is not connected to a business or school, chances are that he will only find the address for a central server and you are safe. However, if you make a habit of clicking on links with tracking IDs from the office, you might encounter an Internet Psycho (IP) and end up with a surprise visitor at work. While this security breach example is extreme, my programmer friend told me, "Only one woman was ever smart enough to look up the registered address for my website." It's time for us to get SMARTer when using 21st century technology!

3. SMART Phone Contact

After several safe email exchanges, you can cautiously move to the next Internet courtship level. Find time to talk on the phone for fifteen minutes and see if the guy passes your communications check. Because you are still dealing with a virtual stranger, you should use safety guidelines for connecting on the phone. First, ask for the guy's phone number and use Caller ID blocking (*67) when you call him so that your phone number is not revealed to him. You can even use Caller ID blocking on most cell phones, so always try using *67 when placing first calls.

If you are ever at the point where you are comfortable giving out your phone number, use a cell phone or alternate number to your home phone. If someone is really creepy and has your home or work phone number, he can get your address by looking up your number on the Internet. Avoid such a situation by taking extra precautions when giving out personal phone numbers.

Trust your gut instincts when you talk to someone on the phone. If someone makes you feel the least bit uneasy or puts you off in any way, eliminate him. It won't get better if you meet in person. Remember there are plenty of other candidates out there. Next.

4. Continue to Put "Safety First" When Making Live Contact

Once a verbal connection is established on the phone, you can schedule a date. I recommend that you always have these first meetings in a public place and make sure you are familiar with the area before you agree to the location. Meet the candidate at the designated venue—never rely on someone you don't know for a ride. Don't accept a ride home even when you feel as though a candidate is on the up and up. If you drove to the meeting, avoid allowing the candidate to walk you to your car. It's best to even keep the make, model, and license plate of your car a secret. My favorite meeting place is a local coffee shop, but not one too close to home. If you schedule a lunch, drinks, or dinner date, use valet parking when possible so that the candidate, who is primarily a stranger at this stage, cannot follow you to your car when you leave. Lastly, hold your cards close to your chest. Be careful about the amount of information you share during these first meetings and phone calls. Never give out your last name or address until you are comfortable with someone's character. There are women who have been stalked and even raped by Internet dates, so you just can't be too careful in the beginning.

5. Consider Background Checks

If you are curious, there are many ways to find out more about candidates. Internet search vehicles can help you find out details about candidates prior to meetings. By searching on the man's name, you can easily gather information about his background. For example, if you use *Google.com*, you might find out about his educational degrees, work history, and personal interests. You can also click on the "Groups" button to learn more about his interests and hobbies. Other options are also out there. You can check genealogy sites for his family history. There is also a new dating site called True.com that offers background checks as part of their basic Internet dating services. The challenge is that these background checks only look for criminal records within the current state where the person lives. If someone commits a crime in one state and then moves, you may be missing important information. And if you get serious with a man, you can even go to the extreme of hiring a professional investigator to check out his history more thoroughly. No matter what you do, take it slowly, ask questions, and trust your gut.

Cautionary Tales—Stories from the Field

No matter how hard you try to be smart and safe, you will probably run into a few wild cards along your Man Hunt journey. While you can meet these men through any dating avenue, there seems to be a higher likelihood on the Internet. You might think you know someone after a few dates and then he turns into a totally different person. Many women shared stories with me about rude, emotionally unstable, and sexually aggressive men who use the Internet simply to get laid. Beware of these jerks, watch for the warning signs, and get out fast.

- I interviewed a 43-year-old production coordinator who had been Internet dating on and off for three years. While she has had two long-term relationships from Internet dating, she also had to weed out a few wackos. She told me about two first dates on which the guys "forgot their wallets." Wallet MIA # 1 was a successful 45-year-old land developer who announced he'd forgotten his wallet upon arrival. She graciously offered to pay for the date even though there was no Chemistry Connection. She added, "I do not need to be taken out to dinner. I'm happy to meet for a walk on the beach or a cup of tea, but this guy had insisted on meeting at the restaurant." They never saw each other again.

The second time she was not as nice. She met Wallet MIA #2, who was a 48-year-old real estate professional, outside his home for their first date. They walked a few blocks to an expensive Italian restaurant that he had selected. At the end of dinner, he announced that he had forgotten his wallet. In this case, she did not offer to pay. The guy finally spoke to the hostess, who told him to walk home and get his wallet. He was embarrassed and angry, and she never saw him again— nor did she care. She commented to me, "I hate cheap men because I am not cheap. They don't have to spend a lot of money, but should be kind and honest."

- Another 37-year-old marketing manager told me about a 42-year-old pornography-industry jerk whom she met on the Internet. He had disguised his career, claiming to be a writer, but confessed to her on the date that he made porno films and was seeking "a conservative woman who wears an apron." This wacko proceeded to quiz her with a list of ethical questions. For example, she said that he asked, "What household chores do you like?" and "If I asked you to have sex right now in the bathroom of this bar, would you do it?" He left after an hour to go to a "porno-related business meeting," and she was relieved to see him leave.

- The most disturbing story that I heard was from a 40-something woman. When she raised a LIFE question with her Internet date, it was easy to label this jerk. She asked, "What would you do if your wife got breast cancer?" His response knocked him out of the running for potential life partner immediately. Without feeling he answered, "I would leave her." When I shared this scenario with other men and women, everyone had a strong emotional reaction. One 42-year-old female commented, "I would have punched him in the face and run for the door."

- Lastly, I know a 26-year-old female financial advisor who had met a 38-year-old acupuncturist online. They experienced an instant Chemistry Connection and the first date ended with a hug and nice kiss. She described her initial impressions of him to me: "He expressed a desire for a relationship, was very complimentary, and had good communication skills." She continued, "He was very sweet, articulate, kind-hearted, and very enthusiastic about connecting with me." He called her every day, and the relationship seemed to be progressing. The couple went out to dinner six weeks into the relationship and she "could feel that something was different." After dinner, he confessed his reservations to her about moving forward. She told me, "His guru told him that he should not be with me, so he broke it off." Another wacko bites the dust.

You Can Find Love Online

Because Internet dating continues to be the best way to boost your dating numbers, ego, and odds, I want to encourage you that despite the need to follow safety tips and rare disaster dates, you can find love online. If you set up an enticing profile, post a great photo, define what you want, write fun emails, and get to coffee talk fast, you can make it happen by playing this numbers game. The key is to be patient and persistent and avoid giving off any needy vibes. You want to know what you want and be ready to take it or leave it.

And if you don't find love right away, don't give up. I interviewed a 40-year-old screenwriter who found her husband after Internet dating on and off for a few years. She told me, "I was learning about me and what I wanted." At first she admits, "I was undecided about children so I would get emails from other people who were undecided." She told me, "How can you look for someone else when you don't know what you want?"

She soon defined her requirements and the dating results were much more successful. She described her Mr. Right this way, "I wanted someone who liked sailing, was clear that he did not want kids, had sisters, was not an only child, and someone who had similar interests. If they described their perfect weekend, I wanted us to be on the same page." I asked her to expand on the "not an only child" criteria. She told me, "I realized that I dated a lot of only children and for whatever reason, I don't get along as well with them. I'm also one of five children." While you might enjoy dating an only child, it was not for her. We should give her a standing ovation for recognizing what was not working and avoiding the same mistakes. SMART Man Hunting is about breaking patterns that are not working so you can succeed. Do you know what to avoid and what you want?

When this screenwriter met her man, she had gone on at least 50 first dates with guys that she met online. Because they were both traveling, she actually emailed him several times a week for a few months. When they finally met, she told me, "I knew right away after my first date that I wanted a second date, but I wasn't sure about marriage until later." The couple dated for a year and a half before getting engaged, and then were together another year and a half before walking down the aisle. Marriage was not as important to her as finding a great connection. She explained, "I was not focused on a wedding, but more on finding a good, healthy, and happy relationship." When she confirmed with him that they were dating exclusively, she said, "That was what I wanted to hear more than an engagement ring."

When I asked her more about why she chose Internet dating as a way to search for love, she told me, "I started doing it for fun. I found it fascinating to see people's pictures and read about them online." She encourages others to jump online to find romance. If someone acts strange about trying it, she is baffled.

If you haven't started dating online, pick a site, set up your profile, and check it out. With 50 million singles online, you can find love online using the SMART Man Hunting dating strategy and techniques.

More Casual Chat Rooms

In addition to Internet dating sites, some people like to meet people through more casual Internet chat rooms. Many of these rooms are oriented to specific topics or subjects so it may be easier to find someone with common interests in them. For example, one man I know meets women exclusively through chat rooms devoted to health. He ascribes to healthy eating and living and so enjoys discussing the latest fads, supplements, and workout techniques.

The problem with chat rooms is you don't see a photograph of someone, though you can ask someone to email one to you privately. Nor can you search for someone with specific characteristics or interests or who lives in a desirable geographic location. In fact, I'd classify the man above as a perpetual emailer. He's happy to have pen pals all over the country so geographic location doesn't matter to him. My guess is that anyone who is serious about finding someone to date is using Internet matchmaking sites, not chat rooms. I haven't used chat rooms myself, but my advice is to be cautious and use all the Net SMART safety tips for your own protection.

Chat rooms are not hopeless, but I would proceed with caution. During my research, I met a couple in their 60s who had met in a chat room. The man was widowed and later met his second wife in a chat room where gardening tips were discussed. By following their instincts, they started a long-distance relationship that eventually led to a happy marriage. It is possible to find someone using a chat room, but Internet dating provides you with much more information about potential dates upfront.

Remember, It's About Patience and Persistence, so K.I.T.

Don't let the numbers game discourage you. It takes a lot of candidates to get down to four or five potential dates. At one point in my Man Hunt, I had received more than 400 email inquiries from four Internet dating sites. I actually decided to talk to 25 candidates on the phone. From this group of 25, I arranged to meet 20 for coffee or drinks and then went out on second or third dates with five potential partners. Out of these men, I dated one guy for one and a half years. With Internet dating, it's about patience and persistence. It may seem like a lot of work to weed through so many candidates, but it can be exciting and fun too. Just keep your sense of humor and adventure and remember to K.I.T. (Keep It Together).

Whatever happens during your dating journey, remember K.I.T. As a survival technique, use this as a mantra. It can help you keep your cool even when you are ready to scream or cry. Dating is not always easy, and you will find twists in the New Era road. However, getting upset is a waste of energy and makes you much less attractive. Despite the dating hurdles you may encounter, you can succeed by keeping your positive attitude and a sense of humor, and remember to just keep saying "Next" until you find a man. It will happen. It is just a matter of numbers and time.

Enter the Widest Web Wrap-up

Connections made through the Internet and online matchmakers have many benefits. As an exercise, it is definitely a great ego boost and will increase your traffic flow giving you great "dating practice." You can find a high quantity of men on the Internet, but you need to carefully sort through the candidates. While I had some strange encounters, I did meet some attractive and intriguing candidates and even had a few relationships. You can attract the dates that you desire using the Profile Makeover and Photo Makeover tips. You can also make your Internet dating experience easier by heeding the advice in Weeding through Email—The Net Selection Process and Net SMART Safety Tips. Have fun with the dating site features and quickly decide when to say "Next" versus when to take a closer look. Save time and trouble by benefiting from the wisdom of women who have gone before you when you use the SMART ABC Man Codes provided in Part IV when identifying your man.

Remember to be patient, persistent, and to continually work on expanding your Home Box. Oh, and don't forget your sense of humor since you will meet some real characters. When I got discouraged, I would remember all the Internet matchmaking success stories I've heard. I'd call my married friends from Arizona who met on the Internet and now live in Washington, D.C. The husband would encourage me to keep trying. When I asked him what he found to be the biggest benefit of Internet dating, he told me, "You have access to people that you never would otherwise. A lot of people don't go to bars anymore, so it is a great way to meet your man."

You will gain more confidence with every dating encounter. One woman told me, "You got me to practice dating by using *SMART Man Hunting*'s advice and it made me feel so much more confident." The more you just do it, the better results you will see.

6

───❦───

Test Speed
Screening Dates

Do you want to know a few Man Hunt shortcuts? After weeks of Internet dating, a friend recommended that I try something new called Speed Dating or Rapid Dating. The idea provides a fast and effective way to get dates and seek a mate in the New Era. You can also quickly assess chemistry with potential dates at a new type of singles event called Silent Dating. These speed screening dates are the most time efficient dating trends in the New Era.

Five-Minute Men

During job interviews, most managers can tell whether they are interested in a candidate within minutes. Similarly, you can probably determine if you want to see someone again within the five- to 10-minute timeframe of these introductory dates. While I was Internet dating, in most cases when I first met a candidate in person, I knew within minutes whether I wanted to see him again. So this fast track approach seems to make sense. It's a SMART way for men and women to go hunting for a mate. *SMART Man Hunting* is about getting out there, increasing your dating volume, boosting your ego by getting attention, and ultimately finding a great mate. Speed Dating is an excellent dating option for a busy woman in the 21st century.

How does Speed Dating work? You sign up for an event where you meet 10 to 20 candidates during introductory sessions of 3 to 8 minutes each. These speed dating twirls are scheduled based on age ranges and can be a great way to quickly increase your bandwidth of potential suitors. While there are many groups offering this service to singles, the basic process follows.

Speed Dating Steps

1. Search the web for speed dating providers in your area.
2. Select a speed dating event and RSVP via the event provider's website.
3. Receive an email confirmation from the host.
4. Bring your smile, confidence, and a positive outlook to the event.
5. Meet men fast in three- to eight-minute interviews during the evening.
6. After each interview, write down the man's first name and circle "Yes" or "No" on a sheet to indicate whether you want to meet him again.
7. Wait a day or two while the host determines whether any of the men you selected want to meet you again too.
8. Receive an email from the host or check on the host's website to find out your mutual matches and how to reach them.
9. Set up first dates with singles who passed your pre-screening test so you can learn more about them.

Speed Dating—A Personal Tale

Speed Dating has been a positive experience for me; here is my tale with some additional insights. I first signed up for a Rapid Dating evening for 28 to 48 year olds in Santa Monica and it was really fun and time effective. Even though I was older than some of the men, I still came out with some great candidates in the end and a potential Mr. Right.

There were about 50 singles at this event. We met at a nice hotel bar and were given an evaluation sheet for the evening's activity. Similar to musical chairs, the event involves rotating places. The men were seated at numbered tables while the women moved to the next guy every five minutes when the bell rang. Our event host told us to simply write down each man's first name and then circle "Yes" or "No" after the five-minute introductory meeting.

Light-Hearted Approach

I decided to take a lighthearted approach and just go with the flow of the event. At first, I made the mistake of being too goal-oriented by asking each man for three things that he seeks in a mate. I found this question to be too complicated and serious for five-minute meetings, so I just started to relax and enjoy myself. Once I started using my KISS (Keep It Simple Stupid) questions that are best for first dates, the results were much better.

Some of the men actually had their own pointed questions for me. One asked me to tell him about the most romantic place that I had visited. I hesitated and then told him Santorini, Greece. Then he admitted, "That was actually a trick question because my most romantic place is anywhere with that special someone." I liked him.

Punchy Talk

By the time that I reached the tenth guy, everyone was getting punchy. At this point I found myself being sidetracked from my main mission and doing stuff like spending five minutes talking about the importance of names and how they can impact some-one's ego. I think that I launched into this conversation because my brother was about to have a second baby and everyone was anxious to find out the new name.

By the end of the Speed Dating twirls, I had met 12 candidates and selected four as "Yes" men. The host explained that we would receive an email the next day listing the contact informa-tion (which is what you decide to share) for our matches if both parties marked "Yes."

The Rapid Results

The next day an email arrived with my matches. All four of my "Yes" men said yes as well. I trusted my gut, was selective, and contacted two of the men. While I found the first match extremely together and attractive during our follow-up coffee date, I was hesitant to date him because of our 12-year age difference. The second match blew me away. It turned out that I'd met him in passing earlier and he'd been thinking about contacting me again. In addition to this previous connection, our personalities seemed to click and I was definitely attracted to his "mojo." When it did not work out with this Mr. Click after three intense weeks, a wise friend reminded me, "If it sounds too good to be true, it probably is the case."

After a recovery timeout, I ended up back in two more sessions of *Rapid Dating* to test out their new age ranges of 25 to 40 and 35+ years. I met more interesting men and made several business connections. The new age ranges worked well for me and both evenings were successes. I definitely recommend this type of New Era dating.

One night, I met two brothers and liked both of them. Brother #1 had a candle and candy hearts on his table. Meanwhile, when I asked Brother #2 what he was seeking in a mate, he told me: "I ask three questions. One: Do they have a happy soul? Two: Does she like herself? and Three: Is she passionate and romantic?" Wow. Unfortunately, because they were brothers, I couldn't

Advice for Speed Daters

- It's a good idea to review Part III, The Dating Assessment Dance, before you leave home. Attend events with a positive and lighthearted attitude. People are attracted to an upbeat personality versus someone who is low energy—so give it your best shot by letting your personality shine!

- Go with low expectations so you can maintain your positive persona. It's a numbers game so you're bound to meet some people who make you turn green. But remember, it is only five minutes of pain. Chances are that you will make at least one connection in an evening.

- Take the pressure off yourself and just try to have some fun. You are there for the evening so relax and be yourself for the best results. I recommend that you use KISS (Keep It Simple Stupid) questions and remember to ask yourself, "Would I ever want to kiss this person?" Ask him about his favorite vacation or what he likes to do for fun versus his resume.

- Dress for success! You don't need to dress for the ball, but wear something that makes you feel good and is "business casual" so no jeans or tennis shoes please! By now you've had your Style Makeover and know your colors. Refer to the bachelor survey comments on fashion for Speed Dating dress success. You are going on a pre-screening date, and while you are selecting a few good men, the guys will definitely be checking you out from head to toe.

- Be open to the idea of meeting new friends or business connections along with potential mates. You might set up follow-up meetings with people you meet during your Speed Dating adventure. You never know how they might help you or how you can help them in meeting dates or business contacts. For example, one evening I met a screenwriter who shared a similar passion for writing. He was working on a screenplay for the Sundance Film Festival at the same time that I was writing this book. I gained a great book cheerleader by attending Speed Dating. You might find supporters too.

A 40-something comedian/actress in New York City met her boyfriend of three years at a Speed Dating service called Hurry-Date. During this event, she was introduced to 25 men for three-minute encounters. She immediately connected with this guy, and found similar interests in travel and movies despite completely opposite careers. Because they share a mutual passion for checking out new countries, he took her to St. Petersburg and Morroco for long weekends. Even though his handicap equipment business has nothing to do with her entertainment world, the couple now goes to the Sundance Film Festival and is talking about making movies. When they visit Los Angeles, it is clear to everyone that they are into each other and a great match.

If you have any hesitation, think about this Speed Dating

observation from a 30-something woman who I met at an event. She told me, "I get more dates out of this type of thing than at parties or bars." She added, "You've got to stir the pot. If you're not out there, nothing is going to happen." Search for an event near you on the Internet, go with an upbeat attitude, and have some fun screening your dates.

Silent Dating—A New Screening Alternative

If you want an alternative to Speed Dating, why not check out Silent Dating as a shortcut for screening dates. It's a hot new dating trend that started in the United Kingdom and is reaching across the States. Did you know that over 80 percent of communication is non-verbal? Why not go to a singles party where you can practice your non-verbal body language signals and maybe make a connection along the way?

Silent Dating brings hundreds of singles to an event where the only rule is—No Talking Please! Now I'm not sure this approach will work in Los Angeles, but it is catching on in New York City and Chicago. You can communicate during the event via hand-written notes, text messages, email, cartoon drawings, and body talk.

I was so curious about Silent Dating that I planned a "research" adventure to San Francisco to check out the first West Coast event. This singles safari was being held on a Saturday evening from 7:00–9:00 p.m. in an art shop/ gallery downtown and was hosted by QuietParty.com. I jumped on a plane three days after hearing about the event so I could share the tale and tips with you in this book.

Imagine walking into an art gallery filled with about 75 attractive singles, with a wine bar set up on the side, music playing, and a crowded table in the middle covered with index cards and scribbles. The only rule on the entrance sign was "No talking until 9:00 p.m." At this point, I even had to write the type of wine that I preferred on my first index card and give it to the bartender. I took a moment to stare around the room and checked out the crowd. With a wine glass in one hand and stack of index cards in the other, my screening dating games began.

The easiest and most common introduction was when strangers would walk up to me with a simple, "Hi" on their index card. If I was interested, I started writing back. If not, I would just smile and keep walking. It was easy to get distracted and start communicating with someone else because it was a full house. After about 15 minutes, I thought to myself, how am I going to make it two hours without talking?

Once the chemistry started charging with two men writing on index cards to me at the same time, I was quickly engaged and lost my sense of time. Do you think two men would both try to hit on you in a bar at once? Suddenly, the room was getting very warm. This Silent Dating strategy was awesome because it was much more inviting than a loud crowded bar scene. One guy wrote to me, "This is like Instant Messenger." The difference is that with IM, you cannot see the other person's facial expressions. In this live scenario, a smile is your best ally.

Silent Dating Scribbles

To give you an idea of some of the amusing "silent" conversations via index cards, check out these scribbled exchanges that I had with different guys in the room. It was fun to see the sense of humor, boldness, and creativity in these connections.

Liz: Where did you grow up?
Guy 1: Alameda, do I seem grown up?
Liz: What do you like to do for fun?
Guy 1: Write on little pieces of paper and meet ladies from far away.

Guy 2: I live in Oakland. Would you like to hike the East Bay Hills?
Liz: I live in Los Angeles, but visit San Francisco often.
Guy 2: Call me if you want (name and phone number provided immediately).

Liz: Hi. So what brought you here tonight?
Guy 3: I'm one of the artists.

Liz: Which pieces?
Guy 3: The wood and metal assemblage on the opposite wall.
   Rhythm piece, music piece, and gold piece.

Liz: How do you like to kiss?
Guy 4: That's a loaded question.
Liz: Slow and intimate or passionate and fast?
Guy 4: Would you like me to show you right now?
Liz: Not here, maybe later over a drink.
Guy 4: I don't drink. What about dinner afterwards?

Guy 5: Hug the person to the right of you. (This card was
   passed around the room.)
Guy 6: Invasive artwork. (He flashed a drawing on his card
   while passing by groups.)
Guy 7: Pick a card, any card, and then you must do what it
   says within two minutes.
Liz: (My card said to ask someone to dance so I quickly wrote
   to another guy and asked him to dance.)

Liz: I think we need an interactive game to minimize the writing.
Guy 8: This is the game. It's called life.

Is this the game of life or animals? When I visited one of my married friends in the Bay Area the day after this Quiet Party, she said to me, "That sounds like animals checking each other out." I thought, wow, she is right. It really did seem like we were animals making advances to check each other out.

This version of Silent Dating could be enhanced with wireless technologies. While I had a blast at this event, it did get a little exhausting to write back and forth on index cards for two hours. If everyone wore nametags that included a first name (or code name) and their cell phone number, we could have exchanged text messages instead of scribbling messages on little pieces of paper. There were several situations where either I could not read a guy's handwriting or he could not read one of my words. Singles could also exchange emails if they were in an Internet café. A wireless approach could add a fun dynamic to this Silent Dating dance.

If you have an open mind and want to practice your non-verbal communication, Silent Dating is an excellent option for singles. After the event, I found out that many participants found the invitation posted on Craigslist.com. Another woman told me, "Curiosity more than anything else brought me here. I'm usually open to new and exciting things." Another passerby saw the crowd, and told me, "I had to see what was happening."

To get the most out of Silent Dating, take your lighthearted attitude, dress for success and focus on having fun. You definitely want to wear something that makes you feel really good inside. If you wear something unusual such as a scarf or unique piece of jewelry, it can also spark conversations. One guy was wearing a hat that said "Boston" at this event so I asked him if he was a Red Sox fan. No matter what you wear, remember that your confidence sex appeal will create the animal magnetism that naturally draws men to you.

When I spoke to the QuietParty.com host after the event, he explained, "We started setting up these events to study group behaviors in different situations." He added, "We tried playing different types of music to see if it changes peoples' behavior." I think people were more bold in this organized non-verbal communications event versus other singles events. The rules were totally different and it was a refreshing change.

As a result of being bold and adventurous, I had two men ask me out via index cards. Two immediate invitations for dates is the fastest results of any singles event that I've attended. One very attractive guy even took me to a cozy Italian restaurant across the street right after the game ended. Okay, I was returning to Los Angeles the next day so he had to move fast, but that was definitely a rapid response. You can find the same results with this type of pre-screening dating option. Search online for a Silent Dating event near you, and then go have some fun, laugh, and maybe meet a few cute men along the way.

Bachelors Are Watching Your Body Language

When I surveyed bachelors to find out what encourages guys to approach a stranger for a date, here's what they told me they are watching.

- "If you get a little eye contact and a smile, that's everything."
- "The way she looks, her style, the way she carries herself."
- "I look for someone who is engaged in conversation because they are usually more approachable."
- "I'm drawn to someone with nice hair, beautiful sparkly eyes, good posture (indicates good self worth), and someone who is relaxed."
- "Girls, I know they kill your feet, but you just gotta wear heels more often. They make you look sexy as hell."
- "A woman who laughs easily with a twinkle in her eye and a bright mind behind it. Couple that with beautiful knees and ankles, no panty lines, and a shapely waist—now don't read any of that as necessarily skinny—pretty much perfect and a turn on."
- "A smile is really important. She has to look happy for me to approach her."
- "Eye contact is the most powerful type of body language. It's a green light."

Sign up for a Silent Dating or Speed Dating event, and then give it your best smile. Consider these screening dates as more practice for making great first impressions. And if you get lucky in love along the way, more power to you.

Test Speed Screening Dates Wrap-up

Speed Dating and Silent Dating are excellent ways to screen dates in a fast-track world where our minutes are even more precious. You might be punchy by the end of the evening after meeting so many men and smiling for hours. You will also probably be pleasantly surprised that you made a connection or two.

7

Consider Using the Professionals

BEYOND INTERNET DATING and speed dating, New Era daters are also hiring professional matchmakers and attending more casual singles events hosted by an organizer, both of which may involve a variety of approaches and different levels of intensity for finding a soul mate. You will need to determine what works best for you. If you test one strategy and it is not working for you, be open to trying another avenue until you find a service that introduces you to the right candidates. Here are a few matchmaker options and personal insights from daters who have tried these services.

Serious Players

If you do not want to go the Internet dating route, there are several types of professional matchmaking services available that offer more thorough candidate screening for a price. While these services charge a much higher fee, you can eliminate some of the misrepresentations by men that go along with the dating game using this more structured approach. Professional matchmakers can be a great choice if you are serious about your search and willing to make an investment in finding a high-quality Mr. Right. Check out different services and ask for references if you want to hear about their success stories.

Partnering with the Professionals

While professional matchmakers operate in ways that are similar to the Internet matchmaking sites, there are differences. Here's how they work:

1. Set up an in-person meeting with a matchmaker's service coordinator to discuss their process and your goals.

2. Define your best attributes, along with what you desire in an ideal mate by completing statistic sheets and writing enticing personal essays.

3. Provide appealing and recent photographs that include a close-up and full-length hobby shot to let your personal attributes shine.

4. Partner with the matchmaker to narrow their pool of candidates by using your statistics and interests as a way to identify most-likely-to-succeed men, and/or

5. Wait until a guy picks you and if you want the men to make the first moves.

6. From this shorter list of candidates, take a closer look by reviewing their photos for a KISS Test and personal essays.

7. Select a few good men and indicate interest in going on a first date. Let the guy or matchmaker make the plans and simply prepare your smile.

8. If the guy passes the KISS Test on the first date, let him take the lead by setting up a second date.

9. If you decide to keep seeing him, do not stop dating other guys until you hear, "I want you and only you," and the feeling is mutual.

Two Experiences with Professional Matchmakers

Do you want to learn more about this option? Here are two stories from women who tried the same professional matchmaking service with completely different goals and results.

Bachelorette #1

A 37-year-old operations manager told me about her experience with a professional dating service. She paid a few thousand dollars versus the $25.00 a month that many of the average Internet dating sites charge for their services. She kept it very quiet, and commented to me, "It was a last resort and I never wanted to admit that I was that desperate."

She was given an extensive packet to complete regarding her background and interests for her profile notebook. She also had a photo shoot with a professional photographer and placed these pictures in her personal profile as well. In addition, the service filmed videos of all candidates, which were housed in a library for prospective dates to access. Once all of her personal data was gathered, she was assigned a reference number versus a name to protect her privacy. To view the folders of men, she had to physically visit the dating center. If my girlfriend was interested in learning more after reading someone's folder, she could view the potential date's video in the center. Once a candidate was identified, she could leave a reply card inquiry at the administration desk for the individual to pick up based on his ID number.

My girlfriend went out on a few dates but did not meet the man of her dreams. She found that both of her dates were more interested in talking about themselves and did not want to hear her point of view. In addition, her timing was wrong. She wasn't really ready to find a Mr. Right, but was only trying out the service to meet new people. It's not worth spending money on a professional matchmaker unless you are serious.

Bachelorette #2

Alternatively, another woman whom I interviewed used the same professional matchmaking service with marriage results. As a successful businesswoman, she applied her business savvy to her search, taking it very seriously. She told me, "I look for talent for a living. In my job, you might find one person in a hundred who fits a particular assignment—and that's probably good odds. I had just broken up with the wrong one soon after my 40th birthday and knew that I had to up my numbers."

Once this winning 40-year-old created her profile at the dating service, she received 200 solicitations from men within six months. She had initially selected four men to approach, but later decided that she wanted men to contact her first. She actually went on dates with 19 men, and wound up marrying one of the 200 who had expressed interest in her.

How did she receive so many inquiries? Her advice to anyone setting up a profile with a dating service: "You have to be sincere, but also sound appealing. You have to find the right balance in your personal profile." She added, "I made every effort to make the pictures and video look good—I thought of it like a marketing tool, keeping in mind that the whole purpose is to attract men."

So what happened next? She shared more insights about her process with me: "I took it as seriously as finding a new job. I went to the dating center every week, checked who picked me, eliminated the definite No's, looked at videotapes, and then narrowed it down. I was picked by about fifteen men a week, I read their profiles, which usually led me to view seven videotapes, from there, I'd whittle it down to about four men who I'd be willing to meet in person."

As far as the dating process, she shared, "You kind of need to be brutal, but I wasn't interested in just dating." A few times after talking to them on the phone, she decided not to meet them. She also bumped into two "creepy guys." However, she ended up going on second dates with five men and married one of these five.

She also had a strict "no kissing" policy until after a connection was made. While this approach may sound odd, her strategy was: "Women need to get themselves more in the driver's seat." She added, "My husband is the loveliest guy, but most men will try to get you in bed early. They will try and take you for granted, and I wanted to avoid that situation."

Her Mr. Right was only six weeks older than her and it took five dates before she started having strong feelings for him. Initially, he did not call for a month between dates, so she just kept dating away. However, after a while they had a more relaxed, informal pool date where genuine connections were made. She added, "I was dating three guys at the time of the pool date and not kissing any of them." The happy couple dated for one year before getting engaged and married six months later.

She explained what she considered to be her top three advantages of using the dating service: "One: Because it is expensive, you have people that are a little more serious and it weeds out the riff raff. Two: I love it that you have access to so many people. Three: I liked the videotapes."

Lunch Men

Do you want someone else to do the homework? Do you have time for lunch? Even if you are busy, we all need to eat so why not consider a matchmaker who schedules singles for lunch dates? This type of service is usually not as expensive as some of the other professional matchmakers and seems like a good middle-ground option. The price may seem high compared to Internet dating, but it's not the highest.

Most lunch men whom I met were busy professionals who wanted to meet women outside their office or client list. I paid an annual fee, which would guarantee me at least 14 lunch dates over one year, which averages out to be one to two lunches per month.

The Lunch Dating Process

1. Meet with a Lunch Dating Coordinator

The first step is to find a lunch dating service. You can search for one in your area on the web. Next, arrange to meet with the service's dating coordinator who interviews every candidate to document individual goals and desires in a relationship. The matchmaker takes your picture for their files, checks your license to make sure you are providing the correct age, and then goes to work setting you up with people whose preferences match your characteristics and desires.

2. Receive Your Man Candidates

The dating coordinator will call you with a list of candidates and will pitch them to you. You evaluate how someone sounds and whether you are willing to have lunch with him. If your interest is sparked, the coordinator will work with both of you to set up a time and place for you to meet. You never have to contact the Man Candidate and he doesn't contact you so this process is much closer to a blind date.

3. Go to Lunch or Drinks

Meet your lunch man at a local restaurant for lunch or drinks. (Sometimes it is not a lunch date.) Again, take a lighthearted approach and do not take the date too seriously. This attitude helps reduce nervousness on both parts and I have found it makes men want you more.

4. The Feedback Loop

After each date, both parties are encouraged to call the dating service to provide feedback. Obviously, the goal is to have satisfied clients and the comments help the service to ensure long-term success. It's a good idea to talk to the coordinator after your lunch dates. By sharing with the Coordinator your likes and dislikes about a lunch date, it will help them find men closer to what you desire when setting up future dates.

5. Hold Option

A positive feature of some matchmaking services such as lunch dating is that you can put the service "on hold." You might want to activate this option when you are already dating so many men that you can't handle any more. Or you may have met a Mr.

Right and decided to date him exclusively for a while. If your Mr. Right or the other men you are dating don't make the final cut, you can always reactivate your membership in the lunch club.

6. Read the Fine Print

When signing up with any dating service, be sure to read the fine print and find out whether you can place your membership on hold and how it works. You will pay valuable money for professional matchmakers so be sure you understand the fine print. If you meet someone special, it is nice to know that you can stop the clock, and then pick up with the service later if your current Mr. Right candidate falls through.

After fourteen lunch (really drinks) dates, I finally found one guy who sparked my interest. The drawback to this dating option is that the matchmaker selects whom they think you will find attractive. Chemistry is a very personal thing so it was a painful process to show up for the majority of these dates and have it be over in five minutes. After providing feedback, the matchmaker encouraged me to keep working with them, and at last there was one guy whom I wanted to see for a second date. Of course this happened within the same week that I met another guy through a smaller local matchmaker who asked me to date him exclusively. Both candidates lived in the same beach town so I had to politely part ways with my Lunch Man.

When selecting a dating service, ask questions about the demographics of their membership (male/female ratio within your age range is key), review the fine print, and decide what works best for your needs before signing the dotted line.

Set Your Own Pace at Singles Events

Along with professional matchmakers, there are many singles groups out there that organize events with a theme. These organized activities can be a great way to get your feet wet in the New Era dating arena. All you need to do is find an event, show up with a smile, and then see if you click with anyone. There is no pressure to perform one-on-one because you are not paired up. You set the pace, take what you want, and leave the rest behind.

Because you are only sharing basic personal information with the event coordinator when you sign up, this route is the safest way to meet people with the least amount of pressure. Simply search on the Internet for singles events near your home, find one with a theme that excites you, and then get out there and check it out. You might recruit a girlfriend to go with you to increase your comfort level, and then go have some fun with this dating option.

The themes of typical singles events are inviting and include everything from ski trips to Academy Awards parties. I found a broad range of singles events options out there including athletic activities, dinners, weekend adventures, and even international travel. Here is a snapshot of some types of singles events:

Singles Event Themes

- St. Patrick's Day Party
- Museum Art Walk
- Academy Awards Party and Dinner
- "Blind" Wine Tasting
- Valentine's Day Mixer
- Las Vegas Weekend
- New Orleans Jazz Festival
- Tennis Social

In addition to the types of events listed above, I discovered during my research that singles dinners are cropping up around the country. I attended a few singles dinners that I found through an Internet date who turned out to be a friend versus a Mr. Right candidate. He recommended a dinner club organized by a woman who had recently moved back to Los Angeles from New York. Our party organizer was interested in meeting new singles and friends. She graciously opened her house for monthly dinners, and asked everyone to bring wine and new faces to broaden the circle.

These singles dinners included an equal number of men and women and often featured a theme. For example, one night we had a wine tasting where everyone brought their favorite Merlot. We rated the wines on score cards and the activity sparked great conversation amongst the crowd. Another evening, we invited an astrologer to share brief personality descriptions about the guests, and then everyone guessed who matched the profile.

Singles events can offer a variety of fun activities for meeting Man Candidates, but how successful can you be if it is a free-for-all mating scene? As in every New Era option that I researched, I came across success stories for singles events. My singles dinner organizer told me a story about a 39-year-old doctor who met her fiancé at a singles dinner. She became engaged to the 35-year-old retail entrepreneur after only 10 months, with the wedding planned for the 14-month mark.

More Casual Dive Dinners

If you're not into organizing dinner parties, why not host a low-key Dive Dinner? During my man hunt, a girlfriend recommended that I check out a networking group who had monthly Dive Dinners. These dinners included a mix of entertainment professionals who were making ends meet with their day jobs while going after their dream jobs (which has been my situation with this book so it felt good to be around people who understood my juggling act).

The only requirement for the Dive Dinner is that the entrees be under $10.00. Every first Wednesday of the month, a designated organizer picks the location and sends out an Evite. While the first night was a little awkward for me to break into the crowd, I felt much more comfortable by my third Dive Dinner. It can take time to build bonds with a new group so don't give up on the first try.

I found these dinners to be very casual with a smart, hip, and fun jet-set crew. When I interviewed one of the founders, he explained, "The simplicity about the dinners is a good thing. No one goes with expectations. There's no purpose other than good friends getting together. If networking or dating happens it's great, but there's no intention or design." There are writers, producers, and actors in this group so the creative energy is contagious.

One night the guy across the table shared with a smile that he was going to be on *The West Wing* that night. Someone asked the restaurant owner to turn on the TV, and there he was on the big screen. The next time I saw him, I learned that he played one of the doctors in the movie *Million Dollar Baby*. This actor also has a production company on the side so we discussed creating dating videos together. It was fun to dream about what could happen, and this crowd was the perfect enabler for creative dreams.

Another guy at the Dive Dinner informed me, "I've sold a movie treatment to someone to make a movie about how many women whom I've dated got engaged to the next guy right after our breakup." Do you want his phone number?

During my third Dive Dinner, our designated host invited us to a bowling alley diner. I sat across the table from three encouraging cheerleaders from a local Los Angeles paper, who suddenly started brainstorming about me writing a dating column for them. I felt like I hit the lottery, and really liked their positive energy. We laughed over our cheap feast of burgers and fries, and then proceeded to disco bowling. Everyone was high-fiving each other and having a blast despite the wide range in skill sets. Overall, the dynamics were perfect for mixing and meeting potential dates and mates.

When I asked the founder about the romance track for this group, he explained, "There has definitely been dating, and I think even a wedding, but not intentionally so. You never know who you might meet and who someone might bring."

Based on this fantastic experience, I recommend starting a Dive Dinner in your neighborhood with professionals in your field. The founder of my dinner added these benefits when we spoke. "It's always an interesting place to eat dinner that you probably would not have thought about and it helps you stay in touch with people who you would otherwise not see." The low budget and low expectations approach takes the pressure off the evening.

It's okay to act like a kid again. Dating is about getting out there and having fun. What a great way to meet new people whom you might date. You will be guaranteed to expand your world by making new connections at the very least. And if you find love along the way, more power to you for taking initiative and positioning yourself for success.

Since these events are group activities rather than one-on-one interviews, singles can take the pressure off, contribute to your numbers game, and significantly increase your chances of finding a man. If nothing else, you are not sitting home alone and should congratulate yourself for being brave and taking a chance. As a result, you might be surprised by how much fun you find and meet a Man Candidate simply by getting out there.

Consider Using the Professionals Wrap-up

Professional matchmakers can be expensive, but the higher quality of candidates may be worth it. If you are looking for professional men with money to burn, these services are right for you. Since the profile pool tends to be more professionals with more money, you can guess that the people who use these services will be somewhat older. Younger guys are still looking for women in bars, though not always. Be sure to ask the matchmaker the percentage of men versus women in your dating age range using their service. Professionals are also setting up lunch dates, singles dinners, travel adventures, and other group-based single activities. And if you prefer a more casual route, start a low-key Dive Dinner with your professional network.

8

―――◎―――

Expanding Your Home Box, Part II

HOPEFULLY, THE WHOLE TIME you're exploring the SMART Man Hunting landscape by trying on different New Era dating options, you've also heeded my advice in the first chapter of this section to continue to expand your Home Box. Not only will broadening your horizons make you more interesting to your friends and Man Candidates, but you'll be having a lot of fun and building confidence. At this point, I'd like to talk about some more opportunities in the New Era Man Hunting Landscape that you may not have considered.

Open Your Mind to International Flux

Global commerce and the world wide web have made the world a pretty small place indeed. Have you ever met anyone from another country who opened your eyes to different perspectives? There is a flux of people traveling internationally or living abroad today. Don't discount meeting men born in or living in other countries as potential dates or friends. Being more international in your outlook is a great way to expand your Home Box and broaden your overall perspective on life.

You can even sign up for an international adventure with a group that specializes in organizing singles trips. And if no one in your travel group is a Love Match (LM), you might just meet him through serendipity on the journey. Would you like to check out Costa Rica for scuba diving, the Greek Islands for island hopping or Florence, Italy, for the art? Go where you can share passions with other singles and perhaps make that love connection. By finding a trip that puts a smile on your face, you will more naturally attract the dates that you desire.

When I was living in Washington, D.C., I found myself meeting a variety of people from all over the world. I worked for a multinational organization, which made it easier to meet and maintain international contacts here and overseas. While you do not necessarily want to date your business contacts, you never know whom they might want you to meet and what knowing them might teach you. Most of the men I've met were nothing more than friends, but I met a few Man Candidates along my journey too.

Broaden Your World with International Travel

International travel is an ideal way to expand your Home Box so consider taking a trip abroad. Not only can it broaden your dating opportunities, but it will enhance your life skills. Travel calls forth any variety of skills and requires you to rise to a number of challenges. Dealing with people of different cultures is great practice for the interpersonal dance we do on the Man Hunt. By staying open while you travel, in addition to meeting potential partners, you'll develop lasting friendships. By asking questions, I learned about new cultures and built business connections that I keep today.

My approach was based on some good advice from my aunt. She told me, "Go as a traveler and not a tourist." Her advice was to focus on learning about a country's culture and values versus just joining the crowd and flocking to popular monuments. Because I took her advice to heart, the personal rewards and knowledge gained while traveling abroad were invaluable.

The Safari Stud

On a business trip, I met a 35-year-old Lebanese safari guide while visiting Dubai, U.A.E. He totally opened my eyes to other outlooks on life and is one of the most positive and happy people that I have ever met. He immediately drew my attention when I first met him on a safari. He started the tour with this statement, "Tonight will be one of the most memorable nights of your life. You will see things that you have never seen before and always remember this tour." He also sparkled with a sense of humor. By clowning around with us, he made us laugh when our four-wheel vehicle got stuck in the sand dunes. A definite Man Candidate, he could barely buy me a cup of coffee, but his confidence and worldliness drew me to him.

During my first three-week visit to the U.A.E., we became inseparable. One night we sat on the beach and played what I called 20 Questions at the time. (This is now part of the LIFE Match Game.) When I asked him to tell me about the scariest time of his life, he proceeded to describe how he almost died in a battle during his conscripted stint in the Lebanese army in his twenties. Dubai was his escape route. I had never met anyone in the United States with this type of story.

When I returned to Dubai five months later, I learned more from this international connection. I scheduled a safari for my training class, and the safari guide took us to a goat farmer's house during the excursion. We sat in the middle of the hot red-sand desert on rugs shielded from the sun by a canvas tent and sipped tea while attempting to communicate through non-verbal sign language with our hosts. Wow, simply by stepping out and setting up this safari, my worldly view was expanded with a new appreciation of western civilization!

His zest for life was irresistible. He shared that, "I have women all over the world who send me love letters and tell me that they want to have my children." I believe it. I often tease him about my code name for this female magnet, Safari Stud. He continues to be my friend today despite the fact that he lives on the other side of the globe.

International Mr. Rights

Have you met any international Mr. Right candidates in your Man Hunt? Because the world has become a much smaller place, you are now more likely to meet a man who is from or lives in another country. One 47-year-old executive told me, "I met my girlfriend at a wedding. She lived in England, but has now moved back to Los Angeles."

In this small world, you never know whom you might meet. One of my Internet dating candidates emailed me, "I am in the South of France. I uploaded my pictures from Singapore. Will be in Los Angeles on Wednesday. Do you want to have coffee?" This email definitely caught my eye because I wanted to meet world travelers.

After speaking on the phone, I met this guy for coffee on a Saturday morning. He explained, "I'm in the process of moving back to Los Angeles from England." We shared many similar interests in both telecommunications and international business. During this meeting, I also discovered that he was a WD (Wounded Divorcé, see more SMART ABC Man Codes in Part IV). He had just left his wife and it had been a very dysfunctional good-bye. When I expressed my interest in getting re-married, he responded, "Does it have to be a marriage?" We parted as friends after three dates.

While that connection did not work, a 35-year-old woman from Tokyo, Japan, who recently moved to the United States to be with her man told me a success story. She had met her partner while working on World Cup events there. He was a U.S.-based photographer assigned to the World Cup while she was working in the medical center. She felt attracted to him, so, thinking fast, she asked him for guidance on how to best use her new expensive camera.

In order to take scenic shots and share her Japanese culture, she took him to visit a temple. She described their adventure and emotional connection, "We went to a small stone temple where memorial stones are placed by women who have lost babies. Once he learned about this tradition, his mood changed. I found out that he had lost a baby many years ago. He wanted to place a stone in honor of his child in the temple. He started crying and decided to buy a stone." She said, from that moment forward, "I knew that I could trust his heart."

After the 57-year-old photographer left Japan, the couple talked on the phone several times a day, often for hours at a time. She said to me with a grin, "We spent a lot of money on the telephone." After two failed arranged-marriage attempts by her mother earlier in Japan, she flew the coop and has landed with her new man in America.

Don't Discount Long Distance

The key thing to remember about International Mr. Rights is that it's a small world. Don't be so quick to eliminate a candidate from overseas. If you meet someone you cannot resist, it is easier now in the New Era than at any other time to entertain long-distance dances with an international man.

The same holds true for men who live in the same country as you but maybe not in your city. Thanks to telecommunications, you are no longer limited by geography in the New Era so that long-distance romances are more feasible.

If you meet someone via email introductions, Internet dating, matchmakers, or business travel, distance is no longer an insurmountable hurdle. As one wise 60-something man told me, "If you hit it off, there is no such thing as geographically undesirable anymore." While meeting someone outside the city walls may not be ideal, modern technology makes it easier today to maintain a relationship.

Long-Distance Quality Time

The biggest hurdle in a long-distance relationship is to find ways to maintain intimacy and time. There are cheap and easy ways to

maintain regular communication today with a long-distance partner. You always have the email option, which is free and elimi-
nates time zone difference considerations. I have also found that
cell phones and calling cards minimize long-distance bills. When
my rock star (see more in the SMART ABC Man Codes section)
was traveling on tour, he used calling cards to reach me often
from Frankfurt, Tokyo, and Sydney. No matter where he landed,
these cards allowed him to stay in touch on a regular basis without paying outrageous hotel telephone fees. These options can
reduce the stress of talk-time limits and lessen the financial
burden. Don't forget about pagers, personal organizers, and text
messages as alternative ways to maintain long distance communications with your mate.

In addition to benefiting from wireless technology, it's still
important to have quality face time with each other. Luckily,
flying to meet a long-distance partner for quality time together is
no longer an obstacle. You can make a long distance relationship
work well when one partner flies to the other's city on a monthly
basis. Despite the delays due to increased security measures at
airports, discount fares and multiple flights make it practical to
visit your mate on a regular basis.

One 30-something male explained his long-distance relationship to me. He said, "She works as a consultant so we alternate
weekends. I fly to her once a month, and then she comes here
another weekend." After two years of dating long distance, the
dynamics of the long-distance dance have worked for them. Not
only is the couple committed to each other, but they share similar cultural backgrounds. Both parties are Chinese and grew up in
Australia. Because their foundation is so solid and there is a genuine respect for each other, they can handle any relationship distance hurdles. These Winning Long Distance Dancers are now
married after surviving a consulting assignment that separated
the couple between Rome and Los Angeles for six months.

Do's and Don'ts for Long Distance

Do's	Don'ts
Give long-distance love a try if there is a strong mutual connection and both parties are committed to give it a go.	Don't waste your time with men who are not serious contenders. Unless the guy is communicating his feelings and making plans to see you again, he is not in this long-distance game.
Use wireless technology to build the bond and sparks through regular communications.	Avoid big long-distance bills by using cell phones, calling cards, email, and text messages for communications.
Make an effort to meet at least once a month in person to allow for quality time and to keep the relationship moving forward.	Don't let yourself get so busy that you can't find time to meet. You might drag out a relationship for months or even years without having regular contact only to find out he is Mr. Goodenough.
Periodically give yourself a reality check about the relationship and make a Go/No-Go decision.	If the guy is not talking about the future after a few months, stop dreaming about what might happen and cut your losses.
Build your own network before making a move for a man so you don't lose your confidence sex appeal.	Never make a move only for the guy. You only want to move if the new location complements your needs.

Making a Long-Distance Move Decision

At a certain point, you need to have a discussion about whether someone should move so that you can be together. The globe-trotting will get old and, eventually, you will need to make a Go/No-Go decision. Set a time limit for making this decision and then periodically monitor your progress. During the long-distance courtship, encourage an ongoing dialogue so you understand each other's expectations.

Moving is a serious milestone and making a move demonstrates a serious commitment. Consider what the new location brings to you as an individual versus moving only for your partner. For women, careers, interests, and friends bring balance to a relationship. Losing these supports can put undue pressure on a personal connection. Start building a support network prior to making a move. My relocation to Los Angeles from Washington, D.C., was prompted, in part, by a long-distance relationship. As soon as I first entertained the idea of a West Coast move, I immediately started building other connections out there through high school friends, college connections, and work associates. I found a new job using the Internet and acquaintances, re-connected with a childhood friend living in Los Angeles, and rented my own apartment in Santa Monica. I wasn't about to put all my eggs in my suitor's basket. I was personally ready for a change in geography for many reasons, not just for the man.

And it was a good thing that I took this "build your foundation first" approach, because once I moved, I quickly learned that my partner was at a stage where he could not handle a relationship in the same city. I was able to adjust quickly and accept that he was not emotionally ready for a commitment. Because I had already built my support systems, I was able to move on more easily.

This story brings up one of the downsides to long-distance relationships. They might work only because they are long distance. In other words, you and your man may both be busy professionals who don't have time for more than a phone friend and twice-a-month weekend date. When you do get together, there might be too much pressure to fulfill a fantasy and reality gets diluted. In fact, someone who regularly gets involved in long-distance romances may not be ready to commit to more than that, like my man friend above.

You don't ever want to move because you think a man is going to fix your life. You need balance to keep your confidence and sex appeal. Always try to keep your interests in mind first when making a move inspired by a long distance partner. In the end, you will have a more fulfilling life and be a better partner. The moral of the story: Keep your Home Box open and keep expanding its boundaries.

Expanding Your Home Box Part II Wrap-up

There are enough long-distance dating success stories, including international ones, to encourage you to stay open to Man Candidates from other countries or cities. It's a global economy these days and that includes the New Era dating options. The key is to be willing to continually expand your Home Box and try different experiences and dating options.

Exploring the New Era of Man Hunting— Start Dating Up a Storm

With this baseline understanding of New Era dating mechanics and opportunities and armed with safety guidelines, you can begin taking advantage of all the expanded dating options to start dating up a storm. These new trends and tools provide multiple angles for success in the 21st-century dating game.

- These modern dating scene themes create endless possibilities for finding your man.
- Email is a blind date enabler and provides an easy way to flirt with your man.
- Internet dating is more accepted, provides the most Man

Candidates, and can boost your ego by the increased dating activity.

- Chat rooms and singles events allow you to set the dating pace and share similar interests.
- Speed Dating and Silent Dating provide the fastest ways to meet and screen potential dates.
- Professional matchmakers can provide more help and higher quality candidates for a price.
- Singles events offer a low-key alternative way to expand your Home Box.
- International mixing can open your eyes to new cultures and Man Candidates.
- Long-distance romance is now more feasible with 21st century technologies.
- Wireless technology now offers endless ways to make virtual love connections.

With all the Man Candidates you're going to find yourself with, your biggest problem now is how to assess and evaluate them. The next section of this book provides you with everything you need for the Dating Assessment Dance—including GUT Instinct Checks, First Date Tests, Quick Qualifiers, Love Match Pre-Test, and the LIFE Match Game—to help you identify your Mr. Right. In short, you will learn how to get the facts to assess your man and how to work with your own instincts to pick the best Man Candidate for you. Using these assessment tools, you can gain insights on ways to be selective versus settling for a nice guy who shows interest. Don't settle for Mr. Goodenough or just anyone who adores you. Remember, searching for a life partner is equivalent to mining for gold. You want Mr. Wonderful, don't you?

PART III

The Dating Assessment Dance—Steps to the Perfect Match

9

❦

What You Should Know Before You Go

DO YOU WANT to save time by learning from other people's dating successes and mistakes? Are you willing to review your Mr. Right candidates thoroughly for the best long-term results? Are you ready to avoid the kind of failures you've experienced before in relationships?

Finding a lifetime man should be taken as seriously as searching for the right job. Forget taking the long road strategy used in Bridget Jones's dating diary. This new Dating Coach's plan can help you know when to say, "Next," versus when to take a closer look on a much faster track. In this section, you'll learn how best to assess your man for the greatest assurance of long-term success. Remember a Man Hunt is like a Job Hunt. In fact, Mr. Right interviews are even more important than finding the most desirable job because a marriage deal is much harder to break.

SMART Man Hunting is all about making the right choice at the right pace based on the broadest range of options:

- SMART is about proactively positioning yourself for dating success.
- SMART means using the right body language to get the right guy interested.
- SMART is expanding your bandwidth and increasing your odds.

- SMART is recognizing the red flags early so you know when to let go of Mr. Wrong much faster.
- SMART is realizing that choosing a partner is one of the most important decisions you can make.
- SMART is making a commitment to yourself to fully evaluate every Man Candidate based on whether *he* fits *your* needs, interests, values, and long-term goals.
- SMART means asking the right questions, listening for the red flag roadblocks, and then taking the time to observe his behavior to see whether he walks the talk.
- SMART is about relationship reality checks and knowing when to cut your losses and say, "Next!"
- SMART means pacing yourself and the relationship so as to enjoy the dating dance versus forcing it.
- SMART is about maintaining your confidence and sense of self as the relationship builds.
- SMART is knowing how to identify Mr. Goodenough versus your Mr. Wonderful.
- And before you start your evaluation, remember SMART is patient and persistent versus desperate, so take your time, have fun, and avoid giving off needy vibes.

It's imperative that you avoid being swept into a relationship based primarily on hormones and make a conscious decision to evaluate the entire package. While you definitely want a chemistry connection in a Love Match (LM), great sex is only one of the critical Mr. Right ingredients. Not only will saying, "Next" to Mr. Hormones only spare you a lot of wasted effort and energy, but it's also apt to spare your feelings as well. Don't waste any more time on Mr. Wrongs. Instead devote your energy to finding Mr. Right by saying, "You're fired" more often—even if it prolongs your search. You will save valuable time and heartache by insisting on a complete complementary package.

How do you go about evaluating your Man Candidates?

Maybe you've never even thought about it before because you've been more concerned about how *they* are evaluating *you*. Believe me, they are. But forget about that for now. And once you get into a relationship, remember to keep yourself together. You don't want to sound like a 34-year-old woman who told me, "My relationship was so much about making him happy and making the relationship work that I forgot about my needs." This Man Hunt is about what you want. This is about being SMART.

Positioning Yourself for Success

You've already positioned yourself for success by trying New Era dating options and jumping into passions where you may meet attractive men. You now have more options and increased confidence due to the ego boost benefit that you are feeling from all this dating activity. But what can you do in your everyday life to attract more high-quality men?

I surveyed bachelors to find out what body language makes them feel invited to make a move if they see a stranger in a bar, grocery store or in the drug store. Because 80 percent of communication is non-verbal, you might want to take a look in the mirror and find ways to enhance your body language to attract more desirable dates. Your eyes, smile, tone of voice, and energy level are all being closely checked out by men. Consider the green lights versus red lights that men consider when approaching a woman so you can position yourself for success.

Bachelor Survey Says . . . When to Approach

Approach Green Lights	**Approach Red Lights**
"Eye contact is the most powerful type of body language. It's a green light."	"If you're not getting any eye contact, it's a shot in the dark. You look like an idiot if you ask her if she wants a drink and she says no."

Approach Green Lights

"I get a general impression in one shot, and then look at more detail. I look for a willingness to engage in a conversation. I like it when a woman asks questions and acts interested."

"If we're in a bar, I'd be checking to see if she's with a guy. She has to look like she wants to be approached. Eye contact is key."

"The way she looks, her style, the way she carries herself."

"Pretty, in shape, smiling, nice hair, beautiful sparkly eyes, good posture, (indicates good self worth), and relaxed."

"If she is laughing with friends or smiling or otherwise seems easygoing (based upon non-verbal behavior or body language) and if she makes good eye-contact with me."

Approach Red Lights

"If a girl appears to be super confident, I tend to think she's out of my league. If she acts like she's hot stuff, it can be intimidating and scares me."

"Overweight, bad breath, bad teeth, bad skin, ratty hair (or hair that is dyed one or more unnatural colors), more piercings than just in her ears, ratty clothing, slouching (only if it is so much that it indicates an obvious lack ofself-esteem)."

"Shapeless sweatpants and sneakers."

"A pinched, sad, and angry face when she thinks no one is looking. Anxious when left alone, overly animated in a crowd, and sweatpants in public are other turn-offs."

"A bad personality or her politics."

Approach Green Lights

"If she takes care of herself and takes pride in her appearance. A great smile with eyes that become animated when she smiles. Her voice is also very important to me. Is it pleasant to listen to or does it grate on my nerves?"

"I observe her and see how she interacts with others, especially with any service staff, that tells me whether I want to meet her or not."

"A brain plus the guts to use it; humor and laughing; simple sexy outfits without much effort or make-up; positive easygoing attitude; kindness; weird off-beat interests; humble, gracious responsibility; self-starters/ entrepreneurs."

"When someone is engaging, confident and a good listener, that's a turn-on"

Approach Red Lights

"Lack of eye contact or effort not to make eye contact and, admittedly, fear of being rejected."

"Very nervous, shaking inside."

"Know-it-alls who talk all the time and try to impress; complicated schedules; too much makeup; materialism; negativity/martyr issues; corporate career-climbers."

"If a woman is self-absorbed and high-maintenance, it is a serious turn-off."

Should Women Make the First Move?

Once you make contact, what's a girl to do about making a first move? Should women make the first move when dating online or offline? Now that we are in the 21st century, why shouldn't we make more first moves? Of course you can wait for a guy to make a move if you are more comfortable, but according to my recent poll, the bachelors' survey says they love it when a woman makes a first move.

In order to succeed, you will want insights on how to manage this delicate dance move. You want to use humor, drop hints, and body language signals to show that you are interested versus coming across as desperate or aggressive. By sending short, personal and lighthearted emails to men, women can especially find success making the first move online.

Men traditionally make the first move when Internet dating. So if a woman contacts a guy online first, they are going to look twice before deleting your message because you took the time to show interest. By using the "wink" feature on many dating sites, you can be more subtle and find more dates that you desire. I tried this approach on Match.com and got a handful of dates because the guys were flattered. Below are survey responses from seven hot bachelors who shared their thoughts on whether a woman should go for it first!

Bachelor's Survey Says . . . Women Should Make the First Move!

Bachelor #1

"*Absolutely!* The earlier, the better. It's best if women wouldn't disguise their intentions."

Bachelor #2

"A woman should make the first move if she feels the man won't and she wants to clearly let him know she wants to exchange more than platonic energy with him."

Bachelor #3

"If there's interest and curiosity, then certainly express it! We're not in a "traditional" culture anymore where men have to make all the first moves. As frank as people are in the business world, we should be aware of our fellow human beings. Press on regardless!"

Bachelor #4

"I think if a woman's interested, she can definitely take initiative, but with discretion. If she doesn't do it right, she'll have all the same things guys face—possible embarrassment, appearance of being desperate, rejection—along with the fact that it's not a cultural norm. What's wrong if she says hello? If the guy's into her, he'll retake the initiative and ask her on a date, and suddenly all the cultural niceties are back in order."

Bachelor #5

"The first move needs to be a very small, 'Hi,' or some sort of very simple greeting that allows the man room to responsively initiate. If a woman is very forward in initiating, it can cause a relationship to occur with an otherwise passive, unmotivated guy."

Bachelor #6

"My answer is, sure. Being essentially very shy I pretty much leave it up to women to initiate contact. If they don't either make the first move or indicate somehow that they want something to happen, it won't. Left to my own devices I'd be a lonely guy."

Bachelor #7

"I'd like to see more women making first moves honestly."

And how do bachelors define the delicate balance needed for women to make first moves?

- "If we are already on a date because I asked her out and then she makes the first move, physically *Great*! Because it signals to me that things are going well and will only get better."
- "If a girl asks me to dance at a club, that's good."
- "If I give a girl my number, then it's totally okay for her to call me and ask me out."

- "I would like it if a woman sent me a drink in a bar. It's a nice and subtle move. I wish it would happen more."
- "It would be over the top for the woman to get my number from someone else without my knowledge and call me for a date."

Here's to a new day when women can feel great about making more first moves.

Man Candidate Interview Practices

So, you've entered the New Era, tried on all its dating options, and the men are lined up at your door for dates. It's now time to be selective. By properly interviewing and evaluating your Mr. Right candidates, you can succeed at a long-term relationship by taking the time to talk through your goals, interests, and backgrounds with potential matches.

Your job is to evaluate which Man Candidates will stick. Whom do you want to see after your first date? Whom do you want to see for a second or third date? And after the third date turning point, who is showing long-term or even marriage potential?

A wise 39-year-old film editor told me, "Dating interviews are all about testing flexibility and negotiating boundaries." By the time you get to the third date, asking LIFE Match Questions, active listening, and observing behavior can help you discover the real man behind the candidate to assess marriage potential. The film editor added: "You need to find out if the person is too extreme for you in certain areas." For example, if someone is a baseball fanatic and you have no interest in that sport, start asking questions to find out whether it is important to him that his partner join him at all the games.

Dating assessment is a three-step dance, one that you are doing with your date. While he's dancing, you're going to be dancing too. Each step is geared to a deepening level of interest in your date as you are opening up with each other. The steps are also about getting the information you need and recognizing red flags

early so that you can make some decisions in the shortest period
of time. Why spend months dating someone only to discover he's
not right for you? With the Dating Assessment Dance Steps provided in this section, you'll be able to make a decision quickly—
usually within the first three to seven dates. Try these steps to
secure a long and happy relationship.

Mining for Gold—Defining Your Mr. Right

You can't mine for gold if you don't know what it is. In other
words, what does Mr. Right look like to you? Before you even
engage in Man Candidate Interview Practices, you have to know
what you are looking for in a Perfect Match. Employers don't
seek to fill a position without a job description, and neither
should you.

Identify your Key Criteria

What's your gold? Ask yourself what qualities and attributes you
want to see in a lifetime man and consider how important they
are to you. Qualities may include honesty, kindness, consideration, intelligence, approach to life, looks—in short, it's any variety of things. (If you need ideas, you can read more about how
others define their Perfect Match at the end of Part III, The
Dating Assessment Dance—see the Perfect Tango story, p. 214.)

Define your Best Attributes

What's golden about you? Be able to define your best attributes,
along with what you desire in a mate. Take a closer look at your
behavior patterns and desires. Search for men who are seeking
your best qualities for greater LIFE Match Game success. While
you never want to make yourself over in an attempt to become
what someone is looking for, you'll have greater success if you are
honest enough to know whether who you are fits what someone is
telling you they want. If a man is looking for a great cook and
take-out is your middle name, it's reasonable to assume that a
match between you won't work. And if he asks you to describe

yourself, you want to make sure you have your marketing pitch down. Remember you want someone to think of you as their gold.

Keep your key criteria in mind during all initial contacts with Man Candidates, whether in email, on the phone, or in person. Be prepared to eliminate anyone who doesn't fit the list. Once you mine for gold in the crowd, your chances of finding Mr. Right will rise significantly. By only meeting the top men, you will have a greater chance of finding a soul mate faster. If you are looking for a long-term relationship, don't waste time with unlikely matches. The opportunity cost is too high and you need to focus your energies on real candidates.

It is important not to force a match if there are major differences. If you identify someone that sounds great, but your key criteria do not complement each other, move on quickly to the next prospect. One 33-year-old financial manager shared this observation, "If you want to believe something, you can believe almost anything. People get lost in relationships and are not objective." You need to be truthful with yourself and objective on the Hunt.

Let Your GUT Be Your Guide

Have you ever noticed how often your friends end up dating or marrying men unlike any of the other men they've ever been with before? Or how often the people you know end up with someone you'd never have expected to see them with? How did that happen? What drew her to that man? I'm not talking about the disasters you can see from a mile away here, but the healthy, yet surprising relationships around you.

The answer is probably the bottom line GUT factor. There is truth to the common wisdom, "Trust your gut." What is your gut telling you about a man. In SMART Man Hunting, your GUT should be alerting you to a potential Mr. Right even if "on paper" he's not what you initially might have envisioned. What is GUT? Try this expanded definition to look beyond the surface early in the game:

Genuine—Is he sincere?

Understanding—Does he actually listen, care, and share his
feelings with you?

Trustworthy—Is he trustworthy, reliable, and of good
character?

Much of this GUT definition is probably on your list of key
criteria above. Everyone is seeking the same core GUT qualities
in a life partner: honesty, trust, companionship, good communication, compromise, consideration, confidence, and fun. You
will find them listed online in the "Hallmark greeting card"
profiles.

So why is it so hard to find? Timing and desire are probably
the biggest hurdles. You need to find someone who is ready, willing, and able to share these core qualities with you. If you find a
man who matches your values, personality and desires, and happens to also be a great Love Match (LM), the wedding bells will
be much closer than spending time with a candidate who builds
fences around himself.

In SMART Man Hunting, it's important to let your GUT be
your guide throughout your dating travels. If you're looking for
a life partner, you're looking for GUT. If you talk to divorced
couples, the majority will tell you that their GUT knew before
they walked down the aisle that it was not the right match. Why
did they take such a major leap of faith? If your GUT is not
good, don't be afraid to jump ship. You might feel alone at first,
but think about the wedding bills and heartache you will save in
the long run.

I interviewed a 40-something marketing manager who met a
sales manager at a networking party in Dallas, Texas. At first, he
said everything that a girl would want to hear. When they started
talking on the phone before their next date, this jerk started talking about sex when he barely knew the woman. He told her, "I
want to do it with you in every position." On another call he told
her, "I bet you are really amazing in bed." She fired this guy

immediately after that phone call. She told me, "I sent him a short and to the point email that I was not comfortable with continuing the conversations or seeing him again." Even though the guy called to apologize for taking their phone conversations too far, she simply deleted his voicemails and never returned his calls. If a guy is out of line, fire him fast. As my close 37-year-old girlfriend prepares for her wedding she told me, "It really matters what you feel when you're with the person. I like who I am when I am with him." She reconnected with a college friend after years of no contact. He was studying to be a minister and planning to visit India. Because my girlfriend had studied in India, he called her unexpectedly in Washington, D.C., from Texas to ask for advice.

After several calls and emails, they decided to visit in person. Within three months, she knew that he was "the one" for her. Her 37-year-old male partner is now moving to Washington, D.C., and has decided not to be ordained. The couple was open-minded about long-distance relationships, listened to their GUT instincts, and found life partnership in the end. When you get a good GUT feeling that your man is genuine, understanding, and trustworthy—you might just throw your Mr. Perfect checklist in the trash.

Start checking your GUT with candidates by asking yourself these questions:

GUT Instinct Questions

- Is he real?
- Does he make me feel really good about myself?
- Is he enthusiastic about getting to know me?
- Is he polite and considerate to me and others?
- Does he share his feelings with me?
- Is he trustworthy?
- Is he reliable?
- Does conversation with him flow or is it a struggle?

- Can we share laughs together?
- Does he make me smile?
- Is he really into me?

Take a closer look at the dynamics of the dance with your Mr. Right candidates. Besides asking them questions, you can learn a great deal simply by observing them. Remember the adage "Actions speak louder than words." What is his behavior telling you? As a wise 34-year-old female marketing manager told me, "If people contradict themselves with their behavior, pointing it out seems pointless. They're only telling you what you want to hear—been there, done that!"

Your GUT reactions want to sound like this dating success story. Six months after ending a seven-year relationship with a good guy, a 30-something TV producer found herself with sparks flying across the room with a serious Mr. Right contender. When I asked her, "How did you know?" she replied, "It was instantaneous—it was like a snowball. It started running down the hill and never stopped." When I asked her to continue, she added, "The best part about it was that he was completely open and honest. He wasn't afraid to call and there were no rules." Her last comment tells it all. She said, "I've just been in tune with him since the beginning." Along with the basic GUT instincts, below are some observation clues. Men often express love and caring more freely through their actions than their words so watch for these good GUT signs and recognize the unspoken messages when identifying Mr. Right candidates early.

Good GUT Man Behaviors

Good GUT Man Action	The Unspoken Message
The guy is always on time or calls if he is running a little late.	He values and respects your time.

Good GUT Man Action	**The Unspoken Message**
He opens the car door and pulls the chair back for you at restaurants.	He is a gentleman. He wants to show you consideration. There is no need for chivalry to be dead in the 21st century. Let him treat you like gold.
The guy turns his cell phone off when he is on a date with you.	This man wants to be with you and only you during dates.
During the initial dance, he picks you up at your place and makes formal plans.	He wants to make an effort to treat you with respect.
The guy follows up the day after a date with a call or email to simply thank you for a great time.	This guy is in to you.
The man is willing to compromise on how and when you meet and what you do together.	This guy is flexible, which is a great foundation for any relationship.
Your date gives you compliments, but does not go overboard.	He likes you.
He tells you about friends and family that he wants you to meet.	He wants to share his life with you, which is a great Mr. Right sign.

You might be surprised by the twists in your Man Hunt road. If the GUT is good with a man you would normally not consider, give him a second look.

Looking Beyond GUT

If you've got GUT, you also want to look beyond your basic instincts. GUT can take you a long way, but you still need to be compatible in core areas and want the same things out of life and love. Even with GUT, you have to be SMART. So engage in all the SMART Man Hunting Interview Practices, Strategies, and the LIFE Match Game to see if your Good GUT Man can become your Mr. Wonderful.

Give Him Three Chances to Enter the Mr. Right Lane

I recommend three dates before knocking someone off your Mr. Right Lane list if he passes the First Date Tests and looks like he could be a good GUT Man. By the third encounter, you'll have gathered enough information to make a solid assessment of the candidate. When you are seeking a new job, employers rarely offer the position based on the first interview. In a similar manner, give the guy three chances to show his true colors, and then continue to monitor for reality checks and red flags as you move on to the LIFE Match Game. If you are not "star struck" by the third encounter, hit the eject button. Just like some guys have been taught that if you don't have sex by the third date, dump the girl, let's create a new third date rule for women. Let's agree to only invest time in the LIFE Match Game when your GUT is really good with a guy at the third date mark. If there is any hesitation, hit the eject button immediately! Let *SMART Man Hunting* empower you to make these Go/No-Go choices faster so you don't waste weeks, months, or even years with the wrong match.

Consider the Importance of LIFE Match

As you evaluate your Man Candidates, one of your main objectives is to find out if your life goals, values, and attitudes match up. One of the reasons so many couples may be divorcing these days is a failure to consider LIFE Match during courtship. LIFE

Match is more than just statements of what you want or are seeking. It's all in the attitudes and actions.

You want to sound like this compatibility success story. From her Manhattan Beach, California, beachfront apartment, this 30-something finance manager found her true love in San Diego, California. This southern California connection was off the charts in terms of compatibility, chemistry, and communication. She reached beyond her city limits to find true love with an old boyfriend. She said, "We want the same type of a relationship and value the same dynamics. For example, we both want our significant other to be our weekend playmate. We love to surf together, go golfing, hiking, whatever. We just like to do it together." A few months after this interview, I received an email from Ms. Manhattan Beach announcing her engagement. When I sent her my congratulations, she replied; "I just couldn't be happier. I have totally found my Prince Charming and feel like the luckiest person in the world."

LIFE Match will show you whether you and your Man Candidate have what it takes to go the distance.

What You Should Know
Before You Go Wrap-up

You're ready to meet your Man Candidates and begin the Dating Assessment Dance. Before you go, it's a good idea to review your key criteria in a man and define what you think is "golden" about you. You know that finding a Mr. Right is about successful interview practices, listening for clues, and SMART observations so pack these skills in your bag. Think about male green lights, red lights, and how to position yourself for success to increase your odds. As a prelude to your KISS Test, use Quick Qualifiers and the other early tests to see if your date has the potential to be a Mr. Right. Keep in mind that your GUT is probably the most important indicator of success when making your selection. Is he genuine, understanding, and trustworthy? Is he really into you? And more important, are you really into him?

10

---~◎~---

The Dating Assessment Dance—Step One: The KISS Test and Coffee Talk

BY NOW YOU'VE WEEDED OUT the undesirables, you've given some thought to what really matters to you, and have a few interested men in line. Are you ready to meet your Man Candidates? Do you like coffee? Even if you don't, find a coffee shop near your home, order something else, and then prepare for your first date screening questions and tests. The coffee shop is the ideal setting because it is a neutral, safe, and public place. The first date is simply about checking each other out and building rapport.

You are simply screening the candidates. Quickly decide whether you would go on a second date with the guy or immediately remove him from your list. Relax, take a deep breath, put on your confidence and your best colors, and avoid first date discussion bloopers. Focus on the following KISS Test in order to maximize results and minimize first date disasters.

The KISS Test

The only thing you should ask yourself on a first date is, "Do I want to kiss this guy?" A 48-year-old personal trainer told me that after a few email exchanges with Internet dating candidates, he often writes, "Don't you think it's time for us to meet at the coffee shop and decide whether we would want to kiss each other?"

As simple as that, this Chemistry Connection check should be your primary objective on your first encounter with someone. One 39-year-old movie producer told me, "My friends have a sixty-second test. They decide whether there is any chemistry within the first minute."

You might want to give the candidate a full hour before making a chemistry Go/No-Go decision—especially if there's good GUT—even though you will probably know in the first five minutes.

Watch the non-verbal communication between you and the Man Candidate during the first date to guess how he rates you on his KISS Test. A 35-year-old paralegal manager reminded me, "When identifying Mr. Right, the number one thing to consider is whether there is mutual sexual attraction." While you will probably know if there is a mutual attraction right away, observe his chemistry clues while remaining conscious of your own signals to him. Remember to be SMART, sexy, and confident. Similar to dressing for a successful job interview, wear something that makes you look and feel good. Your dress and positive persona will make lasting impressions on a candidate. As one 47-year-old bachelor said to me: "Don't dress like you want to go to bed with the guy either." Instead, dress SMART for the occasion and draw him in with confidence versus bare skin.

Non-verbal Chemistry Connection Clues

If you are wondering what the guy is thinking, here are some non-verbal clue questions to help you gauge the man's attraction level to you:

- Is he smiling at you often? Is he leaning toward you? Is he nodding his head when you are making a point?
- Is he making direct eye contact or are his eyes wandering around the room?

- Does he try to make contact by reaching out to hold your hand or touch your shoulder?
- Does he raise his eyebrows to show enthusiasm when making important points?
- Does he open the door for you? Does he try to hug you good-bye?
- Does he try to kiss you when he says good-bye? (I'm okay with this move on a first date if there is a good connection. You need to decide your own boundaries.)
- Is he dressed nicely, or does he look like someone who just rolled out of bed? (Actually, if he is unkempt, this is a clue that this guy isn't all that interested. Next.)

If these non-verbal clues are present on a first date, they are great indicators that the guy is into you. If you find the candidate physically appealing, give him the same type of positive confirmations in return. Because chemistry is a major part of the equation and up to 80 percent of communication is non-verbal, don't overlook the importance of this initial KISS Test exchange.

KISS Approach

While the main point of the first encounter, testing to see if there is a Chemistry Connection, involves a non-verbal exchange, you're also going to have to do some talking. Approach your first dates with a very casual and relaxed attitude for the best results. When engaging in conversation, follow this wise KISS approach: Keep It Simple, Stupid. Your only concern is whether you would consider kissing the candidate in the future so save the details for after they pass Go.

Do not propose marriage on a first date. Never put a guy on trial. While you might be laughing, my Lunch Men dating coordinator told me, "I know women who have gotten very aggressive on their first date. The feedback was not good." You do not need to conduct a federal investigation on the first date. You want to be

SMART about these meetings, and SMART is not desperate or aggressive, so relax.

Use easy and non-threatening questions during your first date to create a comfortable conversation. You are meeting a stranger, so simply take the opportunity to build rapport.

KISS Questions

Here is a short list of KISS questions that you can use during this brief first date meeting to keep things light and positive:

- What do you like to do for fun? How long have you lived here? Where did you grow up? What was your favorite vacation?
- Where would you like to visit if you could go anywhere in the world?
- Have you seen any good movies lately?
- If you could play pool or Fooseball, which would you play and why? (Listen to their why versus the choice for a quick compatibility check.)
- Who is your favorite sports team and why? (This question can tell you a lot about a man's sports extremes before you decide on a second date.)
- What do you think the weather will do today? (A great KISS question for most of the U.S., but not as effective for southern California—sorry to rub it in, but people don't talk weather that often in L.A. unless it is raining.)

KISS Question Warning: Do not ask "How is your dating going?" I cannot count how many men asked me, "How do you like Internet dating?" or "Have you had any success using Speed Dating?" during first encounters. These questions only bring up discussions about other dates and you are trying to avoid First Date Disasters.

Avoiding First Date Disasters

The number one cause of first date disasters is fear, which leads to discussion bloopers and unnecessary anxiety. Remember, you have adopted a No-Fear attitude so you can avoid these clashes on your Man Hunt journey.

What fuels fear on first dates is anxiety over surprises, rejection, or disappointments—and usually it's a combination of all three. I also think a primary cause of first date jitters is societal pressure to be successful. People tend to base self-worth on success in career and family. On first dates, there is extra conversational emphasis on these two areas since most first date questions always revolve around what you do for a living and what your relationship history might be. These questions come dangerously close to pressing low-self-worth buttons.

You need to forget about this pressure for an hour, relax, and focus on being positive. So what topics should you avoid discussing on a first date? Similar to the Internet dating tips discussed earlier, you want to hold your cards close to your chest. Don't share your whole life story. You are in marketing pitch mode so why bring up any dating obstacles?

First Date Discussion Bloopers

Do you want to avoid being added to the First Date Discussion Bloopers Hall of Shame? Then avoid getting too personal on first dates. Remember, your key to success is using a KISS approach. Here are three of my favorite bloopers that you should dodge on first dates:

Don't Bring Up Finances or Big Checkbooks

No one needs to know your financial status on a first date. Nor do they need to try to be impressed by fancy cars and big checkbooks. A woman raised a question at one of my book signings regarding finances. "I am living on disability payments. Do you think that I should tell this to a man on the first date because I want to be honest?" My response: "I believe in honesty, but don't bring it up on the first date. You need to decide whether you want to kiss him before you start sharing anything too personal." First dates are all about chemistry and that has nothing to do with material things. If you talk too much about finances on a first date, you will definitely kill the sparks.

Why Talk About Weaknesses?

Would you ever bring up your weaknesses in a job interview? Why would you ever share your scars during a first date? If you are having trouble dating, don't share that information with a date. You want to be sexy, smart, and confident instead. I had drinks with a guy who told me on a first date, "Liz, I just can't figure out dating. I can't get women to call me back and they cancel plans with me at the last minute all the time." Why would he ever share this information with me on a first date? What a turn-off! This is too much information. Next.

Leave the Exes in the Car

Talking about past relationships is the number one mistake people make on first dates. I think daters feel self-conscious and want to clarify why they are no longer dating someone. I went out with a guy who told me on a first date that he left his wife, then got her pregnant, went back to have the baby, and was in the process of divorcing her again— Check, please! Why bother bringing any negative energy into the equation? You are both single now and on even ground. You want to be beaming with positive energy and make someone feel special so leave the ex in the car for the first few dates. And if you get asked about your ex, just give a nonchalant, casual response and then switch gears fast!

Always accent the positive because the first date is all about marketing yourself to a potential mate. Go back to your key selling points and talk about your passions versus your pains.

What Men Watch in Women on First Dates

While I received many comments about first dates from men, here is an insightful list from a 35-year-old-lawyer regarding what he watches in women on first dates.

- "How does she carry herself?"
- "Is she wearing nice clothes that go together? Are her shoes worn out?"
- "Is she interested and receptive to me?"
- "Can she get my sense of humor?"
- "Can she maintain prolonged eye contact?"
- "Does she smile often? Does she smile and then look away with her eyes in a flirtatious way?"
- "Is she okay with showing that she likes me?"
- "Is she conversational or confrontational?"
- "Is she nodding to show that she is listening?"

His bottom line comment about his observations, "I think a woman who carries herself well is ten times more attractive."

Remember, you want to highlight your strong points (and without being too boastful). First conversations are about using the right balance to present a desirable package. It's not the words so much that matter, it's your attitude. SMART daters avoid dating disasters!

The First Kiss

So how far should you take it physically on a first date? If a guy shakes your hand, that is probably not a good sign. If a guy kisses you on the cheek, he is most likely interested and is a gentleman. But what if he goes for your lips? What kind of first date kiss do you prefer? Here are a few best and worst first kiss stories from bachelorette experts whom I interviewed about their experiences.

Best Kiss

"My best kiss was kissing someone that I had wanted to for a long time and couldn't because he didn't live where I did . . . so after the long build up, it was definitely worth the wait!"

"Believe it or not the best was a light kiss on the lips, and more important, it was what was said right before it. Speaking of the anticipation, he told me, 'It gets harder every time I see you.' I still melt."

"There are different sorts of 'best kisses.' The commonality is that it is a passionate kiss with someone that there's been great chemistry with for some amount of time period. . . . It can be either deep or tender."

"The firecrackers exploded when a guy gently connected our lips and looked directly at me at the end of a first date. The chemistry was intense and this kiss sent chills down my spine."

"My best kiss was a sensual kiss, followed by an

Worst Kiss

"The worst was kissing someone who was way too anxious to kiss me and was sloppy!"

"The worst (and I remember this far back) was at a high school dance when a guy who had been drinking came up to me and stuck his tongue in my mouth and splashed it around. Gross!"

"The 'worst kisses' are when someone forces his tongue into my mouth and it just lays there or there is no muscle-tone to his tongue. (The guy's tongue reminds be of a limp piece of sashimi rather than something a bit firmer, such as cooked eel.)"

"Super wet kisses (as if the guy has hyper saliva production) is a turn-off."

"Oooh, I just remembered a time when this guy I met

immediate compliment and request for a second sensual kiss. Both kisses were sexy and I walked away with a big wow."

"The best kisses are when a guy nibbles on my lips like he is enjoying a fine meal. It makes me feel special versus someone just to fulfill his sexual needs."

playing pool with roommates came to take me out on our first date . . . His kiss tasted like he had been eating British "bangers" for days. Yuck!!! (If you are unfamiliar with bangers, think spicy Polish sausage with grilled onions.)"

"The worst first kiss was when I got mauled by a guy's enthusiasm and slobber. I could not breathe and this first kiss was way too sloppy. I had to ask him to slow down, but it didn't work. His slobber maul kiss was a huge turn-off."

A first kiss can be very telling so listen to the signs and know when to say Next! When I went to survey bachelorettes on whether they thought the first kiss tells you anything about the future of a relationship, the results were mixed.

Bachelorette Survey Says . . . Fist Kiss Signs

- "I think it's a good indicator of the man, what he is like. So actually, if you can kind of tell what a man is like by his kiss, then you can guess what your relationship could be like, then decide the future of your relationship with your man."
- "Yes. Three and a half years later, I am still with my best kiss and very much in love."
- "No, I do not think a first kiss means much . . . that is, unless it is truly horrible. However, I think more men than women think there is some truth to this."
- "Yes in an inverted way. The good first kissers always turned out to be the non-committal type guys. Hence, they become good first kissers, lots of practice."

Listen to your GUT when you give a guy the KISS Test, and if the GUT is good, then you probably want to go for that second date.

The Second Date Hunch

If the candidate has passed Go on your KISS Test and it seems you've received positive signals in return, you can expect that you'll be proceeding to the next date. If this doesn't happen, don't sweat it. Remember there are plenty of other men out there. Above all else, don't take it personally. There could be a thousand reasons why he doesn't want to see you again and usually none of them have anything to do with you. Anyway, if you misread the non-verbal clues and he felt no chemistry connection with you, who cares? Give yourself credit for putting your best foot forward and taking a chance. There will be plenty of men who will feel a mutual Chemistry Connection with you.

The first date is really about screening out who will make it to the second date. If you make it to the second date, pay attention to what the guy plans to gauge his level of interest. What have been your best and worst second dates? Here are some examples to help you gauge your guy's level of interest:

Best Second Dates

- After a first screening coffee date, a guy set up an afternoon horseback riding date. We went out to a polo club and had a private guide take us on a one-hour ride. We went for a nice lunch afterward and shared Caribbean food, which made for an even more special date.

- A creative guy took my girlfriend to a five-star hotel for drinks and appetizers for a second date. They dressed for the setting, which made the date a little more exciting. They shared stories and kissed on the couch near the fireplace. She told me, "This intimate date definitely increased my comfort level."

- Another hot second date was when a guy took me sailing out of the Marina. He encouraged me to take the helm and showed great confidence on this date. We shared wine, cheese, and crackers along the journey, and this date made a lasting impression.

- In another best second date scenario, a guy invited a girl-friend to his favorite dim sum restaurant in Chinatown for a different experience. Since she had never ventured down-town to this area, it was a great adventure and made him stand out in her mind. She told me, "We laughed and swapped international travel stories."

Worst Second Dates

- One of my worst second dates was with a guy who asked me out with no game plan, and then left everything up to me. He told me, "I know I'm supposed to have a plan, but I have not thought about it." He asked me to look up the movies online, and then groaned when I expected him to pay for the movie ticket. Next!

- My girlfriend had a horrible second date with a guy who invited her to his apartment without a plan. Once she arrived, he took her to a diner in Beverly Hills that had hor-rible food. She confessed to me, "I love diners, but this one was the pits and so was he."

- In a different dilemma, a guy invited me to his house for dinner on a second date. I just wasn't ready to be alone with him, which told me that I was probably not into him. I was dating up a storm and was not totally "star struck" at this early stage. I delicately explained that I preferred to go out again before coming over to his casa. He never called me again.

If a guy is into you, he will make an effort. It doesn't need to be an expensive date, but he should at least choose a dive with good food. If you don't see any signs of a plan or effort, you know what to say. Your time is way too valuable for slackers. Pay attention to the creative daters with a plan.

Red Flag Men

From the first step of your Dating Assessment Dance, you should be on the look-out for Red Flag Men. Usually you can only identify these guys in person, but once you do, you will know. Even when there is a Chemistry Connection, Red Flag Men should be avoided at all costs. The KISS Test can blind you to who these men are, which is why I include them here.

This step is where you really need to rely on your GUT so listen to your instincts and if something does not feel good, get out fast. In order to save you time, embarrassment, and possibly heartache, I want to help you recognize these bad eggs. These tales may also bring you a sigh of relief when you realize that you are not alone if you have bumped into these guys in the past. Here are three types of Red Flag Men and the warning signs to look for on your Man Hunt journey:

Sly Schemer

The Sly Schemer is a "player." He is acting a part and will try to deceive you. This guy plays a game using either fancy words or material things to draw you into the bedroom as fast as possible. You need to watch out for the signs early and run for the hills. These actors will tell you whatever you want to hear to get you in bed. They are likely to be playing the game with multiple women at once as well. Watch out for men who give you too many compliments too early. Watch out for the guys with false promises.

In addition to playing with words, a Sly Schemer might shower you with gifts and take you to fancy restaurants for the sole purpose of winning you over so that you will sleep with him quickly. Unfortunately, many men follow a third date rule. If you are not in the bedroom with them by the third date, they disappear. They have found women who let them get away with it, so if they don't get what they want from you, they just keep moving until someone else falls for their antics. If a guy tries to impress you with material things right off the bat, take a closer look. Fancy dinners, flowers, and gifts should not lure you in too fast.

While dream men exist, beware of the guys who give you too much attention too soon. I met a man at a party who immediately locked on to me. He told me, "You look like a really interesting person. I'm hosting this party, but will you stick around so we can get to know each other." Afterward, he ended up taking me to a wonderful restaurant in Beverly Hills for dinner with his boss. We had a fantastic feast and enjoyed talking about the party and mutual acquaintances. After dinner, he proceeded to give me sloppy kisses (first red flag). The next day he flew home to Phoenix, Arizona, and then started calling me almost every other day. While the first calls were positive and complimentary, it started going downhill fast when he tried unsuccessfully to shift to phone sex (second red flag). Okay, we had not even gone on a formal date and the guy wants to talk sex. What a turn-off! When he called to announce his plane reservations, intentions to "stay on my couch," and need to address his "back-up problem" (third red flag), I fired him fast via email. He was a sales manager looking to close a deal, and I had way too many objections.

Watch out for men who come after you like a fast freight train filled with goodies and compliments at lightning speeds. They are not real deals. If it's Mr. Right you are trying to find, jump off this Mr. Wrong train immediately.

Macho Mind

The Macho Mind is a man who places men first, including male friendships, opinions, and activities. These men consider women more as sex objects than as life partners. He prefers spending time on the golf course with his buddies versus taking you away for a romantic weekend. You know these men. They will hang out with the guys over you any day. They place a greater value on hunting, playing poker, and watching football with the gang versus spending quality time with you. Macho Minds don't have female friends so they don't know what they are missing. So when you ask a guy, "What do you like to do for fun?" on a first date, watch for the clues in their answer to see if they have Macho Mind tendencies. If 90 percent of their answer is a list of activities with male buddies, you are probably dealing with a Macho Mind.

In addition, Macho Mind men don't get that when they are out with you they are not supposed to be checking out other women. A great red flag for Macho Minds is that even on the first date their eyes will be wandering to the other women in the room. He should be focused on learning about you versus staring at other women. I don't care if he is cute. If he does not give you his full attention on a first date, forget about him!

While I don't believe couples should have to share every activity and do think that each person should have their own friends, what's wrong with the Macho Mind is the attitude. These guys don't value women or their opinions or ideas, in fact, they don't even *like* being with women. I briefly dated a Macho Mind who told me, "I really value my male friends because we are going through many of the same things and we can talk about our careers." Excuse me? Don't women have careers these days? Valuing a female's opinion is not part of the Macho Mindset. What are these guys thinking? We are in the 21st century and to think that some men don't value what a woman thinks is mind-boggling and scary. You want to find someone who wants to hear your input on important decisions. Why waste time with Macho Minds?

Me-First Man

The Me-First Man is not always easy to recognize initially. This man is totally self-absorbed and preoccupied with his accomplishments, career, workout routine, and anything else that has to do with feeding his ego. Because the natural tendency is to swap resumes during the first few dates, it might be harder to identify the Me-First Man.

Look for clues when he discusses his schedule. Since he just met you, you can't judge him on how he fits you into his time, but what about his family and friends? Does he try to make an effort to make plans with others or does he just wait for the world to please him? How does he describe spending time with the important people in his life? When he shares these encounters, does he describe them only in terms of himself and his needs? Is he set in his ways and his schedule to the point of rigidity? For example, does he need to work out every day at a certain time or he turns into a wild animal?

One of my girlfriends dated a 29-year-old man who was completely self-absorbed. He was fortunate to have grown up in a very affluent family and was handed all the nice things in life way too easily. This Me-First Man stuck to his daily workout schedule at the club across the street, loved playing with his fancy cars, made her drive to his place all the time, and then rarely took time to listen to her interests and needs. When she jokingly commented to him one day, "You are spoiled rotten," he responded by saying, "You don't know the half of it." And if you think this statement is telling, listen to what he pulled on Valentine's Day. Not only did he show up empty-handed two months into the relationship, he didn't even take the time to make a dinner reservation. The couple ended up at a sushi bar and it made her feel horrible to be so taken for granted. Soon after receiving this Me-First message, she got smart and said, "Next!"

If a guy is so self-absorbed that he can't be bothered to listen to you talk about your day or buy you a card on Valentine's Day, what are you doing hanging out with this Me-First Man? Any time you run across this type of Red Flag Man, promptly hit the eject button. There is no give-and-take with these guys so where's the relationship potential?

The Dating Assessment Dance—
Step One Wrap-up

Congratulations, you made it past the first date screening tests, shared Coffee Talk, and trusted your second date hunches. You made small talk while you were checking out your Man Candidate and observing his non-verbal cues about his attraction to you. This fun phase is about marketing, eliminating the obvious "Nos," and enjoying a bit of an adventure. And as one 31-year-old male, who is a financial manager, told me, "You are lucky to learn a little about the person on a first date."

Another active dater, a 42-year-old production coordinator,

shared a similar perspective. She said, "It's basically a look and see. It's a show and tell." So go to first dates with low expectations, play it safe, bring your marketing pitch, and try to have some fun versus fright. Now that you have knocked out the Red Flag Men and selected a few good candidates whom you want to kiss, you're ready to roll up your sleeves and really suss out what makes your candidate tick.

11

---ം---

The Dating Assessment Dance—Step Two: Quick Qualifiers and Go/No-Go Signs

ONCE YOU'VE GOTTEN the first encounter and Kiss Test over with, you can start gathering more details and identifying Go/No-Go decisions. Here are some things to look for as you date your Man Candidate the second, third, and even fourth times. Don't be shy about asking relevant questions, but you don't have to interrogate the guy either. Part of the process is learning if you enjoy spending time with someone and feel comfortable in his presence. On the other hand, give yourself a pep talk every time you go out with your candidate and set your mind on getting some answers so you can determine if he is BA (Bachelor Available), who is ready for a relationship. It's too easy to be afraid to be SMART and just go with the flow. And when you are emotionally ready, test whether he is good in bed as your LM (Love Match) before you go too far. Going with the flow too long is not what this book is about and is not SMART. You need to uncover the common ground and identify the No-Go deal breakers to avoid Mr. Time Waster.

Man Hunt Interview Practices

As you spend time with your Man Candidate, consider that you are also interviewing him. Your aim is to discover as much relevant information about him as possible. Take it easy and don't rush things so you allow room for romance. Also, during the journey, remind yourself that perfect people do not exist so avoid the Perfectionism Ferris Wheel. Develop your interview strategy based on these suggested guidelines and remember, fun and smarts are success keys.

1. Prepare to Tango

Be prepared to share your thoughts and desires with Man Candidates when they ask for your viewpoint. You are entering a two-way street and should be ready to give your answers to the same questions that you ask him. This is a dance and is about getting to know each other, not about you putting him on trial. After all, it is only fair that if you ask him a tough question, you also have to answer a few. Guys like women with opinions and interests so be prepared to add value to the dance.

2. Ask and Listen

One of the most important approaches when interviewing Mr. Right is to use your active listening skills (see more information on p. 189–91) when meeting with candidates. I cannot count the number of men and women who have said to me, "They were so into themselves and trying to prove that they were wonderful to me that I did not get in a word in the conversation."

There is nothing that turns someone off more than when you show that you are not listening to him or her by dominating the conversation. Your aim is to learn about your candidate, so ask your questions and let him do the majority of the talking. Use reflective statements such as, "You told me that you started playing piano at six years old. What do you like the most about playing?" to pull out his personality.

3. Get the Facts First

There are many ways to gather Foundational Facts about your Mr. Right candidates. You should work at uncovering this information within the first few communications and make mental notes as the facts unfold. Basic facts include age, height, weight, family structure, marital history/offspring, career, education, and hobbies. You will often immediately discover deal breakers by simply gathering the facts.

If you use New Era options such as Internet dating or professional matchmakers, most of this data is already provided in a candidate's profile. In this case, you can skip the majority of this research step by quickly eliminating candidates that do not meet your basic requirements.

While, in many cases, guys will openly offer information about their family and friends, you can also start gathering facts using closed questions to make the process less intimidating. A closed question requires a one-word or multiple-choice type of response. Using this technique, you can begin gathering Quick Qualifiers and Foundational Facts. For example, you can ask, "What are your favorite hobbies?" Another closed question might be, "How many siblings are in your family?"

4. Ask for Quick Qualifiers

Do you know your top three requirements in a mate? Can you describe your top three best attributes? Remind yourself to keep the mood light-hearted or you will scare the guy away. Simply ask the guy with a smile, "what are the top three things you want in a life partner?" If this tango does not go well, it is no big deal, it is just time to exit the game. The game is about getting to "Next" as soon as possible to avoid time wasters. Quick Qualifiers can also provide forward movement in the LIFE Match Game.

5. Discover the Real Man

Start using open questions to disclose more detail and look inside the man. You are trying to identify Mr. Right so begin building a comfort zone with a candidate to coax more honest responses to these open questions. For the best results, use LIFE Match Game Questions to discover the real man. (See more about this in Chapter 12.) Start slowly with some ice-breakers. For example, you might ask, "What was the happiest time of your life?" And then when you get more serious, you might ask, "Tell me why you have never been married before." Focus on areas that might help you discover Showstoppers. For example, if you are sure that you are not ready to be a stepmom, check out whether the man has children from a previous marriage early in the process. Once you have uncovered a connection with a potential mate, you can start playing the LIFE Match Game more seriously.

6. Use the SMART ABC Man Codes

In order to provide you with some levity and practical solutions for identifying your Mr. Wonderful, Part IV contains the SMART ABC Man Codes. These valuable codes help you to assess what kind of man you have on your hands and whether you are compatible. Use the questions provided in the codes to confirm your initial assessment of your Man Candidate. Most men are a mixture of codes so you'll find your Man Candidate may be a number of them. You are looking for a BA (Bachelor Available) and LM (Love Match) in the beginning of the game because they are your Go/No-Go signs. You need to require both characteristics in your man. And because you don't want to misinterpret someone, you might want to share the ABC Codes Compatibility Quiz to see how he rates his extremes. Make it a fun exercise and offer to share your codes as well. Since the questions are progressively more personal, use your judgment when trying them out. For example, on a second date try some of the Tell Me or ice-breaker questions listed first. In the end, you might not even need to ask your Man Candidate the answers, but can rely on active listening to learn what you need to know.

7. Mix It Up to Make It More Natural

Because a date is less structured than a job interview, feel free to mix up all of these interview practices. Don't go to every date with a formal agenda or you will kill the sparks. Give it time and let the information come out naturally. As long as you find major red flags early and avoid Mr. Time Waster, you want to give yourself some room for romance. Too much structure will damage the dance. While you can also make a lot of progress via email and phone discussions, avoid spending precious time on the LIFE Match Game Questions at least until after the second live encounter. You do not need to know extreme detail about a Man Candidate until he passes the KISS Test and Quick Qualifiers.

Gather the Foundational Facts

If you meet a candidate through email introductions, international mixing, serendipity, or mutual friends, here are some fact-finding questions for your Mr. Right questionnaire. And again, take it easy because a lot of this information will be openly shared. Taking mental notes versus asking direct questions can be the easiest approach at this stage where you are just getting the facts.

Age, height, weight

How old are you?
What age range are you interested in dating?
What is your height and weight?

Family Structure

How many siblings are in your family?
Where do you fall in the order of the siblings?
Are your parents still together?
Do you have any nieces or nephews?

Marital History/Offspring

Have you ever been married?
Do you have any children?
If yes, what is the custody arrangement for the children?

Career

What have been your professional highlights?
Where did you go to school?
What are your future career goals?

Hobbies

What are your top three interests outside of work?
How many times a week do you like to exercise?
Are you interested in the arts?

A Fact-Gathering Comeback Story

While this foundational fact check may sound obvious, this step might be the most important in the dating game. You should eliminate anyone whose foundation doesn't match your needs way before walking down the aisle. I coached a 38-year-old woman from Baltimore, Maryland, who left her husband due to different foundations. She explained her first choice to me, "I only ended up with him because I wanted to be married. I married him for the potential future that he could be versus what he was at the time. He was bright and I thought he would be successful." Oops!

The first coaching sessions were about how to get through the divorce and deal with her feelings. Once she got over the divorce paperwork hurdles, she admits, "I was only interested in a 28-year-old that I had no business dating." We both agreed this Young Explorer (YE) was a loose cannon. When she found herself bailing him out of jail for a DUI, I think that woke her up. It was nothing more than a Chemistry Connection, which can be very seductive and dangerous. She skipped my "take a timeout" step and immediately started dating, which made her judgment a little off with the first guy. We've all made mistakes. The success key is to avoid repeating the same mistake and knowing when to say, "Next" faster!

Within a few months, she shook off this Young Explorer and found her Mr. Wonderful, who had a much more compatible foundation. When I asked her to describe the major attraction to her new Mr. Right, she replied, "He's from the same stable." Okay, she liked his brown eyes too, but it was more important that the couple had similar life experiences with "money, education and socializing." While she was at first hesitant to date her man, a girlfriend convinced her to take a closer look. This good friend explained to her, "He is called the Mayor of Annapolis because everyone adores him." Because she had a similar social style in Baltimore where she loved to pull friends together, their Social Guru (SG) personalities complemented each other. Her ex-husband had been the complete opposite. She told me, "My ex lived vicariously through me and it was exhausting."

Not only did they both have similar interests in sailing and shared some of the same friends, their families had crossed paths throughout their lives. Both of their sisters had gone to Randolph-Macon Woman's College in Virginia. Her sister was actually the resident assistant (RA) for his sister at one point. Their mothers had also dated the same guy while attending Smith College. When I asked her more about the importance of these connections, she added, "I do not believe that opposites attract. My ex was a shy introvert. If we took a Myers-Briggs personality test, we would be in the complete opposite quadrants."

When I see her with this new Mr. Wonderful, it's obvious to everyone they are a Perfect Match. He is confident, secure, and adores her. The couple is now happily married with a baby boy in Annapolis, Maryland. The new foundation is built to last—more power to her for making this solid connection the second time around!

Quick Qualifiers

With potential candidates, you can quickly determine the likelihood of a match by asking for the top three characteristics he desires in a soul mate. Be prepared to share three traits that best describe you and define your partner requirements list in return. These Quick Qualifiers are essential and can be gathered via email, phone, or in person with prospects. These facts will also help you quickly identify any relationship Showstoppers so you can immediately move to the next candidate.

As a single woman, being on the lookout for Quick Qualifiers helps me identify Man Candidates. For example, I attended a business networking event where I had qualifying discussions with two bachelors. Both men openly shared their thoughts so I was able to ask what they were looking for in a mate. As long as you keep the conversation light, you can find men who are happy to play this exchange game.

Bachelor #1 wanted someone who can cook, is trustworthy, and provides unconditional acceptance. Bachelor #2 first responded, "It's all about chemistry." When I asked him to elaborate, he listed a sense of humor, adventurousness, and playfulness as his priorities in a mate.

I was instantly out of the game with Bachelor #1 because I can barely boil water. Alternatively, my characteristics and needs more closely resembled Bachelor #2's checklist. I look for someone who is worldly, passionate, and charismatic. I would also use these characteristics to describe myself. Not only did our top three needs harmonize, but there was also an immediate mutual attraction with Bachelor #2. Because of these connections, we decided to have drinks the following week. I took a chance by asking these Quick Qualifying questions and ended up with a potential Man Candidate.

Recently, I polled singles all over the country for their Quick Qualifiers. While there are some parallels, the answers show clear differences between the sexes and they are worth presenting here.

What Women Want

My single female friends value personality traits first. The top three things females are looking for are:

1. Good communication skills—ability to discuss, listen, and help problem solve
2. Sense of humor
3. Intelligence

In comparison, males listed sexual attraction as their top priority. Perhaps most women just assume sexual attraction as an obvious qualifier. However, the men were more obvious and blurted out this requirement.

What Men Want

The top three male preferences in female partners are:

1. Sex appeal—chemistry, looks (another reason why you need to be continually updating your style)
2. Sense of humor
3. Smarts—brains, intelligence

Overall, men and women have overlapping desires in a soul mate. So why is it so hard to find your special someone? Perhaps it is because people have different definitions of intelligence, sense of humor, and communication. What might be funny to you might not be humorous to him at all. However, Quick Qualifiers will most likely help you identify connectors and roadblocks faster. Because time is precious, start using these Quick Qualifiers. If your top threes do not complement each other, it is time to say, "Next."

Showstoppers

So what about the Showstoppers? Showstoppers are deal breakers. They may take the form of different goals (a desire to have or not to have children is a big one) or undesirable behavior (smoking is a common turn-off) and they stop all forward movement with a Man Candidate.

I had a win-win discussion with a Young Explorer (YE) who told me on our third date that while he used to think age was a Showstopper, he was more comfortable with older women and preferred their company over women his same age. While I had been initially nervous about the seven-year gap in our ages, this discussion actually cleared up my anxiety about this potential Showstopper. What are your deal breakers?

Have you thought about your Showstoppers? In order to increase your awareness of what might break the deal, I took a daters' poll and received this helpful list of what will make people walk away. There are some clear similarities among the sexes and great insights in their comments.

Dating Dealbreakers

She Said Showstoppers	He Said Showstoppers
"Caught lying"	"Someone who is an actress"
"Bad manners is one of the most important parts of dating. No manners, no more dates"	"Lacks empathy"
"Extremely cheap"	"Too anxious to have marriage and kids"
"An arrogant man is a turn-off"	"Name droppers"
"Couch potato"	"No professional ambition"
"Rudeness to others"	"Overly talkative. And/or never reciprocates questions"
"Making last-minute plans can be a red flag"	"Women who stress out and/or always talk/never listen"

She Said Showstoppers	He Said Showstoppers
"Obese"	"Poor grammar/writing in online situations"
"Lack of knowledge about basic etiquette"	"Charmless—her personality was boring"
"He should have a purpose or direction in life, not be wondering"	"Debt—I found out she was swimming in consumer debt"
"Excessive drinking, illegal drug use"	"Substance abuse of any kind: drugs, booze, cigarettes (can't stand 'em!)"
"Definitely smoking is a big red circle with a slash through it for me"	"Cigarette smokers are a definite turn-off."
"Unkempt hair and lack of personal hygiene. His clothes should say that he thought to look nice for me"	"I wouldn't date someone who doesn't take care of herself, i.e., smokes, doesn't eat healthily, and doesn't exercise regularly"

Quick Qualifiers and Showstoppers— Top Three

You can avoid wasting time with Man Candidates who have different agendas or conflicting requirements from yours by using this worksheet as a guide. Don't take this sheet to your date, but throw out these questions in a lighthearted, almost "let's play a game" tone. You are in the early stages of dating so it's not time to get serious. Ask him for a list of his top three needs in a mate. Be willing to share your lists in return and remember to keep it fun versus placing the guy on trial.

A. What are the top three characteristics that are really important for you to find in Ms. Right?

    1.

    2.

    3.

B. Here are my top three characteristics that I use to describe Mr. Right:

    1.

    2.

    3.

C. My top three best attributes include:

    1.

    2.

    3.

(In case you are asked to describe yourself, prepare for this one and practice delivering it with a non-boastful tone.)

D. Are there any characteristics that are Showstoppers or deal breakers for either of you? Swap Showstoppers and give him some examples to spark the conversation.

    1.

    2.

    3.

Emotional Readiness Pre-Test

An all-important test at this stage of dating is Emotional Readiness and it's a real Go/No-Go. Here's where you honestly ask yourself whether your Man Candidate is truly available. You're not just looking for clues as to whether he's involved with other women here, what you're looking for is whether this guy is *emotionally* ready for a real relationship. If he is not a BA (Bachelor Available) seeking a relationship, you are wasting your time and energy. A 32-year-old male entrepreneur who also shared this perspective told me, "A guy will make himself available if he truly wants to be with a woman." So if he is not talking feelings or future with you within a reasonable start-up phase, maybe you are just not the right one for him and it's time for the check, please!

The Emotional Readiness gauge can immediately make or break a long-term relationship deal. If you overlook the importance of Emotional Readiness, you might spend weeks, months, and years fooling yourself with an unavailable candidate. There is a lot of truth to the statement, "Timing is everything." You don't want to be looking back five years into the relationship with a Relentless Renter (RR), who plans to rent forever and never buy.

Gauging Emotional Readiness is usually achieved by analyzing his responses to less direct questions. You probably want to tone down these statements on the first date. Avoid blurting out, "Are you ready to get married?" Using a direct question right off the bat may scare him, so watch for more subtle signs. For example, you might say, "I am tired of dating multiple people and really want to find a long-term relationship." If he responds with a similar viewpoint, then you know that you are in warm waters. You can also ask, "What has been your longest relationship?" Depending on the length of his past relationships, you can gauge his readiness. Guys who have recently ended a long-term relationship will usually find a new partner fairly quickly because that is their comfort zone.

Approach Emotional Readiness lightly, by commenting with a big smile, "I promise that I won't ask you to marry me today, but I want you to know that I am trying to find a long-term partner." I tested this approach during Speed Dating and no one seemed to be taken aback by this comment. The success key is a non-needy delivery of the message.

You can also try asking him with a smile:

• Are you having fun dating or would you rather be in a relationship?

- Do you think marriages can last today with the high divorce rate?

If he does not seem interested in responding to either of these statements, you are probably dealing with a player and you know what to do with these Sly Schemers: just say, "You're fired."

Look for signs of Emotional Readiness as early as the second date. I met a 40-something financial manager who told me on a first date, "If we start dating, I'm looking for a long-term relationship with a monogamous partner." I almost fell out of my chair when I heard this blatant BA (Bachelor Available) confession. We dated for over a year, and it felt great to have this commitment confirmed by him.

So long as you see *some* indication that it might be there, you can give him until the third date for further confirmation. If the potential partner does not seem interested in playing monogamous ball with you early in the game, it is time to find another opportunity. If you see signs of a Wounded Divorcé (WD) who thinks marriage is a hoax, run for the nearest computer and get back online so you have more dating options. You are seriously seeking Mr. Wonderful and cannot afford to waste precious time and energy on someone who is not emotionally ready. You want to be saying what my 40-something girlfriend told me about her husband-to-be, "There was no doubt in his mind that he wanted to be in a long-term committed relationship."

Look for these signs when gauging the Emotional Readiness of a man:

Emotional Readiness Go Signs

- He is calling regularly to check in and ask about your day.
- He shows enthusiasm to see you by constantly setting up next dates.
- The guy shows a genuine interest in getting to know you and wants to hear your opinions.
- He becomes a cheerleader for your goals and interests.

- The guy makes you feel special. He goes out of his way to bring you happiness and makes a habit out of saying and doing nice things.

- The guy tells you that he wants to take sex slow so you can build a bond first. (He is tired of playing the field and wants to get serious. I received a marriage proposal from a guy like this.)

- His actions match his words. He means what he says.

- The biggest sign of Emotional Readiness is that he tells you that he wants a relationship and/or a future with you.

Pay Attention and Listen for the Answers

SMART Man Hunting is not only about asking the right questions at the right time, it is also about knowing when to just listen for the answers and pay attention to someone's behavior. Many times you don't even have to ask direct questions. The guy will hand you the answers and clues in conversation to help you make the right choices. While you can use the questions in this book directly, you can also find many answers in his statements and actions simply by raising your awareness.

Remember, you don't want to sound desperate or aggressive so this passive approach can be very effective and make the good GUT and red flag information come to you more naturally. I'm not saying don't ask questions. There are certain areas and times where you should probably be more direct (for example, when asking if someone is interested in a monogamous relationship). However, you can gather a lot of information without ever having to ask by actively listening and being honest with yourself about what the signs are telling you.

Throughout the Man Hunt interview process, make mental notes and don't overlook the importance of casual conversation and actions. While someone may not have had a long-term relationship with you, their interactions with others can teach a lot about the person. Here are some examples of statements and signs revealed in casual conversation that can help you read between the lines.

Active Listening Examples

Casual Man Statements	Major Man Signs
"I watched the basketball game last night with my family. The game went into overtime and it was a blast."	This guy is a family man. He can have fun with his family, which is always a good sign for interpersonal relationships.
"The people at work drive me nuts because everyone has crazy ideas. I don't get why no one ever listens to my recommendations.	Watch out. This guy might not have the best interpersonal skills. He might have a tendency to blame others for his faults.
"I took my mother out to lunch today for Valentine's Day."	He is a potential keeper. He has a good relationship with his mother, which is always a good sign.
"I have a bachelors' party weekend coming up. We are renting hotel rooms in Las Vegas. I don't know when I'll be back, but it should be a blast."	Warning—Warning—Warning. This guy might be a Macho Mind, and we don't like guys who always place men first and treat women as a second priority.
"When my father got really sick no one could tell us what was wrong so I kept calling friends until someone got me to the right doctor with the right diagnosis."	This guy is willing to stand by your side when the going gets tough. He is more likely to be there when you are old and gray so take a careful look at this man.
"I am having dinner tonight with friends and can see you afterward for coffee."	This guy is not serious about you. He wants to keep you around but is not willing to share his life with you. Get out fast.

Before you go too far into a relationship and The LIFE Match Game, you are going to need to hit the mattresses with a guy to determine whether you are a Love Match (LM). If the sex is not good, this should be a Showstopper for your relationship. Of course you want to have safe sex and get physical at your own pace, but your final pre-test for the LIFE Match Game should be in the bedroom. Don't wait months or years before you hit the mattresses with a potential Mr. Right.

Love Match Pre-Test

You don't want to walk down the aisle with someone unless they are good in bed. He might be the nicest guy, but if there are no sparks in the bedroom, then he is not your man. I've made deep emotional connections with several men who unfortunately were not matches when we hit the mattresses. This compatibility challenge can be the most frustrating situation. If you stay in the relationship despite this roadblock, it will most likely go bust later in life. If he is not making it happen in the bedroom, get out fast so you can get closer to finding your Love Match. If you want to keep the guy in your life, you will increase your chances of maintaining a friendship by making this quick decision.

This Love Match Pre-Test is your second Go/No-Go indicator and should be given sooner versus later. You need to decide when you are ready within your own comfort zone. Most guys would love to have sex with you on a first date, but honestly, what is realistic? I've met couples who had sex on a first date and later got married. However, most men say that women should wait if they are looking for a long-term relationship. When I surveyed my Bachelor Board of Advisors on this timing question, the results were very mixed.

Bachelor Survey Says . . . Have Sex
When It Feels Right

- "If the woman wants a commitment, she should never have sex on the first date. If she does, the relationship will always be primarily about sex. Should she wait two months or until it feels right? I don't think anyone should ever have sex with anyone unless it feels right."

- "If she is a sexual being and the energy is there, she should have sex by the third date. You don't want to overthink it— if it's real, it's real. Any long-term relationship that I've ever had, sex happened early. If the sex is a drag, then you want to know and confront it or move on. You won't want to marry someone that you hate having sex with."

- "You can't have sex soon enough."

- "You can have great sex with the wrong person. You might as well wait until you find out if they're the right person before you have sex because you can have great sex with more people than are likely to be a great partner. If you want to have better than average sex, then 49 percent of the people will probably qualify. Of the people you meet, how many are likely to be a great match for you? It's probably one out of 80. Focus on finding a great match before you go to bed with them. If you wait until after you get to know them, you also have to be ready to walk away if it's bad sex."

- "The answer is when it feels right. I don't agree with the waiting until the third date routine. It makes me mad when a girl withholds sex just for the sake of withholding it. My current girlfriend and I have been dating for over a year now. We slept together the night of our first date, and we've been in love ever since."

- "When she is comfortable with him *and* feels he wants the same thing. After all, if he tells her that he is seeking a commitment on the first date, she still might not be ready for sex."

- "Have sex when it feels right. If there's mutual chemistry just go with it. So what if it doesn't work out long term; live in the moment and enjoy your life. The most important thing is to be honest with yourself and others about your motives so everyone is clear about expectations. Personally I've had sex early in some relationships and waited months (my choice) in others. It didn't make any difference—they all ended sooner or later for other reasons (mostly my problems with intimacy). Better to have loved and lost. My wife and I had sex the first weekend we were together romantically, although we had known each other as friends for about six months before there was any spark."

- "This is one of the tough questions with an easy answer. There is no one answer. I would say it's something women wish had an answer. The most important thing is that the woman finds a man who is looking for a committed relationship. In general, the first woman who happens into his life when he tips into this side of the relationship pool, will be the one who gets him."

- "If a woman just enjoyed dinner with a guy . . . she should have sex with him and then, if he's a decent lover, profess her desire for a committed relationship. He will be so relieved that it was that easy he may just ask her to marry him right then. I guarantee he will think about it. With any man who is not at this point . . . he will be Blanche White and gone when the sun rises regardless of whether the woman waited two dates or two years."

- "It doesn't make any difference to me. I had sex with my first wife on my first date, but then, maybe that's why she was my first wife."

- "The dating standard is have sex within three dates, but I think people hold back sometimes just to play by this rule."

- "I think it's good to hold back because you might just have a bunch of sex, but I don't think it makes for a great relationship start. If you pick the right person, then it's ok, you're sleeping with the right person, but you only know them as the person you're sleeping with. If you pick the wrong person, it means you're probably going to sleep with the wrong person for a month before you figure it out."

My advice is wait until it feels right. What is your GUT telling you about the guy? Is he genuine, understanding, and trustworthy? Until you have a good gauge on the guy, stay out of the bedroom. You want to know if there is a Love Match (LM) before the relationship goes too far, but don't let a guy pressure you just because he needs his sexual fix. Guys often look at sex as nothing more than a physical need, where women usually want to make an emotional connection first. One 39-year-old teacher told me, "I meet woman online all the time. We have sex often on the first night and to me, it's just something that I do like playing basketball." While he might be an amazing physical fix, you are probably going to feel lousy when this player walks. Make a mental connection before hitting the mattresses with any guy to protect your emotions.

How can you predict if a guy is going to be good in bed? Are there any clues that will help you gauge his sexual skill level before you hit the mattresses? I went out and surveyed bachelorettes on this hot topic to gather insights for you. Check out these hints for whether a guy is going to please you in bed.

Bachelorette Survey Says . . . Signs That a Guy Is Good in Bed

- "Anyone who eats exotic food and is into enjoying it is a great sex partner. If they like a lot of different foods, they're good in bed."
- "If he likes to garden, he's good in bed. Any man who has given me flowers gave me more foreplay than other men. These guys appreciate women and show it in bed."

- "If they are a good dancer, they know how to move their bodies in bed."

- "I look at their hands. You can tell how big or little they are by the thumb and index finger."

- "Look at their shoes. The shoes are a tip-off of a Go or No/Go for sex. It's all part of a bigger package for me."

- "For me, it's all about how well they flirt. I would have known when the guy kissed me."

- "His confidence level is a good indicator of his size."

- "I think it's a combination of how he touches you and moves."

- "A guy that doesn't hug you closely is probably not going to be good in bed. If he's stiff, he's probably bad in bed. If he's comfortable getting close to you with his hug, he will probably be good in bed."

- "It's consistent. A sloppy kisser is sloppy in bed. A sensual kisser is sensual in bed."

- "If a guy is open-minded and comfortable talking about sex within boundaries, he's good in bed."

- "If they pay attention to you in conversation, then he will pay attention to your needs in bed."

- "A guy who is comfortable with his body. It doesn't mean that they have to be hot, but comfortable enough to take a shower with you."

- "It's a chemistry thing. If there is great chemistry before you get in bed, it enhances everything in bed."

- "I've found that men who when they were in their early twenties (or even late teens) dated women in their thirties-plus tend to be really attentive and have very solid skills. I think the key to this is when a guy says 'I used to be really into women who were older than me.' It indicates: I learned a lot about how to make a woman happy."

Sex is a very important Go/No-Go part of the package that should not be compromised. If a guy cannot give you pleasure, let him down easy and move on quickly. Hot Man Hunting is totally different than SMART Man Hunting. Hot Man Hunting is about finding good sex—SMART Man Hunting is about finding the total package. You're looking for a guy who can pleasure you in bed, is emotionally ready, plus someone who complements your style. Don't let the hormones make you lose your head about going for the total package!

The Dating Assessment Dance— Step Two Wrap-up

The second step in the Dating Assessment Dance is all about uncovering red flags and determining with whom you'd consider to enter the LIFE Match Game. (You are literally determining not only who you might be inviting into the bedroom, but into the rest of your life.) Once you have completed your fact-finding mission and pre-tests, you should be able to make a Go/No-Go decision about your Man Candidate at this stage. No-Go decisions will probably involve Showstoppers such as substance abuse or rudeness to others, or your belief that the candidate is not emotionally available. Or maybe you've run across a Red Flag Man. However, if the Foundation is right, the Quick Qualifiers work, he is ready, sex is great, and the GUT's good, use The LIFE Match Game Questions in the next chapter so you can take a closer look inside, continue to observe his behavior, and identify your man.

12

The Dating Assessment Dance—Step Three: The LIFE Match Game

HAVE YOU KNOCKED OUT all of your Mr. Wrongs? Are you ready to go to the mattresses with the real players? By now you know that you must find chemistry with a guy who is Emotionally Ready (See more on the Bachelor Available and Love Match in Part IV's SMART ABC Man Codes) or you are wasting your time. The Quick Qualifiers and Showstoppers told you if there was potential for going the distance. By using closed questions to unveil Foundational Facts, you determined whether or not you want to dig deeper. You also eliminated the Red Flag Men and listened to your GUT about non-verbal warning signs.

Once you have identified a potential match who has passed all of your pre-tests, it's time to use LIFE Questions to take a closer look inside the man. In the words of Penelope Cruz's father in the movie *Captain Corelli's Mandolin*, "Love is like a temporary madness. It's like an earthquake that erupts and then subsides." Once the dust settles in your relationship, you want to find out if there is a compatibility foundation outside of the bedroom. While you might have great sex, a partnership based only on hormones is extremely dangerous. You need to come up for air and look at the bigger picture before you tie the knot.

You are now trying to identify Mr. Right candidates, and this can be the most challenging dance step. Remember that it is better to get this important information before you enter a life-long partnership. A recently married man shared his insights on identifying the right partner by saying, "You want to find some-one who is upbeat with moderation. They don't need to make everything rosey because every joke is not funny. Instead, you want someone who can be diplomatic when pointing out your joke might not be funny." Gauge your Life Match Meter based on how your Man Candidate responds to these questions and then avoid blinders by taking time to observe his behavior. Is he a real deal? And most importantly, what is your GUT telling you during this dance step?

Play the LIFE Match Game

If the candidate has made it this far, it's time to play the LIFE Match Game. LIFE Match is about getting to know your Man Candidate on a deeper level in order to evaluate whether he could be a "life match" for you. By the third date, you should be com-fortable enough to start asking these more revealing questions. LIFE Match revolves around gaining the following information:

L Lessons Learned—What has he already learned in life?

I Introspection—Can he be introspective and articulate his view on life and his feelings?

F Flexibility—Can he be flexible? Is he willing to compromise?

E Extremes—What extremes exist in his life? Is he extreme about work or hobbies? Do you share his interests?

The LIFE Match Game is important for these reasons:

• It helps you further assess whether your Man Candidate is truly ready for or looking for a long-term commitment. If someone doesn't want to play LIFE Match, he's no match. I went out with a guy who told me on a third date, "Ask me

any question you want. I am not afraid to answer anything."
Remember, attitude is key, especially at this stage. If someone does not want to play, he is not real deal potential.

- You will learn what is important to your Man Candidate and
how he views life. His answers to LIFE Match questions will
enable you to determine the "fit" between you and your
partner. LIFE Match will reveal glaring differences in life
views as well as areas of agreement.

- LIFE Match reveals more than his answers. The most
important part of the LIFE Match game is observing all the
non-verbal clues your Man Candidate exhibits as he answers
LIFE Match questions. As you play LIFE Match, realize that
the answers lie as much in his actions and in what he doesn't
do as in what he says. If you want to be SMART, you'll look
for this important information.

- Your analysis of LIFE Match willingness, questions, and
nonverbal clues further helps you identify the SMART ABC
Man Codes of your man. The ABC Man Coding keeps you
from losing your head as you get to know your Man Candidate better. Realize that remaining clear and confident
ensures greater long-term success. Take the ABC Codes
Compatibility Quiz with your man to see how your extremes
match up for life. You need to play the game with finesse,
and that means maintaining a non-desperate vibe. So be
ready to take it or leave it if things start going south. Don't
try to force a match or the right answers. The purpose is to
avoid the "D" word, so why try to close a deal that has the
wrong foundation or missing parts?

How Do You Play the LIFE Match Game?

1. Begin a Dance Dialogue

You are about to enter into an ongoing dance dialogue with a
Mr. Right who could be a potential mate. This dialogue is a like
a negotiation since you'll both be presenting your points of views

and then deciding what you can and can't live with. Realize that with this more personal level of exchange, you will begin building a solid foundation for a long-term relationship. If he is willing to play ball, start looking at the real man inside. Discuss your feelings, clarify your expectations, and ask him more about what he is feeling. Explain your personal goals. One 40-something girlfriend told me, "Tell him what you want in a non-threatening way and then see if he steps up to the plate."

2. Watch for Willingness in the Candidate

You are seeking a life partner, so anyone who does not want to start sharing on a deeper level at this stage is obviously not in the same ballpark. This step is a fork in the road and requires some decisiveness on your part. You're either going to stick to your SMART Man Hunting guns by getting the information you need to fully evaluate someone or you risk wasting time on a Mr. Wrong. If the candidate is not willing to communicate and discuss life views, he is probably not sincerely interested in you as a partner or in having a long-term commitment in his life. Decide whether he is working with you or avoiding the LIFE Questions. If you are not getting the results and respect that you desire at this point, take the nearest exit.

One 34-year-old recruiter made this observation about her serious relationship with a 45-year-old writer. She said, "We both agree that a relationship is a vehicle for our own personal growth. Most men don't even understand what that sentence means." While you might not get this extreme buy-in from a man, look for the readiness clues.

If your Man Candidate is genuine and willing to engage in a LIFE Match dialogue, I recommend limiting LIFE Questions to in-person encounters. It's the non-verbal clues given during the dialogue that are critical during this stage so it's best to keep communication face-to-face.

3. Trust Your GUT

Based on his verbal and non-verbal responses, you will get a good sense of the person. Watch how he treats you and pay attention to how he makes you feel inside to determine if he's got good GUT—is he Genuine, Understanding, and Trustworthy?

Don't stop checking your basic GUT instincts, even after the Emotional Readiness and Love Match Pre-Tests. What are the dynamics between the two of you as the dating dance continues?

Check your GUT regarding the way he works with you. You can use these GUT Interaction Questions to test your tango.

GUT Interaction Questions

- Is there a good give-and-take exchange in this relationship? Does he actively listen to your concerns? Does he do what he says he will do?
- Does he treat you with kindness and consideration when you are together?
- Does he make your dates a priority or allow them to be interrupted by cell phone calls?
- Does he show good character when he interacts with people?
- Does he complement you both mentally and physically?

If you're going to grow old with Mr. Right, these interpersonal dynamics become even more critical. You want a life partner who can work with you, and the way the two of you interact is an essential success factor. As my 45-year-old male CEO friend added, "Ask yourself whether you would want to get on a boat for a two-month sailing trip to Hawaii with the guy. Would you be better off as a couple in the end?" The reality test is about how the two of you work together as a team. The sexual passion may fade, and you need to be more concerned about what is going to last a lifetime.

You want to sound like this success story from Ms. Manhattan Beach, who found her Mr. Wonderful. She described her Mr.

Right further to me with these examples. "He hides little notes or cards in my stuff to surprise me. He'll call me in the middle of the day just to tell me he's thinking of me; not every day by any means, but every now and then. These are gifts from the heart, not a store, and make me feel so loved and safe."

While perfect people do not exist, you can find a Perfect Match. Be SMART about selecting a man who will be there for the long haul.

4. Look Beyond Your GUT

Even if the GUT is good, it is still your job to uncover any potential major obstacles by asking the LIFE Match Questions. When my 30-something girlfriend was invited to move in with her boyfriend, she told me, "I need to ask him some of your LIFE questions first. We need to have more conversations before I move into his house. I'm not sure if we share the same long-term goals of marriage and children." A man can have great GUT but may still see or want things differently from you. In fact, you should be even more careful when there's GUT because this candidate may truly be "the one." But you won't find out if you don't continue to play LIFE Match.

5. Accept that There Are No Right or Wrong Answers

There are no right or wrong answers to LIFE Questions so it's not fair judging anyone on what they have to say. Remember you're just looking for a match. The right answer depends on your needs and desires. How do you mesh with this candidate's views? Does his way of life complement your lifestyle? Can he be flexible? These are the questions for you to ask during this interview phase. And always check the GUT factor.

6. Round 1: First Look Inside

You can start with icebreaker questions to ease into the game. Discover how the guy has handled the ups and downs on his life's journey. Find out more about his viewpoints by using this "Tell

Me" method. Because you cannot predict the future, Tell Me questions illuminate how the candidate has handled various situations in the past and whether he is able to learn from his mistakes. Use these LIFE Match Game Round 1 questions to start your review of the Total Man. You can even make a game out of this exchange. Offer to share your answers if he agrees to enter this tango with you. And don't forget to listen for the answers along the journey. He will probably tell you the answers to some of these questions without you even asking.

Round 1 Tell Me Questions

- Tell me what you like to do on the weekends.
- Tell me what activities you like to share with your girlfriend versus the guys.
- Tell me how often you attend sports games and who usually goes with you.
- Tell me about your happiest moment and what happened.
- Tell me about your scariest time and what happened.
- Tell me about your greatest personal achievement and why it was so important to you.
- Tell me about the most exciting time of your career.
- Tell me about the most challenging time of your career.
- Tell me about what you think makes a great friendship.
- Tell me about someone whom you were able to help with a problem.
- Tell me about your hero(s) and why you admire them.
- Tell me about what you think makes a great marriage.

7. Round 2: ABC Man Code Analysis

While gathering information with Round 1 Tell Me Questions, you will start to learn more about the ABCs of your Man Candidates. In Part IV, you'll find the SMART ABC Man Codes that apply to your Man. These codes provide more food for thought and shed light on situations using real-life scenarios as examples.

You may want to go back to Round 1 and ask more questions before proceeding to your Final Man Analysis. You will also find the ABC Man Codes help you develop success strategies for working well with your Man Candidate.

After months of dating the wrong men in Los Angeles, I created these Man Codes as a way to bring levity to my search for Mr. Right. These male dating codes are not based on science and are intended to provide you with some reality checks by asking you to think more clearly about a Man Candidate. In these descriptions, you will find a balanced array of personalities that include both desirable and undesirable guys. You might find that your personality also fits one of the codes. Many of the ABC codes are not gender specific even though the examples in this code book are all male. Interestingly, many men have asked, "Tell me, what is your code?" It's easy to apply these codes to women. For example, a BA can be a Bachelor Available or a Bachelorette Available—so be prepared to join in the fun and share your codes with a man.

The definitions, true-story examples, and strategies in the codes are designed to help you quickly determine whether a candidate meets your needs. What works for you might not be a match for somebody else. You might find a Man Candidate represents several of these ABC man acronyms. Use the LIFE Questions recommended in the codes to disclose his patterns and priorities. The goal is to find a male with a code(s) that complements your personality while avoiding the rotten eggs or elephant in the room. You want to hit the eject button as soon as a guy unveils the red flags in the bad codes.

Use these SMART ABC Man Codes to gather additional insights and make better and faster Mr. Right decisions. Extremes are especially important. As one 30-something woman commented about the codes, "It's hard for some people to clear out the cobwebs and impressions get clouded. The codes help you tune in to your radar." Even though someone expresses an interest in a hobby or is career-oriented, you will not know the extreme until you ask for more information. You also need to take time to get to know the person to see if his behavior corresponds with his answers. One Man Candidate asked a woman I know to marry him. An avid sailor, he neglected to consider or reveal his long range plan of devoting the rest of his life to his hobby. He saw nothing wrong in leaving his partner behind for weeks or months at a time "holding down the fort." If you ask about his dreams early, you can quickly evaluate the long-term potential and minimize surprises.

8. Gauge Your Life Match Meters

At this point in the game, it is time to check the gauge on your LIFE Match Meter with Mr. Right candidates. It's time to decide how long you want to play the game with a particular candidate. If you are not sure about a man, one 40-year-old girlfriend told me, "Write a Pro and Con list." You are not going to find Mr. Perfect because he doesn't exist, but you may find Mr. Perfect Match. Decide whether the pros outweigh the cons.

Give your potential match a rating on a scale of 1–10. If he receives at least a 9, then you may have found a life mate. Guys have been rating women for years on the front steps of fraternity houses and inside locker rooms so why shouldn't we do it? Only this time, the rating is much more important. We now have SMART strategies to help us make good choices versus simply reacting to a guy's appearance walking down the street. Similar to the corporate world where 95 percent is a typical goal for quality, you need to set high standards and mine for the gold. Anything below a 9 is not okay with me.

You want to sound like this 30-something woman who described what makes her relationship work. "We want the same type of a relationship and value the same dynamics. We just like doing things together. Other men I've dated were more interested in spending time with their guy friends during the day on the weekends, seeing me only at night. That isn't what I like so the dynamic was always stressed." She quickly recognized this match and is now happily married to her Mr. Wonderful.

Start gauging the results of your LIFE Match Game. Do you

want the same things? Do you have the same values? Does he want to make it work with you? Can you live with his approach to life?

If your gauge is leaning heavily toward a Match, but you still need more information, go back to Round One. If your Gauge and your GUT tell you that this could be "the one," proceed to step 9, below. If he did not receive at least a 9 on the LIFE Match Meter, he is not your man. It's time to go back to SMART Man Hunting.

9. Review the Total Man—Final ABC Man Analysis

The Life Match Meter helps you to gauge the guy's long-term potential, and then the Final Man Analysis uses the SMART ABC Man Codes to review the total man. Let these true-story examples shed light on your dating experiences and reinforce what to look for in a guy. These Man Codes and examples are based on a balance of good and bad male encounters. Use the codes to save yourself from wasting weeks, months, and even years with Mr. Wrong. The most important part about the Final Man Analysis is not just deciding when you have a Mr. Right on your hands, but being honest with yourself when someone is a Mr. Wrong. The sooner you make this decision the better. In the 26 A-Z codes, you'll find good guys, bad guys, and mostly maybe guys because it depends on whether you complement or clash with a guy. There is a description of each code in Part IV and a compatibility quiz in Appendix I. Here is a sneak preview of the SMART ABC Man Codes that you can use as a quick reference guide during this LIFE Match dance step.

Sneak Preview Guide— SMART ABC Man Codes

Good Guys	Maybe Guys	Bad Guys
Bachelor Available (BA)	All Sports Fanatic (ASF)	Hello Goodbye Guy (HGG)
Confident Metro Male (CMM)	Dysfunctional Guy with Issues (DGI)	Internet Psycho (IP)

Good Guys	Maybe Guys	Bad Guys
Keeper of the Fire (KOF)	Executive Search Seeker (ESS)	Justifying Juggler (JJ)
Love Match (LM)	Fitness Extremist (FE)	Married but Available (MBA)
Nourishing Nester (NN)	Guy With Offspring (GWO)	Questionnaire Perfectionist (QP)
Virtual Lover (VL)	Overachiever Obsessor (OO)	Wounded Divorcé (WD)
	Post-Traumatic Soul (PTS)	
	Relentless Renter (RR)	
	Social Guru (SG)	
	Tasmanian Traveler (TT)	
	Underestimated Ally (UA)	
	X-Ray Eyes (XRE)	
	Young Explorer (YE)	
	Zodiac Zealot (ZZ)	

You want to be able to quickly identify the combination of man codes and recognize any deal breakers for these 26 types of men. Your goal is to keep moving toward finding your Mr. Wonderful versus settling for Mr. Goodenough. You can find him faster if you know when to say, "You're fired," versus when to say, "You're hired!"

Mr. Wrong Case Studies

In order to help you avoid prolonged heartache and know when to walk away, here are three Mr. Wrong Case Studies. Each case illustrates a very common mistake women make in the dating game. If you make these mistakes don't sweat it. And don't let it stop you from being proactive. Remember, there are a lot of men out there and every dating dance gets you a little closer toward identifying a Mr. Right. You are getting SMARTer every day.

Mr. Wrong #1—The Elephant in the Room

Watch out for the Elephant in the Room, or the man with the overlooked undesirable code. Check out this combination and tale.

ABC Codes:

- Bachelor Available (BA)
- Confident Metro Male (CMM)
- Keeper of the Fire (KOF)
- Social Guru (SG)
- Questionnaire Perfectionist (QP) (the elephant)

Sometimes what makes the Final Man Analysis so tricky is that a Candidate will fall into one or more good code categories while also exhibiting one or two undesirable code categories. It's too easy to overlook the latter because you're so happy to have found the former. Remember all these codes are usually present from the get-go. It's about being honest enough with yourself to admit that they are there. For example, this Mr. Wrong came off as everything a woman could want. He was available (BA), comfortable in his masculinity and open to female friendship (CMM), a devoted romantic (KOF), and social (SG). This example illustrates what happens when one trait that doesn't work for you can negate all the other positive traits. Don't ignore the elephant in the room or you'll regret it later.

This dreamboat had his Ms. Right on cloud nine for years, even down the wedding path. But soon after marriage, the bride in this case was forced out of the clouds when her mate's personality extremes and his QP (Questionnaire Perfectionist) tendencies destroyed the relationship. This man was unwilling to compromise from his requirements checklist. For example, he wanted his wife to cook dinner at home every night during the week to save money and spend quality time together. When she offered to compromise by sharing dinner three times a week, this solution was not good enough for him. Ultimately, this demanding perfectionist's expectations affected all areas of the marriage and became the unavoidable elephant in the room.

Mr. Wrong # 1 Moral: Look for all the codes and never deny the existence of the less attractive ones. They're always the most important and will grow to elephantine proportions eventually.

Mr. Wrong #2—The Too Perfect Transformer

What about the guy who changes his tune? He might have great codes, but give it some time and he might just blindside you with a new attitude.

ABC Codes:

- Bachelor Available (BA)
- Confident Metro Male (CMM)
- Keeper of the Fire (KOF)
- Nourishing Nester (NN)
- Hello Goodbye Guy (HGG) (What happened?)

You know those children's toys that look like action heroes but with the flip of a few parts transform into gross insects? That's what this guy is. This Too Perfect Transformer is an example of someone who seems to be a real Mr. Click. He has all the right codes and the actions to back them up. While dreams do come true, beware of the men who are too perfect. Mr. Click took his date to a great French restaurant on the first date, brought her one of his favorite CDs on the second date, and arrived with flowers on the third date. He called every day to hear about her day and indicated that he had a strong interest in a relationship. After three dates with Mr. Click, he showed all the promising signs of the SMART ABC Man Codes above.

However, three weeks into intense dating with Mr. Click, he suddenly turned into an HGG (Hello Goodbye Guy). Without any explanation other than a busy work schedule, he suddenly dropped off the face of the earth, leaving his date to wonder why. It may have been because she refused to sleep with him on the third date, which actually makes him a Sly Schemer. (See Red Flag Men in Chapter 10.) On the other hand, anything can send a HGG scurrying for the hills. The point is you'll never know why he changed his tune.

Mr. Wrong #2 Moral: Always take the time to allow a man to reveal his true colors or codes. A wise 32-year-old girlfriend who is happily married said to me, "You need to give it time. Ask questions and then observe to see if they do what they say, and avoid salespeople."

While you do the dance, don't put your eggs all in one basket and keep dating, even if he is a Mr. Click. And when a Mr. Click turns into a transformer, don't let this mind-boggling unexpected twist get you down. Don't give yourself a hard time because your intuition was wrong—simply move forward. Better to find out sooner rather than later that Mr. Click turned out to be Mr. Wrong.

Mr. Wrong #3—Missing Ingredient

Beware of men who seem great, but are missing key ingredients. Don't forget to wear your glasses when making a Final Man Analysis.

ABC Codes:

- Confident Metro Male (CMM)
- Nourishing Nester (NN)
- Post-Traumatic Soul (PTS)

Sometimes a key code will be missing in a Man Candidate and for some reason you don't notice. Usually you're blinded by what's going on in your own life or due to strong desire to make the relationship work. When a Man Candidate's other codes fill a need in us, we'll miss a salient point, like whether he is Emotionally Ready.

Take, for example, the story of a 37-year-old business executive who met a same-aged TV producer during the week of the Northridge earthquake in Los Angeles. A long-distance relationship ensued for months afterward. The couple spent hours on the phone talking about the 6.7 earthquake and helping each other through the recovery period. So what happened? She wasn't paying attention to her code book. She wasn't asking the right LIFE Questions. That's because this guy was filling an important need for her. Both people were experiencing a case of post-traumatic stress disorder and needed an intimate friend at that time. This type of connection happens quite frequently. After months of conversations, the woman finally admitted what was there all along: that the TV Producer was not a BA (Bachelor Available.) Yes, he liked her, but he had no intention of walking down the aisle with her anytime soon.

Mr. Wrong # 3 Moral: Be aware when you're having some issues or unmet needs because that's when this type of Mr. Wrong is going to walk into your life. You can deal with your needs on your own or you can date this Mr. Wrong. There's nothing wrong with this comfort man. Just be clear about what is happening and don't talk yourself into thinking a guy who happens to be there when you need him is a Mr. Right. Be grateful for what you receive and move on without regrets. You've probably made a pretty good friend.

Who Is Mr. Perfect?

We all have a conscious image of what we think we want in a perfect match. However, as my 45-year-old male CEO friend clarified to me, "The reality is that we are often ruled by the subconscious that is driven by the heart." We have all been influenced by the media to create a Mr. Perfect image in our minds, but our reality man may be something very different.

In the final analysis, sometimes your Mr. Perfect has to give in to GUT considerations. In the three examples of Mr. Wrong described previously, each woman was misled by her belief that the man in question matched her idea of Mr. Perfect. In the end those Mr. Wrongs did not have the crucial combination of GUT and LIFE Match. This oversight serves to illustrate the importance of GUT over Mr. Perfect as well as how important it is to continue to play the LIFE Match Game throughout your dating journey with a Man Candidate so you can continually check on his GUT—and yours.

Who is Mr. Perfect to you? What real life traits or actions do you look for in your search for Mr. Right? Here's what some daters have to say about what tells them they've found Mr. or Ms. Right.

The Right Stuff

She Observes Mr. Right

"Little things like small touches, cooking, going to places, events, outings he really isn't interested in just because you are there."

"Consideration in everyday parts of life, whether it is holding the door, cooking dinner, or other."

"Other stuff, a good dancer, good taste in general, clothes, music, manners, does he believe men open doors?"

"He watches you (you see him, but he doesn't know you've caught him) doing mundane tasks."

"Either sits too close or too far away. (I want them to have a sense of space.)"

"Must be confident enough to maintain eye contact when talking to you."

He Observes Ms. Right

"Listening is big with me. Someone who will listen attentively."

"Do they present themselves well? Are they stylish, but not overly so? Are they attractive but not flamboyant?"

"A sparkle in her eyes and softening of her facial features when I enter the room."

"I look for smiles—people who smile a lot are usually happy people—I like happy people."

"It's manners. Eye contact, touching, listening, enthusiasm, and the way she carries herself."

"How they interact in social settings. Do they mingle? Are they comfortable talking with strangers? Do they listen?"

"He is focused on us and not scanning the crowd for something better. He appears confident and at ease."

"Mr. Right must be sensitive and touch me once in a while when speaking."

"Being a nice guy in traffic. Showing restraint when matters get tough, at the airport, or when someone is really being slow behind a counter somewhere."

"Someone that makes my heart race when the phone rings and it could be her. Someone who I look forward to seeing more every time we spend together."

"It's the way she likes you even when you're wrong."

"It's a turn of the wrist or flip of the hair, a timbre in her voice, a sparkle in her eyes."

Mr. Perfect Only Happens in the Movies

Let's go to the movies for a good example of a fantasy romance. Only Hollywood can produce this kind of Mr. Perfect. He doesn't exist in real life. But this Mr. Right does pass all the SMART Man Hunting tests, so let's have a look at him anyway. The characters played by Meg Ryan and Hugh Jackman in the movie *Kate and Leopold* share a passionate Love Match immediately. Not only that, there are many signs of an excellent match. You can see that he clearly passes the Emotional Readiness Pre-Test when, in their first few scenes together, the eye contact is powerful and he expresses a strong desire to get married. You can also look at his ABC Man Codes to explain why Leopold is a dream match.

Mr. Fantasy Codes:

- Bachelor Available (BA). He expresses a desire to get married, but to the right one. He shows a genuine interest in finding a soul mate.
- Keeper of the Fire (KOF). Leopold is a pro in the romance department. He sends her a romantic letter with a formal

invitation to dinner on the rooftop. The next day he makes her toast with butter and strawberries for breakfast. When she leaves for work, he helps Kate put on her coat. These are only a few of the countless KOF examples in the movie.

- Nourishing Nester (NN). He cooks her gourmet dinners and carries Kate to bed when she is tired. He is sincerely concerned for her welfare.

So what about the GUT feeling Kate has for Leopold? When she presents him as an actor candidate for a butter commercial to her advertising agency, she tells her boss, "He's a dream. He's handsome, honest, courteous, and stands up when you walk in the room." Leopold's advice to Kate's brother also shows signs of good character. While the brother prepares to call a woman for a date, Leopold tells him, "Women respond to sincerity."

This is a Mr. Perfect indeed. Trouble is you're only going to find him in the movies. Clearly, movie producers, writers and directors know what women are looking for and can create fantasies for them on the big screen.

Check the Core GUT for a Perfect Match

So how do you recognize a Mr. Right? Let's take a look at a Real-Life Perfect Match with all the right ingredients for long-term success.

The Perfect Tango

Remember the story about my piano teacher who met her life partner taking tango dance lessons in the "Jump into Your Passions" section in Chapter 4. She was engaged in ten days, living with him after three months, pregnant at seven months, and married on the date of their son's birth. This couple represents the Perfect Tango. Based on the dynamics of their dance, you can understand why she rates her Mr. Perfect Match as a ten on the LIFE Match Meter.

When the couple met three years ago, she was a 34-year-old pianist and he was a 46-year-old entrepreneur. Both partners exuded great confidence and a sense of self. They were experienced daters, which made it easier for them to identify their soul mate.

Both parties passed the Emotional Readiness and Love Match Pre-Tests on the first date. After ten days, they were engaged. How did the couple know so fast that they had found their soul mates? When I asked her to describe why she knew, her first response was tied to a GUT reaction: "I knew that he was honest with good intentions, and not pretentious." She continued by adding, "He didn't talk about himself. He was very interested in my ideas and was a patient and attentive listener."

If you ask him to explain it, he says, "I was good at developing radar for a good match after being on the dating circuit for five years and after having married twice for the wrong reasons. I knew pretty quickly that she had all the ingredients. After ten days of dating, I knew that I had found my life partner."

When I asked whether she used any LIFE Questions to review his character and go beyond the GUT, she explained this observation, "Well, he had a great relationship with his mother that was really balanced and strong. He treats his mother with great respect, and that was very appealing to me." The couple also shares the same sense of humor and a similar interest in marketing. He added, "We were so compatible. I could finish her sentences and she could finish mine." She added, "We shared the same morals and value systems."

So what type of SMART ABC Man Codes does she use to describe her perfect match?

Mr. Perfect Match

- Bachelor Available (BA). He was definitely emotionally available for a lasting relationship. After five years of dating, he was ready to settle down with a mate.
- Nourishing Nester (NN). He genuinely cares about her best interest and enjoys spending time with her at home. He said

to me, "I don't need to be at parties and events. Being with her is enough for me."

- Keeper of the Fire (KOF). She thinks he is very romantic at heart. He told me, "I continually try to maintain and earn respect from her. I like to hold doors for her, help her with the groceries, and never ignore her at a party even if there are good-looking women there."

- Confident Metro Male (CMM). She told me, "He is very nice to other women and has female friends." He sets boundaries with his female contacts, and the interactions make him a more balanced male.

- Guy with Offspring (GWO). Mr. Perfect Match had two seven-year-old twin girls from a previous marriage when they met. When I asked her how she felt about the kids, she commented, "I wasn't concerned because I loved him so much. I would be more concerned if he was a 46-year-old that had never been married."

- Love Match (LM). There was "irresistible chemistry" between this couple. They had sex on the first night that they dated. The couple was very upfront about their magical love connections in bed.

What has made their relationship remain so strong after a wedding and baby boy? First, she commented, "There is a mutual respect for each other. He is one hundred percent behind me and I completely back him. If you are both striving to make your partner look good, you can't go wrong." In addition, the couple highlights their flexible approach to life as a key to their success. In reference to give-and-take, he noted, "It is natural between us. There is no scorecard. There is no manipulation or lying in our relationship, and it feels great."

While it may be hard to believe, she explained, "We've never had an argument or a fight." He added, "Sometimes we joke yell at each other and pull pranks, but we know it is not serious because we just don't fight."

In reference to previous partners, he told me, "I don't have problems with ex-boyfriends as long as they were nice to her. I'm not the jealous type, but there are many out there who are that way."

She explained their marriage dynamics further to me: "We would do anything for each other, but would never take advantage of one another. There are just too many selfish people out there, and so many relationships get destroyed by an accounting approach of continually keeping track of who did what for the other."

In the end, the happy husband summarized this Perfect Match by stating, "I'm so satisfied with her that I would never be tempted by another. She is really my number one priority in life and maintaining our relationship is a continual process." Her final statement to me was "I don't want our story to seem like a fantasy. We're not perfect people and we don't have perfect lives. We deal with life issues every day, but I'm glad that I'm in the game with him." Based on the Final Man Analysis, this relationship is clearly built to last.

The Perfect Match Exists

While there is no such thing as a Perfect Person, there is a Perfect Match out there for you. Look for good GUT and always check LIFE Match. It might also be time to let go of your ideas about Mr. Perfect. Sometimes our fantasies keep us from the Perfect Match since we eliminate perfectly good Mr. Rights over missing Mr. Perfect qualities. As a 50-year-old female CEO put it: "We can rationalize our way out of anything as an adult and never make a decision." At a certain point, you will need to decide if you are willing to take a chance to go the distance.

Be Proactive

If you want to find your Perfect Match, you have to be proactive. One of my closest girlfriends set a goal on her 40th birthday to be married or engaged by the end of that year. She bumped into someone special through serendipity during the same month. She actually had met her Mr. Right ten years earlier at a wedding. My 40-year-old girlfriend had great success with this man because she used SMART Man Hunting techniques to evaluate her Mr. Right. She made her goals very clear out of the gate, kept an open dialogue, no bull policy, and found herself engaged by the end of the year to a genuine and considerate 44-year-old real estate professional. His comment to me at their engagement party was, "I think she is wonderful. Even though we have differences, I don't even think about changing her. I love her for the way she is, and that is all that matters."

Another 35-year-old financial manager, whom I coached, set a goal to date 10 men between April and December one year. Simply by stepping out and actively dating, she boosted her ego, met more high-quality men, and ended up walking down the aisle two years later with one of the guys she met on her Man Hunt journey.

The Test of Time

Why are GUT and LIFE Match so important? Take a look at my parents' 40-year marriage. My mother always told me that she had a really good GUT feeling when she met my father on a blind date. And they continue to be madly in love after all these years. You can just tell because they laugh out loud often, enjoy surprising each other romantically, and do the marriage dance with the right balance and respect for each other.

When you ask my parents how they lasted so long, my mother will respond, "The only thing that is certain in life is change so it is all about how you handle the turns in life together." Because my parents are both flexible and have compromised over the years, they have created a lasting give-and-take relationship. They have been able to weave their way successfully through the partnership journey. And as my father told me, "It's all about your attitude towards life. When you think you've got it made, it all goes bad. When you think it can't get worse, it always gets better. It is important to find someone whom you love and who can roll with the punches. Your mother and I love each other and have fun together. We adjust in life."

In the end, it is the dynamics of the dance that makes a relationship go the distance. Dating assessment is a dance too, one that reveals how a potential Mr. Right will do the dance of Lifetime partnership. If the dance isn't going well in the dating phase, it won't work in marriage either. That's why the Dating Assessment Dance is the way to go to be SMART.

You Go, Girl!

If you boost your confidence, take chances, smile, ask the right questions, pay attention, present a positive persona, and know when to quit, you will have a successful Man Hunt journey. Use your new SMART dating skills on top of what you already know to achieve better results.

The New Era Dating Options provide women with endless possibilities for finding the right life partner. Expand your bandwidth, learn from your mistakes, and start searching smarter and safely because you are now SMART Man Hunting Certified for success! And if, in the end, you meet Mr. Right through serendipity, with all the practice you're going to have from SMART Man Hunting, you'll know how to quickly find out if he's your Mr. Wonderful. In the meantime, more power to you for getting out there, boosting your dating numbers, ego, and the quality of your dates. You now know when to say, "Next" versus when to take a closer look faster. You might just look back in five years and say to yourself, "Wow, that was a great journey."

And if people tell you that men don't want to get married anymore, do not believe what you hear. Here is an insight from a 29-year-old consultant who is engaged to a 32-year-old woman. He shared a secret with me: "People say guys are terrified of getting married. I think they're only scared if it's the wrong person." Well, you be too. Follow the SMART Man Hunting plan for success and you'll ensure compatibility for the long-term.

With these new insights, SMART ABC Man Codes and Interview Practices, you are ready to meet the challenge of proactively searching for Mr. Right. You were already smart, but now you are SMARTer:

Search proactively for Mr. Right with confidence sex appeal using New Era dating options.

Meet more high-quality men, boost your ego, and position yourself for dating success.

Assess potential candidates to identify your Mr. Wonderful versus Mr. Goodenough.

Review the Total Man using the SMART ABC Codes as Compatibility Guide.

Trust your GUT instincts and LIFE Match results to know when to say, "You're Hired!"

PART IV

The SMART ABC
Man Codes

Comic Relief and Compatibility Checks

ARE YOU READY for some comic relief and compatibility check shortcuts? Do you want to learn from the successes and mistakes of other dating experts? Use these SMART ABC Man Codes, definitions, true-story examples, and strategies to identify patterns, encourage healthy dialogue, and have some fun along your dating journey. You don't want to overlook important characteristic complements and clashes when identifying Mr. Right so let this code book be your compatibility guide.

Because dating can be a struggle, give yourself a few breaks and have some laughs with the code names. Hopefully, you can also laugh at your mistakes by using these dating story reminders. We have all made mistakes so don't be hard on yourself. Applaud yourself for getting smarter with every relationship and allow room for laughter. It's the best survival strategy for dating.

What are these SMART ABC Man Codes? How can they help you with your Man Hunt? This code book will help you identify Man Candidate characteristics and to create a dating success strategy. You now have Man Candidates. Are you ready to take a closer look inside to determine whether your needs match his priorities, style, and desires? The 26 A–Z Man Codes in this section provide both humor and reality checks to help you quickly recognize your Mr. Right. Similar to the acronym soup used to reference corporate departments and organizations, these ABC abbreviations provide women with their own shorthand for dating. Each code is an acronym for a type of Man Candidate. It is supported by a code definition, true tale, and recommended strategies and questions for this type of Man.

These Man Codes are based on the experiences of female dating insiders and will save you time and energy in your Man Hunt. By recognizing the types of Man Candidates out there, it helps you cut to the chase in your Dating Assessments and Man Interview Practices by helping you gain clarity on the Mr. Wrongs, Mr. Good-enoughs, as well as the Mr. Rights. Refer to the dating strategy guidelines to avoid lengthy dating disasters that damage your ego and steal you away from checking out other opportunities. This SMART ABC Man Code Book can help you find your soul mate faster with a much greater ROI (Return on Investment).

The Man Codes do not have to be read in A-Z order. If the code for a potential mate jumps right out at you, feel free to go directly to that description and its recommended strategies. You can even share this reference guide or the ABC Codes Compatibility Quiz in Appendix I with a potential match. Ask him to identify his codes and then see how your perceptions compare. I shared these Man Codes with one potential candidate and compared notes. While I thought he was an OO (Over-Achiever Obsessor), he defined himself as a KOF (Keeper of the Fire) and PTS (Post Traumatic Soul). Because of the tough loss of an old girlfriend whom he almost married, he was just not ready to be a BA (Bachelor Available). I learned a lot about him from this discussion and we grew closer as a result.

And don't forget, even though the examples are all male, the codes can apply to women as well. Take an honest look at your own priorities and preferences when reviewing these male types. What are your woman codes? How do they mesh with your man's codes? For example, if you are a NN (Nourishing Nester) who prefers quiet time at home, you might clash with a male SG (Social Guru) who thrives in a crowd.

Use the ABC Man Codes to gauge your Man Candidate on the LIFE Match Meter and as you do the Dating Assessment Dance. Use the LIFE Questions in the Codes or formulate your own to identify what codes belong to your current Man Candidates. You want to uncover similar goals and then address anything that does not sit well now versus later if you are headed down the wedding-bell path.

Selecting a Mr. Right is not easy. It's a delicate two-way dance. In addition to the LIFE Questions, the dating strategies will give you another way to observe his behavior and listen for the red flags. Remember to use the Winning Hunter's Toolkit by packing your skill set of confidence, patience, and persistence versus giving off desperate or needy vibes to lead you to success at this juncture. Even though you are further along the dating journey, you can still gather vital information without being too serious.

For fun, I've shared celebrity examples of the man codes from romantic comedies. To give you a complete list of celebrity examples, I came up with the following SMART ABC Man Codes Hollywood Quick-Reference Guide. This quick hit list is based on movie characters and provides a fast introduction to the codes. You'll see that guys can fit more than one code so you need to look at the Total Man. And as a good friend told me, "It's all about the package."

SMART ABC Man Codes
Hollywood Quick-Reference Guide

ABC Man Code	Celebrity	Movie
All Sports Fanatic (ASF)	Tom Cruise	*Jerry McGuire*
Bachelor Available (BA)	John Cusack	*Serendipity*
Confident Metro Male (CMM)	Mel Gibson	*What a Woman Wants*
Dysfunctional Guy with Issues (DGI)	Richard Gere	*Pretty Woman*
Executive Search Seeker (ESS)	Pierce Brosnan	*Laws of Attraction*
Fitness Extremist (FE)	Slyvester Stallone	*Rocky*
Guy With Offspring (GWO)	Tom Hanks	*Sleepless in Seattle*
Hello Goodbye Guy (HGG)	Vince Vaughn	*Wedding Crashers*
Internet Pyscho (IP)	Jude Law	*Closer*
Justifying Juggler (JJ)	Jamie Foxx	*Ray*
Keeper of the Fire (KOF)	Will Smith	*Hitch*

Love Match (LM)	Joseph Fiennes	*Shakespeare in Love*
Married But Available (MBA)	Dennis Quaid	*Something to Talk About*
Nourishing Nester (NN)	Johnny Depp	*Finding Neverland*
Overachiever Obsessor (OO)	Richard Gere	*Pretty Woman*
Post-Traumatic Soul (PTS)	Christian Slater	*Untamed Heart*
Questionnaire Perfectionist (QP)	Jack Nicholson	*As Good as It Gets*
Relentless Renter (RR)	Ewan McGregor	*Down with Love*
Social Guru (SG)	George Clooney	*Oceans 11 and 12*
Tasmanian Traveler (TT)	Leonardo DiCaprio	*The Aviator*
Under-Estimated Ally (UA)	Bill Pullman	*While You Were Sleeping*
Virtual Lover (VL)	Tom Hanks	*You've Got Mail!*
Wounded Divorcé (WD)	Billy Crystal	*When Harry Met Sally*
X-Ray Eyes (XRE)	Hugh Grant	*Bridget Jones's Diary*
Young Explorer (YE)	Jude Law	*Alfie*
Zodiac Zealot (ZZ)	Matthew McConaughey	*The Wedding Planner*

Are you ready to have some fun in the final phase of your Man Hunt journey? By placing these codes and dating strategies in your purse, you will not only have some comic relief, but be able to make faster man choices. Have fun with the codes. They can only make you SMARTer and increase your odds of identifying Mr. Wonderful, and that's what this journey is all about.

ASF All Sports Fanatic

All Sports Fanatic Definition

The All Sports Fanatic (ASF) is completely consumed with following his sports heroes, tends to be a season ticket holder, and usually lives and dies by the won-lost log and box scores. Every weekend, ASFs are either at the game or in front of the television. His conversations mostly concern upcoming sports events, game results, and player statistics. He has a sport for every season and constantly looks for opportunities to discuss this fixation.

Depending on your sports fanatic tendencies, this guy can either be a great match or a nightmare.

All Sports Fanatic Examples

Recently, a girlfriend in her 30s married a 38-year-old ASF. Although he has had a successful financial accounting career, his real passion is following football and basketball.

She knew from the beginning that he was an ASF. All weekend activities revolved around meeting his buddies to watch the games. Sometimes the girlfriends and wives were included, but mostly they were all-male rallies. While she enjoyed watching sports, my friend was also interested in movies and cultural activities. As a result, she was able to find a balance by giving him room to go off with his fellow fanatics.

When they got engaged in February, I asked her if we could go to dinner to celebrate. She responded by saying, "After college basketball season in early April." An even bigger surprise was that she didn't seem to mind the wait to accommodate her fiancé's tunnel vision. Apparently, that was just the way the ball bounced.

Later, I learned more about the seriousness of this obsession when my boyfriend and I joined the couple at University of Maryland basketball games. The ASF got so consumed with his team's performance that if they were behind it would ruin his entire evening. He would be silent throughout the game and depressed for several days if they lost. This ASF also placed basketball bets in Las Vegas over the Internet. Overall, he takes the game a little too seriously for me.

The couple is still happily married with a baby boy. Not only has my friend accepted her mate's lifestyle; she has become great friends with his buddies' wives and maintained her own interests. Although she will deny it, they have named their son after the University of Maryland basketball coach. More power to her and to you—that is, if you don't mind jumping through hoops for your ASF.

In another ASF case, I dated a baseball fanatic with extreme tendencies. In 2004, when the Red Sox won the World Series for the first time since 1918, I dated an ASF who openly shared his obsession with me. He taught me about the key players, and because I knew baseball from following the Baltimore Orioles for years, we had fun enjoying the games together. However, when the Red Sox progressed in the playoffs and World Series, he pulled back and told me, "It's like a religious experience so I need to watch the games alone." While I was really happy for him and the team for their long-due victory, he took the game just a little too seriously for me. While I continue to follow the Red Sox, this extreme was one of the deal-breakers for us.

All Sports Fanatic Strategies

ASFs are as loyal to their sports teams as if they have given birth to them. Don't fool yourself that once you are married, things might change. If you have zero interest in sports, the ASF is so extreme in his fandom that you probably should not consider this candidate as a long-term partner unless you don't mind sitting on the bench a lot. On the other hand, if you are a cheerleader for the same teams, you could be ideal for each other. As long as you can have fun watching your teams together, you are probably in the same ballpark.

The best way for you to successfully date or marry as ASF is to accept his lifestyle and build your own interests. If you find yourself entering a relationship with an ASF, test the waters by seeking compromise with some shared activities. For example, ask him if he is willing to go to the theater with you occasionally. You do not need to do everything together. However, you should establish a give-and-take relationship with compromise so that it is a win-win situation.

In addition, consider giving him a separate room for his hall-of-fame autographed pictures or you may find yourself living in a replica of Cal Ripken's locker. This sports memorabilia may dominate your walls. An extra bedroom or den might be a great way to contain the sports paraphernalia your guy lives to collect.

Because ASFs may have many redeeming qualities, they can be

excellent partners despite this addiction. Don't allow this one element to halt a relationship but do consider the full package.

All Sports Fanatic LIFE Questions

1. Tell me about the sports teams that you follow.
2. Tell me how many times a week you like to watch games.
3. Tell me about your favorite sports hero and why.

BA   Bachelor Available

Bachelor Available Definition

A Bachelor Available (BA) is someone who is mentally and emotionally ready for a long-term commitment. These men are not always easy to find, but once a connection is established BAs openly tell you their intentions. You often find BAs using Internet dating or Professional Matchmakers because most men will not try these options until they are serious about finding a soul mate. BAs usually have the best intentions in mind and will value you as an individual. The BA is a Go/No-Go code. He must be a BA or you need to say, "Next" fast.

Bachelor Available Examples

I have two examples of BAs to support the notion that willing and able prospects exist.

The first BA candidate was someone I met through an Internet dating introduction. We shared similar interests in horses, photography, and travel. He showed genuine interest in and concern for my needs, an approach that was a refreshing change from some of the other men I had encountered.

Dates with this BA were unique and romantic. He made a great effort to organize fun activities that interested both of us. For example, he took me to a private museum tour on a Tuesday during lunch. Because he desired a long-term relationship with me, this BA was also willing to move at a pace that was comfortable for me physically.

The second BA candidate was more blatant about his intentions. He had been primarily a friend, who later started asking me out. After two dates, he told me at lunch in a busy restaurant, "I am ready for a commitment so you just let me know when you are ready." I was so blown away as well as uncertain about my feelings for him that I did not know how to respond. Eventually, I realized that I did not have romantic feelings for him, and have fortunately been able to maintain a valuable friendship with this BA.

Bachelor Available Strategies

If you feel a mutual mental and physical connection with a BA, he is an ideal mate.

You should only consider serious relationships with BAs. If a prospect is not emotionally ready, you are wasting your time even if there are other good code connections with him.

However, strategies with BAs will vary depending on your connection with the candidate. Even though you may not be as certain about the match right out of the gate, if there is any potential, don't walk away immediately. Because it can take time to fully appreciate someone, you may learn to adore this individual. Now that you are looking for a lifetime mate, other things become more important than just a physical attraction, and BAs are hard to find.

On the other hand, if you are confident there is no future with your BA, be delicately honest right away. BAs can be more vulnerable because they generally make their intentions clear up front. If you drag things out, it is like a slow torture for these often sensitive men. Let them go so the BA can move forward with someone else that shares a mutual connection.

Bachelor Available LIFE Questions

1. Tell me what type of relationship you want.
2. What do you think makes a really good marriage?
3. Tell me about your long-term goals for a relationship.

CMM Confident Metro Male

Confident Metro Male Definition

The Confident Metro Male (CMM) is another great catch because of his balanced personality and sense of style. These males are confident and comfortable with their own masculinity—yet also enjoy the company and interests of women. CMMs often grew up with strong bonds to sisters and mothers, and, as a result, value female relationships. Such men will choose dinner with you or other couples over a guys' night out. CMMs will go to the movies or theater with you, but will also have male friendships. Because CMMs represent balance, they can be ideal mates.

Confident Metro Male Examples

My 35-year-old girlfriend dated a classic example of a Confident Metro Male. He is an athletic 39-year-old CEO of two businesses. While this CMM shares his passion for extreme sports with male friends, he is equally enthusiastic about calling female friends to go roller-blading. He grew up with a brother and sister and had a devoted relationship to his mother. During my friend's relationship with him, this CMM was comfortable discussing his feelings and regularly compromised on activities so both of their needs were met.

For example, on a typical Saturday, this CMM might go to the spa with my girlfriend, and then later ride horses at the track with his buddies. He also organized group dinners and activities with both male and female friends. An example of this CMM's natural curiosity about women is that he offered to attend the *Vagina Monologues* with his girlfriend and her mother. He was not uncomfortable or intimidated by this situation. This CMM has many female friends and greatly values their opinions.

Because CMMs are more in touch with how women think, these men tend to have a great sense of style. I dated a CMM from the San Francisco Bay Area who made great first impressions inside and out. For Saturday night dinner dates, he often wore pressed dress shirts with an open collar, pressed pants, and a sports jacket. I also noticed his shiny leather shoes and elegant silver watch. His smooth style matched his confident personality and fit in perfectly to the San Francisco singles scene. He did not take himself too seriously and we shared many laughs. We often joked about his offer to go on Oprah with me (when other men would run when asked). The conversation was easy. This CMM was a great listener and cheerleader. Along with an appealing presentation, his positive attitude gave him two thumbs up in my book.

Confident Metro Male Strategies

These candidates are ideal mates for a female who also has balanced interests and maintains friendships with both sexes. Women who can enjoy watching a football game with a mate as well as the ballet can find these bonds mutually fulfilling. Men and women are clearly different and this individual is willing to learn about you.

Don't worry about his female friends. CMMs are more balanced because of friendships with the opposite sex. If you get jealous easily, you may damage the bond and then miss out on a wonderful connection. Try to evaluate the situation and understand the person better before walking away. As long as he sets boundaries and lets his female friends know he is totally devoted to you, it can be an asset to date a CMM. These traits can actually be the basis for a foundation of mutual respect and lifelong commitment.

When checking out a guy's style, consider whether his presentation matches the date and location. Are you going out for drinks on a Wednesday night or is it a Saturday night dinner date? When I interviewed one CMM in Los Angeles, he told me, "For drinks, I wear two colors. For dinner dates, I always wear three primary colors." He expanded on the dinner date dress, "If I wear tan khakis with a deep green shirt, then I will wear a matching brown or black leather belt, shoes and cashmere sports coat." Ask yourself, are his shoes clean or scuffed? Does he have good hygiene? Does he naturally draw you in with a nice cologne? Does he carry himself with confidence? All of these details will help you quickly identify a Confident Metro Male.

Confident Metro Male Questions

1. How do you feel about having a girlfriend who has male friendships?
2. Tell me about your female friends and interests that you share with them.
3. Where do you like to shop for shoes?

DGI Dysfunctional Guy with Issues

Dysfunctional Guy with Issues Definition

A Dysfunctional Guy with Issues (DGI) is most likely a male over 35 who has never been married. Everyone is dysfunctional to a degree, but there may be more baggage if someone has not made a commitment by 35. DGIs are often resistant to partnerships and can be frustrating candidates if you are seeking someone with whom to go the distance. This definition is a broad and general one based solely on age and commitment history. You will need to dig deeper to determine the complexity of the dysfunction.

Dysfunctional Guy with Issues Example

I dated a successful journalist who, at 47 years old, appeared to have it all together. This DGI was charismatic with a great career and solid friendships. He was intelligent and witty with a full list of outdoor sports and cultural interests.

He told me about several long-term relationships in his past and it seemed odd that he never had made a marriage commitment. In one case, he dated a woman for two years, found an apartment to share with her, and then suddenly asked her to move out after just a few months. He never explained why, but I tried to overlook these issues because I was nuts about him.

We spent an intense four-day weekend away together and it

was magical. His eyes were teary when I left, and it seemed to me that a powerful connection had been established. But instead of taking the relationship to the next level, this DGI began to make up excuses why it would not work and basically backed away.

When I looked deeper, I found that he had a non-traditional family with many divorces, step-siblings, and half siblings. However, he had a good relationship with his mother. I took the latter as a positive sign, but clearly there were too many hidden issues. After an agonizing year spent trying to make the relationship happen, I finally waved the surrender flag. In an email, he apologized for being "less than a gentleman," said I deserved better, and wished me the best of luck. My friend who set us up has told me repeatedly, "He is just not marriage material." This DGI has remained single.

Dysfunctional Guy with Issues Strategies

When you come across a male over 35 who has never made a real commitment, give serious thought to looking elsewhere. If you decide to proceed anyway, ask questions about his relationship history and family dynamics to uncover any potential patterns. Avoid playing the caretaker and making up excuses for him because it can be exhausting with little payoff. In addition, don't think that you can fix him because old habits are almost impossible to break at this age. Somebody else probably thought the same thing before you.

Perhaps he has just not met the right one. However, you will need to decide how much time you want to invest in a potentially unavailable candidate. I wasted a year.

Dysfunctional Guy with Issues LIFE Questions

1. Tell me about your parents. Are they still married?
2. Can you describe your last important relationship?
3. Tell me why you have never been married.

ESS Executive Search Seeker

Executive Search Seeker Definition

Executive Search Seekers (ESS) are professional men who only want to date career-oriented women. These men are obsessed with their own work, and need a companion who can understand this passion and is equally driven. ESSs have a myopic definition of their search parameters. They tend to be over-achievers and require similar traits in a mate. Because ESSs are clear in their expectations, they can be a great match for success-driven women.

Executive Search Seeker Example

I exchanged emails with an ESS candidate whom I met via Internet dating. We later spoke on the phone for over an hour before our first live encounter. He played a leadership role for a very successful management-consulting firm and made it clear that this job was his life. This ESS typically worked over seventy hours per week. This prospect was direct in his requirement for a companion who could understand his lifestyle and career focus. We exchanged experiences working with Fortune 1000 clients and discovered that we shared similar management philosophies.

At the end of this lengthy introductory call, we decided to meet the following evening during his airport layover in Los Angeles en route back to his home in Orlando, Florida. In preparation for our meeting, he gave me homework. This ESS asked me to analyze his company's website and be prepared to give him feedback. Because of my e-commerce experience creating website content, I accepted the challenge.

During our brief meeting, the candidate dominated the conversation with the results of his client meetings that day. He was extremely wound up and passionate about his work. When it came time for my website analysis test, the ESS was disappointed that I did not have more comments on the graphics. At the end of this 30-minute meeting, he gave me a follow-up assignment that consisted of more website reviews.

When I left the airport, my cell phone rang. It was the ESS. He said that he enjoyed our brief meeting and was looking forward to receiving the results of my second quiz. I felt exhausted by the encounter and knew there was no chemistry. I wanted to find an ESS, but this guy was just too intense for me.

In a second scenario, I dated a passionate creative director, who was a great cheerleader for my book dreams. He had worked for a top advertising agency in New York City and recently moved back to Los Angeles. On our first date, he had reviewed my website and was excited to offer branding ideas for enhancing my messages. I was impressed by his research and interest. This ESS was reading books about how to start his own business, had directed a movie as a side project, and traveled the world extensively. We clicked in many ways through our career goals and executive backgrounds.

Executive Search Seeker Strategies

For a career woman, there are many benefits to sharing your business passions with a mate. However, it needs to be a balanced give-and-take. An ESS can be very self-focused and too absorbed in his work to create a mutually beneficial bond. Because women are multi-taskers, they can usually do a better job balancing career and relationship needs.

An ESS male may create an emotionally lopsided partnership because he is unable to separate from his work. Evaluate the dynamics of the relationship and decide if your ESS provides complementary traits or is simply a drain on your energy. With the right dynamics, you may find a great relationship with a career cheerleader.

Executive Search Seeker LIFE Questions

1. What types of jobs do some of your female friends have?
2. How important is it to you that your female mate has a successful career?
3. What information do you like to discuss with a partner about your work?

FE   Fitness Extremist

Fitness Extremist Definition

A Fitness Extremist (FE) is obsessed with regular workouts and healthy living. If he does not exercise at least five times a week, the FE is disappointed in himself and feels his muscles turning into fat. His diet consists primarily of vegetables and protein, and it will be almost impossible to break this regimen.

An FE is so absorbed by this healthy lifestyle that he most likely needs a woman with similar workout and diet routines. FEs are totally body conscious and will probably demand the same focus from their mate.

Fitness Extremist Example

One of my 30-something girlfriends dated a 41-year-old Fitness Extremist who was a professional bike racer. His entire life revolved around a strictly defined diet, eating schedules, and regular prolonged workouts.

There was no breaking this routine. If she wanted to go away with him for the weekend, he needed to be able to access a gym and continue his extreme diet. Whenever she found herself enjoying a piece of tiramisu, she was always alone and feeling guilty. She also felt that her own body never met his expectations.

Her FE's diet prescribed no wheat, sugar, or carbohydrates. His favorite foods were sushi and skinless chicken. Some of her favorite foods were at the other extreme—and included pasta, ice cream, and Captain Crunch.

After months of trying to make the relationship work, she realized that this FE was not a candidate worth pursuing. She could never match his fitness obsession and did not want to live with the pressure and guilt.

Fitness Extremist Strategies

Fitness Extremists can be great mates if you have similar workout and diet goals. If you enjoy regular aerobic activities and monitor your eating habits, the FE may be the man for you. He will probably ask you to join him in his exercise routine. If the gym is also your thing, take a closer look at this guy.

Alternatively, if you are not an FE, be honest with yourself and walk away. This relationship will only frustrate you. You will drive yourself crazy by feeling a self-imposed pressure to eat and exercise the FE way.

If this FE is the man of your dreams and you want to pursue a relationship, ask him to share his fitness expectations for a partner. He may surprise you. If he seems less demanding than your perception, set a timeframe to test the relationship out. Periodic reality checks will give you opportunities to make Go/No-Go decisions.

Fitness Extremist LIFE Questions

1. What type of diet do you think is important?
2. Tell me more about how often you work out and the importance of these sessions.
3. What parts of your health regimen do you like to share with a mate?

GWO Guy with Offspring

Guy with Offspring Definition

Meeting a Guy with Offspring (GWO) happens frequently today with the soaring divorce rates. Obviously, these candidates are men with children from a previous relationship. You may also be a GWO with children whom you share with an ex. The GWOs will vary greatly in terms of time commitments to their family. Some parents share custody so the children stay regularly at his home. Other GWOs have children who live in different cities and only see them during holidays and on special occasions. The relationship with the former partner also has a major impact on parent-child dynamics and your interactions with him.

Guy with Offspring Example

My 35-year-old friend married someone with a two-year-old daughter from a previous marriage. This GWO was extremely dedicated to his father-daughter relationship. In this case, my friend found it was easier dating a GWO with a young child versus a teenager. However, an irrational ex-spouse complicated their interactions.

In this case, the ex-spouse initially made it almost impossible for her husband to maintain a healthy bond with his child. The mother was a control freak, holding most of the emotional trump cards, which created great heartache for my friend and the GWO.

My friend had to be very supportive of her GWO husband due to a difficult ex-spouse. She was flexible with her time and commitments. Initially, the newlyweds were never certain when a visit would be allowed. As a result of her willingness to openly address the situation and support the GWO, the experience has enhanced their marriage by bringing them closer together.

Guy with Offspring Strategies

Anyone dealing with a GWO needs to ask herself difficult questions about the impact of a child on the relationship. In order to be fair to the Man Candidate and his child, be honest with your answers. If you have kids and know the routine, you are in familiar territory and are better equipped to deal with the myriad aspects of custody. If you do not have kids, evaluate the relationship and whether it is worth your time and emotion to invest further in this GWO.

Beware of the GWO who feels guilt for not spending enough time with his children. You may end up feeling that your relationship is in competition with the parent-child bond. If you find the GWO always canceling dates at the last minute to be with his children, you should reconsider whether this relationship makes you feel good.

Whenever children are involved, there is a required level of compromise. Determine whether you can handle the level needed by the GWO. Ideally, you want to find a mate who can balance relationships with you and the child. Continuous open and honest dialogue can walk you through the issues and make the bond stronger.

And if you are a single mother, set your own boundaries for his interactions with your children. A 40-something divorcé told me a shocking story. He explained that the first night that he spent at a woman's house, she let her four-year-old daughter get into bed with them. He told me, "I was really uncomfortable even though the mother was in the middle." This comfort zone broke when the woman got up to take her shower in the morning and left him in bed with the daughter. He told me, "When the daughter accidentally touched my bare bottom, I felt really awkward." He added, "This experience ruined the relationship for me. I could not get excited sexually about her anymore." While the mother told the daughter that mommy was just having a sleepover, the scenario was not okay with him. As an outside observer, I think this guy should have left as soon as the daughter entered the bedroom. The dating dynamics are much more complex when children are part of your life. Proceed with caution and boundaries to protect everyone.

Guy with Offspring LIFE Questions

1. Can you tell me more about your relationship with your children?
2. What role does each parent play in raising the children?
3. Can you describe the dynamics of your relationship with their mother?

HGG   Hello Goodbye Guy

Hello Goodbye Guy Definition

The Hello Goodbye Guy (HGG) will convince you that he is genuinely interested in moving forward at first. You make connections with him easily, and he seems like a strong prospect.

The Hello Goodbye Guy is very polite, full of compliments, and leaves you with the impression that there is a future.

However, after only a few encounters, he suddenly vanishes with no explanation, leaving you checking your deodorant, neuroses, sex appeal, and everything else to find out what went wrong. HGGs will avoid all future contact, leaving you blindsided and baffled.

Hello Goodbye Guy Examples

My first example of a Hello Goodbye Guy is from an Internet dating experience. There are many HGGs on the Internet dating scene who will email you back and forth diligently at first, ask you personal questions, and lead you to believe that you have made a meaningful connection.

This guy asked me to tell him about why I moved to California, whether my divorce was amicable (which it was), and to describe details about my family relationships. He was forthcoming with answers to the same personal questions from me. After a week of openly sharing long emails regarding family values and relationship histories, he suddenly stopped writing with no explanation. His disappearance left me feeling empty and confused.

Another example of a Hello Goodbye Guy was someone whom I met through mutual friends. I probably trusted him more because of the association. This 44-year-old candidate made special efforts to find out my phone number, was a complete gentleman, and immediately scheduled a follow up date. We had four awesome dates with what seemed to be mutual mental and physical attractions. I was convinced that we were heading into something with great potential. After a few days with no contact, I started to wonder. After a few weeks of additional silence, I realized he was a HGG and knocked him off my pre-conceived pedestal.

Hello Goodbye Guy Strategies

Even if friends introduce you, take it slowly in the beginning with any candidate. Interview him thoroughly and avoid making assumptions too soon. Because HGGs are often charmers, it is not always easy to pace the emotional and physical interactions. Control yourself to protect your ego and maintain your dignity.

If you are fooled by an HGG, use the experience as a learning opportunity and don't beat yourself up over it. Avoid taking it personally because it is not your issue. HGGs can be slick masters of deception. Next time, remind yourself that first impressions can be misleading. If he sounds too good to be true, there is probably something hidden behind door number three. Take time to assess the candidates and avoid making hasty assumptions.

Rejection from an HGG can feel like a kick in the stomach. Why do guys act this way? One 40-something bachelor, who is famous for his HGG moves, confessed to me, "Guys will do almost anything to avoid a woman getting upset with them. My friends and I have used this strategy for years. We make women mad by avoiding them so they have to do the breakup." Yikes! These HGGs are scum in my book. If they can't make an attempt to cut things off diplomatically, they do not deserve a minute more of your time. Remember, you are a hot ticket who only deserves the best. Next!

Hello Goodbye Guy LIFE Questions

1. What is the longest relationship in your past?
2. What aspects do you enjoy about being in a relationship?
3. How long do you think it takes to determine if someone might be "the one" for you?

 Internet Psycho

Internet Psycho Definition

Internet Psychos (IPs) are rare and dangerous men who seek thrills by antagonizing women they meet through the latest technology. Extremely bizarre behavior is common among these men, and they will invariably shock and disappoint you. IPs take advantage of the anonymity of Internet dating to fool and victimize women who don't exercise extreme caution.

Internet Psycho Examples

If you receive an email that resembles this one, check to see if you can block the email address, and hit delete because you know you are dealing with an IP: "I would like to undress that sexy body of yours by your fireplace, rub strawberries all over you, and . . ."

Some IPs are less obvious so try to avoid the mistakes that I made while Internet dating. My second example is frightening and I definitely learned a lesson about never giving out your home phone number to strangers over the Internet. I received an email from an Internet dating candidate who was a 38-year-old actor living in Beverly Hills. His photos were impressive studio black and whites. His essay responses were direct and witty, which sparked my interest. His first email was a one-liner that said, "I liked your profile, send me your phone number." Initially, I responded by asking more questions. His second email response asked again for my phone number. I had a weak moment and made the mistake of giving it to him.

During the first call, he asked me, "When are you coming over?" I told him that I was not and that he should go to the next person on his list.

The IP continued to persist by stating that he did not do the "Starbucks thing" and that I would have to do that with other guys. I continued to tell him no thank you. He then had the nerve to comment, "Well, if you change your mind let me know because I have four or five women who come over every week." I remained calm, giving him no reaction, and quickly got off the call. Fortunately, I never heard from this Internet Psycho again.

The third IP example was less obvious and surprised me. While I had been warned to watch out for IPs, I still unwittingly managed to set up a date with a crazy man. I exchanged at least ten emails with him, shared photos, and we discussed our careers and personal interests. He seemed like a stable divorced father who was a 44-year-old professor at a top-notch university where several of my friends attended business school. When he invited me to dinner via email, I accepted the invitation without bothering to check the location or question whether I should have confirmed on the phone.

As I approached the restaurant, it was clear that I was in fact nowhere near my Santa Monica bubble. It was a bleak neighborhood where the homes had bars on windows and doors. I repeated my Los Angeles mantra of K.I.T. (Keep it Together) in my head and proceeded with caution. The IP date was for 7:00 p.m. and when he didn't show by 7:20 p.m., I was a little concerned. I tried calling him and left a message stating that perhaps Friday night traffic was delaying him and asked him to call me. By 7:45 p.m., I decided it was time for my exit.

The next day I received an apology email from this IP with the lamest excuse. The IP stated that he was not used to meeting for dates without talking on the phone with a candidate prior to the engagement. He also made an obnoxiously weird comment about "getting back to my ski trip and broken ankle." I didn't have a clue what that meant, and I responded with a short email stating that his apology was not accepted and that I felt sorry for anyone who encountered him. How would he feel if someone stood up his daughter in a bad neighborhood?

Another word of caution. When you start using Instant Messenger, watch out for the wackos who are only seeking thrills online. When I first jumped into the IM game, I had a guy ask me if I wanted to be in the "movies." When I asked what type of movie, he responded with "adult." Other guys will try to get very graphic by describing how they plan to arouse you in bed and much more. If you want to get into this sexually graphic game using Instant Messenger, go to the "intimate" sites. However, if you are looking for Mr. Right, these short-term players clearly have a different agenda.

Internet Psycho Strategies

Watch out for Internet Psycho warning signs when you are setting up dates online. Never give out your last name or home phone number until you have had a first meeting as a precautionary measure. If the psycho is obvious, see if you can block his email address immediately.

I also recommend at least one phone conversation with Internet dating candidates prior to any meeting, to help you detect wackos. Remember that you need to ask the guy for his phone number and use Caller ID blocking (*67) when you place the call. If you sense during the call that you're dealing with an IP, run as you would from a telemarketer from hell. Avoid all future contact with this individual.

If you have a persistent harassment problem, you may also want to consider other security precautions or to contact your local law enforcement authorities without delay.

Internet Psycho LIFE Questions

1. Tell me about your Internet dating experience.
2. Have you met anyone that you liked through Internet dating?
3. Where do you like to go for third dates?

JJ Justifying Juggler

Justifying Juggler Definition

Justifying Jugglers (JJ) will date and have sex with as many women as possible at the same time—and do not even try to hide it. The JJ will try to convince you that his juggling act is acceptable behavior. These men love women and fill their lives with multiple relationships. The JJ is extremely self-focused and narcissistic. He truly believes that everyone should love him and has no concept of commitment.

Justifying Juggler Example

My 32-year-old girlfriend dated a dance instructor with pronounced JJ characteristics. He was incredibly charming and possessed an exceptional understanding of women. This 36-year-old

JJ was also extremely sexy and oozed charisma. He had the gift that caused females to tolerate or at least overlook his unconventional lifestyle.

She knew this JJ had dated many other students from the dance studio, but it just didn't matter. Everyone adored him and accepted his behavior. My friend felt safe as long as she did not get emotionally involved. She knew the game, and had no qualms about his intentions. There was zero chance of commitment or change in his behavior.

She saw the Justifying Juggler every day in dance studio classes. He was extremely passionate about every aspect of women. The JJ made all females feel special with continuous and sincere compliments. Even the ones that were less than physically stunning he made feel like goddesses as long as they were good dancers.

The Justifying Juggler made no effort to hide his attractions to, affections for, and appreciation of other women. As a result, my friend had to accept his preference for multiple partners. Their relationship accommodated his world. She enjoyed their time together, kept her expectations in check, and does not regret her experience.

Justifying Juggler Strategies

If you can handle a relationship with no commitment, the Justifying Juggler can be an ego boost and a ton of fun. However, because you are seeking a lifetime mate, there is probably little room or desire to entertain these charismatic charmers.

Evaluate your personal needs and preferences carefully to avoid situations that can be time wasters. Avoid misinterpreting his intentions. You are kidding yourself if you think the JJ will suddenly have a change of heart and lifestyle on your account. The Justifying Juggler will never be "the one." Because of his passion for women, he will probably never settle for one partner. These men are not potential life-mates. If you decide that you cannot resist a JJ, set realistic expectations and make sure it is a win-win situation.

You will find many JJs disguised online because everyone is playing a numbers game. If you decide to get serious with someone whom you meet through an Internet dating site or matchmaker, ask about his level of commitment before you jump in bed with him. I received this email from a fan who uncovered a JJ online. "My twin sister, who has been on Match.com, just used the codes in your book to identify and eliminate a flaky suitor. He was a Justifying Juggler and boy does she feel better to have shed him. Thanks again!" Because she was focused on finding Mr. Right, this JJ was a complete waste of her time, not to mention dangerous to her health because he was sleeping around.

Justifying Juggler LIFE Questions

1. What are you seeking in the dating arena?
2. Have you ever fallen for more than one person at a time and what happened?
3. Do you think a monogamous relationship is possible today?

KOF   Keeper of the Fire

Keeper of the Fire Definition

Who says Valentine's Day only happens once a year? The Keeper of the Fire (KOF) is a romantic who will perpetually maintain interest by intermittently stoking the flames with unexpected pleasures. These men will regularly remind you of their devotion. They enjoy making an effort and gain satisfaction from making you smile. The KOF does not need to spend a lot of money to sustain sparks. KOFs will find creative and often inexpensive ways to keep the fire going.

Keeper of the Fire Examples

My 38-year-old friend was dating a textbook example of a Keeper of the Fire. He brought her a gift every time they went out, which added surprise and sparks to their relationship. The KOF gifts were not extravagant, but showed great thought. For example, he gave her a CD of his favorite music. Another night he brought her a gift certificate for a massage after she had just managed avoiding a lay-off at work. This romantic wanted to recognize that she had had a tough day. His kind gestures had a powerful impact, and the couple was happily married within two years.

Another KOF example was the 39-year-old artist that I dated in Washington, D.C. He showed his appreciation through acts of kindness and little gestures. For example, while I was on a business trip for a month, he cleaned my apartment, including scrubbing the bathroom tiles. This KOF also loved cooking dinner on the grill for me on summer Sundays. He left me cute notes and cards, while moving very slowly with the physical interactions. He communicated his preference for building a loving long-term relationship prior to having sex. This KOF was a serious Mr. Right contender.

Another 40-something lawyer told me about her KOF boyfriend's out-of-the-box romancers. She explained: "One night he recommended that we share a glass of champagne before a movie. I liked that he came up with a different idea and thought it was very romantic." She continued with another example of his devotion. She added, "When he saw that my bike had a flat tire, he brought me a bike pump." It's the little things that add up in today's fast track world.

Keeper of the Fire Strategies

KOFs are great romantics and excellent matches for women seeking a sincere partner. At this stage in life, it is time to evaluate the core and not be dazzled by the resume. It's important to find someone who appreciates you, and attitude is key. Eliminate effortless dates sooner if they show zero creativity and add no spice. You should be tired of playing guessing games with guys who take women for granted.

If you are fortunate to find a KOF, let him spoil you. Don't feel that you need to return every gesture either. Instead, look for opportunities to surprise him when the timing is right. You want to find the right balance. One night, I took a guy a bag of home-made oatmeal raisin cookies after going to a girls' *Sex and the City* party close to his apartment. He was so surprised and excited that he talked about these cookies for six months.

Even if you feel uncomfortable with a KOF, take a second look. Be open to his acts of romance and carefully evaluate the potential before you end the relationship. KOFs are not easy to find and can bring you a lifetime of little joys. After the sexual intensity fades, the KOF keeps the fire burning with his constant reminders that you are "the one." This guy is a keeper so don't walk unless there are major obstacles.

Keeper of the Fire LIFE Questions

1. How would you define romance?
2. How do you think married couples keep the sparks alive over the years?
3. Can you describe your idea of a romantic evening to me?

LM Love Match

Love Match Definition

Love Match (LM) is a Go/No-Go sign in the Chemistry Connection department. A Love Match can provide you with many physical pleasures in the bedroom, which is a must-have for your Mr. Wonderful. To make a connection last, you will want to find a balanced relationship in the bedroom where there is mutual satisfaction. You will know this guy because he makes your heart skip a few beats when you see his Caller ID on the phone. You will start daydreaming about your sexual interludes with a LM and be ready to make him a priority.

The best sexual partners are more concerned about your needs versus their own. They know how to take their time and wait for you to have pleasure first or experience extremes with you. They recognize that sex should not be over in ten minutes and enjoy cuddling with you afterward. A Love Match will relish the opportunity to go for hours with you. As you get more comfortable with each other physically, it will get better in and out of bed. Not every man is going to please you so don't be afraid to walk away from a bad sex partner, even if everything else lines up.

Love Match Example

When I interviewed a 39-year-old sales executive about sex with her second husband, she said, "We were like rabbits at first. It was summertime. We were going new places on the boat. We just had so much fun that we were very relaxed with each other physically." She continued her Love Match story by sharing, "The emotional attachment made the physical more intense." She admitted that it took her years to get comfortable enough to really let go in bed. When she finally combined her sexual confidence with his technique, it just clicked for her the second time around.

Their first kiss was a great indicator of their future relationship. She expanded on her Love Match find by explaining why the first kiss was a great sign. She told me, "The first kiss was awesome because it had been building all summer. It was a very highly charged evening and we were definitely into each other. We were all over each other. We left a party and made out in the car for hours. It was a lot of fun." Within a year, she was tying the knot with this Love Match. A year after marriage, they had a baby boy.

Similar to this woman's story, I did not discover real sexual pleasure until after my divorce. Perhaps it was the excitement of being with someone new or just being more comfortable with my body—or perhaps it was the guy. Yes, it takes two to tango, and the sexual dynamics need to be right in the bedroom for you to walk down the aisle with any man. But what if you don't know what great sex means? If you find a guy who lets it go too quickly and you are always faking it so he thinks he has pleasured you, he is not your man.

Another 30-something technology manager told me, "I met this gorgeous and intelligent guy and the sex is amazing." When I asked her to tell me more, she expanded, "He rolls over at 3:00 a.m. and we can't resist each other. He spoons his body perfectly around mine. I never experienced such intense orgasms from any man." She was open to trying new things in bed with him because of a high trust level and attraction. When it feels right, you should sound like this woman. And don't be afraid that the sex will fade away over the years.

While it might take a commitment by you and your partner to work on perfecting the art, sex can stay exciting over many years. I interviewed two married couples who remain ecstatic about their sex lives after being with the same partner for years. One 40-something entrepreneur told me, "I didn't realize that sex can just get better and better." Another 40-something actress told me, "Sex is still awesome with my husband after ten years of marriage. It always has been."

Love Match Strategies

If your guy cannot give you multiple physical pleasures, you need to say, "Next" fast. Who wants to fake it for the rest of their life? You want to find someone who is skilled in the bedroom. A wise girlfriend once told me, "I prefer the good-looking guys because they are confident and nice to women." While you don't have to date Mr. GQ, you do want someone who is comfortable in his skin and behind closed doors. I actually think Mr. GQ may be spoiled so skip the guy on the cover of *Men's Fitness* magazine, but go for the guy who feels really good about himself.

And what's a girl to do if a guy is just not responding? One 30-something woman told me, "For certain guys, it can be a big turn-on if you take control. I used to watch a guy do his thing and direct him. It was a huge turn-on for him." Another woman told me her strategy in this case. She advised, "If a guy is MIA, all you have to do is get totally turned on and eventually, they will be straight up." Anything you can do to please yourself will let him know that you are turned on and take the pressure off the guy. Once he is feeling better and more relaxed, you might be able to turn the tide in the bedroom.

You also want to see if your styles are compatible. For example, if a guy is an OO (Over-Achiever Obsessor), he probably wants to let the woman take over in the bedroom since he is in charge all day long. A 37-year-old entrepreneur shared this observation. She said, "A successful guy wants to be dominated because he gets to surrender and stop being in control." If you prefer playing this lead role, then you should go after this type of Love Match man.

Warning: When you come up for air, make sure you do a reality check on the situation. You do not want to prolong a relationship just because you are having out-of-body sexual experiences. One 38-year-old marketing manager shared with me, "I started dating this young hottie, who was the best lover that I ever had. The problem was there was nothing on the inside. He didn't have a job, started taking me and my money for granted, and then had the nerve to tell me he was still in love with an old girlfriend." Excuse me. Next! Remember, listen to your GUT. It will tell you if the guy is a real deal or just another Sly Schemer.

Let yourself go in the bedroom if you have a good GUT feeling. You want to show some enthusiasm and excitement. When you find a guy that is stimulating you in ways that you have never felt before, remember to ask him how he likes to be pleasured so there is mutual satisfaction. Make sure you are comfortable with what he wants you to do, and then relax and enjoy. One 20-something guy told me, "It's all about balance. Show me that you're enjoying it and be honest in your emotions and noises." With the right give-and-take, you will be beaming in the morning. Your friends will soon be saying, "I'll have what she's having." If you find a Love Match, hold on to him tight. If he is a BA (Bachelor Available) and a LM (Love Match), then you are in the money. No paycheck can ever offer you such a wonderful package of sexual and emotional intimacy.

Love Match LIFE Questions

1. What do you enjoy most about sex?
2. How do you like to pleasure a woman?
3. How would you like me to pleasure you?

MBA   Married but Available

Married but Available Definition

Married but Available (MBA) suitors are married men with no plans for shucking their legal bonds even though they are willing to have an affair or relationship with you. These players are very open about their intentions and are content to let you decide if you want to accept their terms. Depending on your culture, mindset, and value systems, responses to MBA proposals can vary. Some experts estimate that as many as 30 percent of online dating members are actually married. Look for the marriage signs and red flag clues when meeting any stranger or testing New Era dating options.

Married but Available Examples

The first example is a 44-year-old film buyer from Holland who was extremely open about his desire to have a fling with me. I met this MBA at a trendy film industry party in Los Angeles. We danced to 70s disco music for 30 minutes before I noticed his wedding band. The chemistry connection was clearly there, but my conservative upbringing prevented all thoughts of an affair. He tried to convince me that his definition of marriage was different from mine and allowed him to have a fling with impunity. This MBA wanted to leave the party with me and was quite persistent. I maintained my ground and he did not understand why.

Another 36-year-old healthcare entrepreneur started having an affair with a married British dude down the street. The guy was doing business with her housemate, and frequently visited their home for meetings. When the couple enjoyed intense sexual intimacy, she decided to let down all barriers and take the relationship for what it is—good sex. She explained to me, "I don't care. He gives me what I need and is a cheerleader for my business goals." This MBA is also a romantic who leaves her a flower every morning in their "secret place." This blind affair continues and she understands that he is never leaving his wife.

In a third scenario, I interviewed a 26-year-old teacher who fell for an Italian pilot whom she met online. She was suspicious from the beginning that he was married, but got blinded by his romantic actions. When she asked him whether he was married, he claimed that he was divorced three years ago. He was on a fast track with her and declared his love on the second date (Warning! Warning!). She found herself getting swept away by his lines and fancy weekend getaways. She explained, "He was extremely attractive, charismatic, and knew what to say to women." She continued, "He came to visit my school, and then all the single women started Internet dating because he was so cute."

When she made the mistake of moving in with this MBA, the warning signs started to be more concerning. Her biggest surprise was the wife showing up on a Saturday morning at 8:00 a.m. while they were still snuggled in bed together. Her Prince Illusion went outside on the deck to speak to his wife while she watched an argument get out of control from a distance. In the end, she investigated his files when he was away; he claimed to make $75,000 a year, but had not cleared $20,000 the previous year. She also checked with his flight school to see if he really had a job (he did), and set up a key logger so she could get his passwords and get into his accounts online. She checked out his phone bill to find out how many times he called his wife. She soon discovered that his separation was actually filed six weeks after they started dating. She also found out that his wife was paying all his bills. The relationship ended the day the wife called her cell phone to talk. The wife explained, "He cannot support himself and we've been together for nine years." She was fed up with his deceptions and immediately broke off the relationship after this call. Why did she wait so long?

While European men tend to be more open about affairs, MBAs are usually not as public in the United States. My 37-year-old married friend in Los Angeles, who frequents a gym three days a week, provided more prime examples to me. She has developed associations with many of the other gym regulars. Married men openly share stories about and pictures of their families with her, all the while dropping hints that despite their marital ties, they are interested in her. These men often make insinuations indicating that an affair would be acceptable.

"Being monogamous is difficult when you are married," said one MBA to my friend. This MBA asked her to stop by his bar for a drink. Another MBA asked about the status of her marriage. She responds to such thinly veiled invitations to infidelity by joking her way out of it. Despite her defenses, these domestic MBAs are relentless in their pursuit.

Married but Available Strategies

There are several questions you need to ask yourself when dealing with an MBA. The first is whether you are interested enough to go down this dangerous path. The second question is whether you want to deal with the emotional consequences of getting involved with someone who technically and legally belongs to another woman.

If you are interested in a fling, remember that this MBA is not leaving his wife. The encounter will only provide temporary entertainment and can result in long-term heartache. Avoid building an ongoing relationship with an MBA. You might waste years dreaming about him leaving his wife while he enjoys the best of both worlds. If you must go there, keep it short and stay detached.

Your best bet is to forget all thoughts about MBAs. These men are trouble and will only complicate your life. MBAs will steal valuable time and emotions that could be spent looking for Mr. Right. You want someone who is totally into you—not a man with a wife on the side. Next!

Married but Available LIFE Questions

1. Tell me why you got married.
2. What is your definition of marriage?
3. Have you considered leaving your wife and why?

NN Nourishing Nester

Nourishing Nester Definition

The Nourishing Nester (NN) prefers spending quality time at home with a mate and will feed your soul with goodwill. These men thrive on building their nest. NNs are content being in their environment with their small circle of close friends and loved ones. These candidates would rather be with you one-on-one than in a large crowd. Nourishing Nesters tend to be family-oriented even if they are not married.

Nourshing Nester Example

Through an Internet dating service, I met a Nourishing Nester (NN) who was a 49-year-old TV producer. All of our dates were one-on-one. On our third date, he invited me for a full tour of his home. This NN proudly explained the meanings of his photographs and paintings during the visit. On our fifth date, he invited me over for sandwiches and the Super Bowl. He made it clear that his preference was to be at home rather than in a crowd for this major sporting event.

This NN was very close to his family and spoke warmly about them frequently. There were pictures everywhere of his parents and siblings. He took great interest in my personal well-being and my family. When I hurt my back, he called every day to check on me. When my brother came to Los Angeles, he invited us to visit his house. He made it clear from the beginning that he wanted a relationship with me. All of his actions were directed toward building a nest with me. Unfortunately, I was distracted by stronger feelings for other potential partners at the time, which ultimately cut off this NN's path.

Another 28-year-old marketing manager told me about a classic NN whom she dated for over a year. Since he knew cooking was not her specialty, he often brought her unexpected gifts from the grocery store. Two of his favorite offerings were fresh strawberries and homemade granola "just because" he was thinking about her. This NN loved spending time in his nest one-on-one with her. This guy enjoyed spoiling her with homemade spaghetti dinners with his special sauce. This NN was a keeper.

Nourishing Nester Strategies

NNs can be great long-term partners and potential fathers. These relationships can be fulfilling because you know the NN is sincere. These men will be there for you in good times and bad, which is exactly what you want in a lifetime mate.

Consider whether his lifestyle works with your personality. If you need constant large group activities, this mate may clash with you. However, if you want to create a family nest, the parties can wait. When you grow old and gray, the NN will stay by your side when the crowds are long gone.

If you are not ready for a NN, be honest with him. He will appreciate the candor, and it will enable him to devote his nurturing efforts toward finding someone who shares his priorities.

Nourishing Nester LIFE Questions

1. Tell me more about your home. What do you like the most about it?
2. Would you rather spend time at home or out in the crowds?
3. Tell me about a time when someone in your family got sick and you were able to help them.

OO   Overachiever Obsessor

Overachiever Obsessor Definition

The Overachiever Obsessor (OO) has spent his entire adult life adding medals to his career trophy case. He displays them proudly on his resume for the world to notice. His primary focus has been on collecting achievements versus building a marital relationship. OOs take great pride in earning advanced degrees and steadily moving up the corporate ladder with promotions. OOs tend to get a wake-up call in their 40s when they suddenly see a need to find a romantic partner. Although these OOs will never give up their obsession with career success, they will eventually start seeking a mate to fill the one gap in their life.

Overachiever Obsessor Example

Briefly, I dated a 39-year-old OO, who later became a good friend and confidant. This OO has an MBA, JD, and a Masters in technology from Ivy League schools. He has a long list of career achievements to complement his education and now sits on the boards of over ten companies. Because of his tremendous career victories, he is also very comfortable financially. He has extensively traveled the world and is now seriously seeking a mate.

This OO started approaching his search with the same intensity of his career achievements. Similar to a requirements document, this OO created a checklist in his mind for a suitable mate. He first contacted friends and then used his industry networking resources. In addition, he took advantage of Internet dating sites. He set up multiple dates with women in the same week for one-hour coffee talks similar to the way he scheduled business meetings.

Several times he felt as if he had met "the one" only to discover that this hasty approach was pushing him to force a match. After jumping into two short-winded serious relationships, this OO slowed down and began taking time for more upfront dialogs about partnership expectations and dug deeper than his checklist.

As a result, he found a potential life partner. He has been dating her for over six months and I hear wedding bells.

Overachiever Obsessor Strategies

OOs tend to put their business goals before personal relationships so you should be careful getting involved with one. You will not be the top priority unless he has reached a personal turning point where seeking a mate is just as important as his career.

Even with a commitment to make a relationship work, the OO will continue to show overwhelming passion for his work. If you don't need a lot of attention and are a good listener, you may be very OO compatible. These partners can provide excitement and financial stability.

In addition, the Overachiever Obsessor can make adjustments to find room for a relationship. Evaluate whether the OO is Emotionally Ready for a partner. Take advantage of his goal-setting tendencies by using interview questions that uncover his relationship expectations.

In addition, if you are an OO, this match will either be ideal or a complete clash. Carefully assess the dynamics to determine the likelihood of complimentary mindsets. Some OOs will want a companion who can relate to the demands of their passions, which means they are also an ESS (Executive Search Seeker). Others will want to come home to a work-free dinner conversation.

Overachiever Obsessor LIFE Questions

1. Tell me about your personal and career goals.
2. Tell me how you balance your career with personal interests and family.
3. Tell me about your biggest personal achievement and why it was important to you.

PTS Post-Traumatic Soul

Post-Traumatic Soul Definition

Post-Traumatic Souls (PTS) have been shaken by a recent life-altering event. The experience makes such a significant impact that the individual starts re-evaluating his priorities. The PTS may be withdrawn and usually limits his interactions to a close circle of friends. The pivotal event may be the loss of a loved one, a physical injury or illness, or some other mental hardship.

Post-Traumatic Soul Examples

The first and most dramatic example of a PTS that I have encountered was someone I met while stranded in New York City during the week of September 11. I met this 37-year-old rock star through mutual friends during a dinner. We immediately connected and consoled each other emotionally. While the rest of our group wanted to dance all night after dinner this PTS asked me to join him for a more high-quality drink and discussion. He shared his story with me while we sat on couches in an empty bar on 14th Street (the closest point to Ground Zero that you were allowed to go at that time). This PTS was concerned about his father, who worked at a school across from the World Trade Center. While his father turned out to be all right, the rock star was emotionally shaken and upset about going back on the road for another band tour with the looming fear of another terrorist attack.

After returning to Los Angeles, this PTS went on tour in Asia. He called me from Melbourne, Sydney, Auckland, and Tokyo. We talked for hours. Because he could not keep the time zones straight and it was important to stay connected, I accepted his calls even at 3:00 a.m. This PTS was constantly watching CNN and alternating phone calls between his parents and me. He told me that it was important for him to stay in contact with those close to him no matter where his job took him. This PTS clearly was going through a life-changing event and reached out to me for support. Our romance eventually turned into a friendship due to distance and rock star travel schedules. This PTS remains one of my closest allies and cheerleaders.

The second example of a PTS is a 40-year-old lawyer I dated in Washington, D.C. About four months into the relationship, he received a call that his mother had been suddenly killed in a car accident in Chile. I immediately left my new job to join his family, who were in serious shock.

The PTS was visibly devastated and it changed the dynamics of our relationship. Suddenly, I became more of a counselor and tried to help him deal with this tragedy. While I consider myself a good listener and loyal friend, the PTS demands continued to be a drain and I ultimately ended the relationship a year later. He was a good guy, but our timing was just not right.

Post-Traumatic Soul Strategies

When you find a life partner or long-term mate, you will eventually face life-altering events together that can make or break the relationship. These changes will eventually result in a relationship re-evaluation. Consider the strength of the bond and your emotional status. Look at how the relationship dynamic has changed and the potential long-term impact of the situation.

Without open communication, the relationship is over. You need answers to difficult questions. This dialogue will help you identify ways to support the PTS rather than pushing you apart. Recognize your limitations and do not take the PTS actions personally during this period. You may even want to set a personal timeframe for how long you can continue in this relationship and then see if the dynamics begin to improve. Unfortunately, the situation may be out of your control and the relationship may not survive the tragedy.

However, these situations can also strengthen a bond. Carefully consider how the PTS responds to you and whether he lets you help him. If he demonstrates trust in and respect for you, these can be great signs for a potential life partner. You may want to support the PTS through the hardship. In the end, you will be a stronger couple with greater chances of long-term success.

If you encounter a PTS on your dating journey, be careful to give yourself regular reality checks on the situation. While you want to be supportive, you need to be honest with yourself regarding the impact this dynamic is having on your life. These situations are not easy and require great care and grace. It's all about finding the right balance, and if you can't, knowing when to cut your losses when dating a PTS.

Post-Traumatic Soul LIFE Questions

1. Have you ever suffered a great loss? Can you tell me what happened?
2. How did you cope with your loss?
3. What stages of grief did you experience when you suffered your loss?

QP Questionnaire Perfectionist

Questionnaire Perfectionist Definition

The Questionnaire Perfectionist (QP) has a defined list of mate requirements. He is seeking an ideal partner who matches 100 percent of his criteria. While some QPs will make a small allowance for differences, these men tend to reject anything that is not close to perfection. Their questionnaire details will vary depending on what is important to the QP. Some critical checklist items may include age, politics, religion, money, priorities, hair color, height, weight, fitness, and hobbies.

Questionnaire Perfectionist Example

I married a QP at 30, who is now no longer my husband. Initially, I was blinded by the strong mutual physical attraction and desire to get married. We were so in lust that the details were never discussed. However, I soon found out about his list of requirements for a mate. When we first dated, we overlooked core priorities because our time was spent sharing mutual interests in biking, hiking, and the arts.

Once we started living together, the QP began to reveal critical needs that he desired from me as his mate. His list was non-negotiable. For example, the QP declared that he wanted to go camping at least once a month with me. As a compromise, I offered to go camping twice per year and encouraged him to go more often with his friends. However, he would not accept these terms. While this issue may sound trivial, it was very important to him and became a serious conflict. When he wanted to go camping for our honeymoon, I should have recognized this extreme interest pre-wedding bells.

This QP also expected me to spend every Saturday at home working on the house with him. Because I worked all week, I wanted to play on this day off. I had no interest in painting and scrubbing the house. This conflict in priorities and interests created another major relationship clash.

As the QP expectations grew, we ended up in counseling. We each made a list of our needs, but he was not willing to compromise. His demands were black and white and any proposed shade of gray was not acceptable to him. The QP requirements created so many roadblocks that there was no other choice but to part ways.

Questionnaire Perfectionist Strategies

As soon as a relationship begins to get serious, start asking some detailed questions to uncover whether this potential mate is a Questionnaire Perfectionist. Once you understand his expectations, it is easier to determine whether you can fulfill any non-negotiable needs.

If you are lucky, you may discover that the QP shares your priorities and interests. In this case, you are fortunate to have found a match. However, I would still hesitate before getting too serious with any QP because what if you change and he can't compromise?

Alternatively, if the QP reveals expectations that you cannot meet, don't overlook the potential long-term issues that may result. QPs will not give up their list, and it is hopeless to try to change them. If you ignore the importance of his requirements, you may end up divorced or trapped in a lifetime of conflict. Avoid letting hormones, peer pressures, and time clocks push you to marry a QP. If a guy cannot compromise on things that are important to you, say, "Next!" fast.

However, if you are comfortable making some changes to meet the QP needs, proceed cautiously without giving up your own sense of self. Test compromises and take periodic reality checks to make sure that it is a mutually beneficial partnership. You want to take a close look at a QP before making any life long commitments.

Questionnaire Perfectionist LIFE Questions

1. Tell me what you consider to be a perfect match for you.
2. Tell me about the aspects of a relationship that you think can and cannot be compromised.
3. What qualities in a candidate have been deal-breakers in the past and why?

RR Relentless Renter

Relentless Renter Definition

Relentless Renters (RR) are men who want to have a relationship and will even live with you long term, but will avoid the ultimate commitment of marriage. The RR is monogamous and a good partner, but has a genuine fear of lifetime agreements. Relentless Renters prefer to have all the benefits of a relationship without the legal bonds.

Relentless Renter Example

A girlfriend of mine has been dating a doctor in his mid-40s for a significant period of time, and there are still no signs of wedding bells. His plans are as clear as the scribbling on his prescription pad. This Relentless Renter has a pattern of long-term, non-marital relationships.

Prior to his relationship with my friend, he dated someone for seven years and never popped the question. As in this RR's prior relationship, my friend lives with him, shares pets, and holds joint bank accounts. They are both very involved with each other's families. In her view, this Relentless Renter is faithful, giving, supportive, and a good partner.

However, my friend is now almost 40 and wants to be married and have children. She has discussed her intentions with him, but he continues to avoid the ultimate leap. The couple has been together for over a year, and she is planning to leave him if the situation is unchanged at the two-year milestone.

Another 34-year-old actress had been dating a guy for over four years and he would not propose marriage. In her words, "I think men always think, 'What if something better comes along.' After meeting with me for coaching, she took a more radical approach and informed her RR that she was leaving him. When he didn't believe her, she packed up his things in boxes with nice labels and placed them in her guest room. She told him, "I need to get back into doing things that interest me. This relationship is not growing. We are at the fork in the road and we're going down different paths so let me go."

Not only did she start going out with girlfriends, she actively dated other guys, which made this RR very nervous. Almost two years later, this RR took a complete turnaround by proposing marriage, paying for her nursing school, and returning to his old romantic ways with her. With a ring on her hand, she told me with confidence, "Women have the power to stop it, take the power from within, and not allow guys to waste your time."

Relentless Renter Strategies

Even though the Relentless Renter is a committed partner, recognize that these men will steer clear of marriage proposals at all costs. Avoid giving ultimatums because you will lose. Instead, take the non-needy and non-aggressive road. Get back into your own life and remind the Relentless Renter of what he might lose if he doesn't change his tune.

Ask questions early with a smile and positive tone to uncover his preference, and then communicate your desires. Walk away with a "I can take it or leave it" attitude so you can re-evaluate whether you are willing to continue dating this guy. If you get emotional in front of him, it will only push him away. Instead, go talk it out with your close allies who know you best. If you are in your 30s or 40s and want to be married with children, RRs will only delay you in meeting your goal.

On the other hand, keep in mind that many people are now replacing traditional marriages with this modern version of a long-term commitment. If you are comfortable with this progressive partnership, your RR may be a good match. Many women who have been previously married might prefer a Relentless Renter versus the potential of another divorce. It's your choice. Decide what you want out of the relationship, and be brave enough to walk if he's not meeting your needs.

Relentless Renter LIFE Questions

1. Have you ever lived with a partner? What did you enjoy most about being together?
2. What is the longest time that you have lived with someone and why did it end?
3. Do you believe in the concept of marriage?

SG Social Guru

Social Guru Definition

The Social Guru (SG) is the life of the party. He thrives on social interaction with diverse groups of people. The SG likes to be the center of attention, and feeds his ego off the crowd's responses. He prefers to have a special someone to be on his wing. These individuals can be great diplomats with high energy and confidence. SGs can also be very entertaining and have a great zest for life.

Social Guru Examples

A 40-something girlfriend dated a financial manager who completely clashed with her Social Guru tendencies. This compatibility conflict ultimately ended a relationship that had the right ingredients in every other aspect. Her first clue was his confession that he was not comfortable in crowds. He would constantly make up excuses for why he needed to miss birthday and holiday dinners with her friends, and then offer to take her out alone to celebrate. He never took her to parties to meet his friends, and justified it by saying that he didn't want her to share that they met on the Internet. Hello. It's the 21st century and 50 million singles are dating online. She never really understood his extreme preference for one-on-one dates and felt left in the dark about his world. Because she values interactions with a diverse group of friends, there was just no middle ground to be found for this couple.

Alternatively, my 30-something girlfriend lived with a Social Guru who just turned 43. He is the CEO of a dot.com who thrives on social interactions. He is always organizing group activities. This Social Guru frequently calls friends to join him for bike rides on the beach, bowling, movies, and dinners.

This SG enjoys meeting new faces and encourages his close friends to invite strangers to these gatherings. He likes learning about other people and always asks many questions to gain knowledge about their experiences. During these activities, this SG loves being the cruise director, shares amusing tales, and often facilitates the discussion. In contrast, my friend is very shy and prefers spending quality time alone or with small groups.

As a result of these different preferences, they both learned to find a balance between social activities and quality time. He cut back on his frequency of organizing events. She made an effort to participate when he planned a gathering and even took an acting class to get more comfortable with social settings. Within a year, the couple was married in front of a crowd of 120. Within another year, they became the proud parents of a baby boy and could not be happier with their relationship. Because they genuinely wanted to make the relationship work and found reasonable compromises, they made it happen—more power to them for overcoming this SG hurdle!

Social Guru Strategies

If you enjoy meeting people and do not need to be the center of attention in a group, Social Gurus can add fun and enthusiasm to your life. As long as you communicate your need for one-on-one timeouts, a relationship foundation can be built for a win-win situation. You can create a happy balance with this mutual understanding and compromise.

However, if you shy away from social settings at all costs, this relationship may be a struggle even with the right foundation. Consider the SG's needs carefully and recognize that this interaction is essential for him to feel whole. If you try to eliminate these group activities, it will only build resentment and damage the relationship.

If you happen to be a female Social Guru, there may be a clash with this potential mate. Evaluate whether you think your styles complement each other or create a competition for center stage. How do you interact as a team at parties? Leave time to listen to each other's social needs and observe the dynamics to determine whether your dating dance is meant to last.

Social Guru LIFE Questions

1. When you go to a party, do you tend to stay with your date or divide and conquer the crowd?
2. How much time do you spend at social gatherings versus one-on-one situations?
3. Do you enjoy being a crowd leader and why or why not?

TT | Tasmanian Traveler

Tasmanian Traveler Definition

The Tasmanian Traveler (TT) is always on the move and tends to live his life on the runway. The TT constantly travels for business and pleasure. These men tend to be on an airplane at least once a week, and it is difficult to keep up with their itineraries. Although the TT may want a relationship, his time is consumed by this hectic agenda. Most TTs are outgoing and open-minded. They can easily adapt to diverse groups in various settings.

Tasmanian Traveler Examples

The first example is a TT that I met through Internet dating. This 50-something man initially emailed me from Australia, and we started scheduling a visit during a planned stopover in Los Angeles. The TT was going to be in Los Angeles for a week before heading to Canada to see his children, and then eventually returning to his island home on Anguilla in the Caribbean. Although his agenda made me dizzy, I was seeking someone who was worldly so I stayed in the game.

After several email exchanges, he took it to the next Internet dating level by calling me from Australia. The TT explained that he writes novels, which allowed him to keep a fluid travel schedule. The conversation was upbeat with multiple mental connections, so we decided to meet in Los Angeles.

Over coffee, the mutual chemistry test was passed. We shared similar passions for international travel and writing. This TT had been a hotel chain owner before picking up his pen full-time. When he sold his hotels, the deal included significant discounts for him everywhere he traveled. With that incentive, he liked to travel around the world at least once a year.

Needless to say, his travel schedule was insane. Connecting again with this TT became almost impossible. I also became suspicious that he had a woman in every port. I did not see any potential for a lifetime partner here and quickly bid "ta-ta" to this TT.

The second TT example had a less hectic domestic travel schedule and managed partner communications much better. My girlfriend dated a 40-year-old TT who owned a paper recycling business in Los Angeles. His passion for riding in steeplechase races took him back to the east coast weekly in the spring. Because they shared this hobby and both traveled frequently, there was a level of understanding that made this demanding schedule less of an issue for them.

Despite his travel whirlwinds, this second TT continued to be attentive and maintained a solid relationship. The couple was constantly in contact using modern technology such as email, cell phones, and Blackberries.

Another 30-something woman told me how she makes it work with her TT fiancé who travels about 50 percent of the year for work. He is a superintendent for a major oil company, and while he makes a good income, he needs to be on-site for jobs almost half of the year. The couple makes it work by reserving ample quality time together while he is home and by keeping in close contact when he is traveling. She loves her own life and goes to school full time to complete a law degree. By having her own goals, she maintains a high level of self-esteem and confidence. His generous income is paying for her education and they are committed as a couple to making things work.

Tasmanian Traveler Strategies

Because Tasmanian Travelers have extreme tendencies, consider whether you want this type of relationship. Ask yourself if you can handle being separated often and whether you are comfortable being on your own. Is there enough communication and quality time to make this relationship go the distance? If you are independent and enjoy having some time on your own, the TT may be an ideal mate. Some couples think they become stronger by having temporary separations. The question is how much separation can you handle.

While you may prefer someone who comes home every night, you should not immediately eliminate the TT from consideration, because he can bring other qualities to the relationship that make it worth being flexible. If you take advantage of modern technology to maintain communication, you will greatly increase your chances for success with a Tasmanian Traveler partner.

Tasmanian Traveler LIFE Questions

1. Tell me about your travel schedule.
2. How do you keep in touch with close friends and family while traveling?
3. Tell me about the importance of communications to you while you are on the road.

UA   Underestimated Ally

Underestimated Ally Definition

Most of us have had close male friends we never considered as potential lovers. The Underestimated Ally (UA) continually gives you his time and energy, and may actually be your perfect match in disguise. He will sincerely be sensitive to your peaks and valleys. UAs will always be supportive in a crisis and are often viewed as big brother types. Sometimes it is difficult to tell if they have any love interest in you because they never ask for anything in return.

Underestimated Ally Example

My 30-year-old girlfriend had a 34-year-old UA in her life whom she did not view as a future mate. She was dating someone else and it never crossed her mind that her UA could be "the one." When she broke up with her boyfriend, it was not long before she realized the importance of this Underestimated Ally.

He was supportive through the break-up and made her feel wonderful with ego-boosting comments. The UA told her that it was the ex-boyfriend's loss and she was better off without him. Throughout the entire transition period, he was genuinely concerned about her well-being. They spent hours together sharing meals, going for runs, and talking through her feelings.

After a few months, it dawned on her that her UA relationship was evolving beyond friendship. Neither of them had ever discussed his or her feelings for each other. She did not know how he would respond if the issue was raised, but decided to take a big risk and share her thoughts with the UA. When she disclosed her feelings, he responded favorably and it was the beginning of a lifelong partnership. They were married two years later and have now been together for more than five years.

Underestimated Ally Strategies

Don't underestimate the value of a male friend because he might just be "the one" for you. You could be spending a lot of time with a male companion and overlook this potential. Even if you have been friends for a long time with no sexual interaction, it doesn't mean that it could not develop into something more.

These UAs can be great lifetime candidates because the foundation is already there. The UA has been there for you through the good and bad times, which is what you want in a partner. He is reliable and sincerely cares about you. So what are you waiting for before making a move?

While you may be worried about ruining a friendship, if you have true feelings it is worth taking a chance. By notifying him that your interest has gone to a new level, you may be pleasantly surprised to find that the feeling is mutual. If not, the friendship should be strong enough to withstand your confession.

Underestimated Ally LIFE Questions

1. Have you ever had a female friendship turn into a relationship? How did it work out?
2. What do you value in our friendship?
3. Have you ever thought about us as more than just good friends?

$\boxed{\text{VL}}$ Virtual Lover

Virtual Lover Definition

The Virtual Lover is the man you meet through an electronic venue. It might be an email introduction from a friend, instant messenger, a chat connection, mobile flirting or someone you meet online through an internet dating site. As technology continues to advance, you might meet him through a videophone greeting or video disc jockey. The possibilities are endless for meeting a Virtual Lover (VL) through 21st-century technologies.

Virtual Lover Example

The hottest new way to flirt with a Virtual Lover is through Text Messaging via your cell phone or blackberry. It's easy, romantic, and let's the other party reply when they have time. I dated a guy who loved to send me text messages. When I left his house one day, he sent me a cute message using fun shorthand, "Thx 4 a gr8 time together. Cheers to you! ♪". Because both of us were often in meetings and living in different cities, we found text messaging the best way to catch each other.

You can also access millions of men online who are potential Virtual Lovers. After testing seven different dating sites, I found a guy through an online matchmaker whom I dated for over a year. I knew instantly by his profile that we shared the same sense of humor, East Coast roots, education, and interests, which gave us great potential as a match. This story can happen to you. If you play this dating numbers game long enough, something is bound to hit.

I met a pharmaceutical district manager at my friend's birthday party in Los Angeles who found love online. This guy was beaming from ear to ear about how he met his wife online. I immediately wanted to interview her to get the full story. She is an attractive 40-something lawyer, who hesitated for years jumping into the online dating game. She told me, "I watched my girlfriend date online for four years before I decided to place an ad on Aol.com." When she reached a peak in her career, she explained, "I found normal avenues for meeting guys tapering off. I was no longer going to bars and was working long hours as a lawyer. If someone wasn't walking through my door at 10:00 p.m. when I got home, it wasn't happening." Instead of giving up, she entered the online numbers game.

When she finally decided to go for it, she said, "I knew what I wanted by that time. There were things that were really important to me." Her strategy was to ask important questions in several emails before agreeing to meet for coffee. She started by insisting on a picture and gathering foundational facts. She expanded, "I would weave my East Coast education into the emails, check to see if they had a career versus a job, and find out whether they were geographically desirable." Not only was she gathering this data before going on a date, she emphasized the importance of creating a profile that represented her honestly so guys would know what to expect on dates. For her pictures, she explained, "I added a photo that was good, but not great. I was honest about me versus calculating to get someone to like me."

So how long did it take her to find Mr. AOL.com? She actually got very lucky fast in my book. After 70 email responses to her profile, she narrowed it down to five men to date, and married the fifth guy. They moved in together at the four-month mark, were engaged after one year, and married just after the two-year milestone. And what about her checklist? She admitted, "He had about 50 percent of what I wanted, but it was much more about the gut response that worked and there were no difficulties."

How did this guy stand out? Why did she have a good GUT feeling about him? Mrs. AOL.com explained, "I loved his email style. It was lyrical and fun." When I asked her how soon she knew he was it, she explained, "Everything was very easy. He was eager and he wasn't playing games." When they went out on their second date, she said another couple made a very telling observation. After dinner, strangers came up to their table and commented, "It's really fun to see a couple having so much fun together."

Four years later, she is very happily married to her Virtual Lover. You can do it too, but you need to get out there. Mrs. Aol.com made this final comment to me, "It's really just a numbers game. If you throw yourself out there, something will work for you or for someone else." Several years back she placed her first personal ad in a newspaper. While this first attempt did not work for her, it eventually connected two other couples. Because she refused to give up, this lawyer eventually found her Virtual Lover online.

Virtual Lover Strategies

Check out the tips in the virtual love connections and Internet dating sections of this book for many different VL strategies. Your three most important tactics are be selective, don't wait too long to meet in person, and trust your gut instincts. If something does not feel right, immediately hit the delete key without hesitation. Decide on your key criteria and check out their profile for key statistics that meet your needs. If you have a graduate degree, and the guy did not attend college, you might have a few hurdles in the education department.

You also want to follow the Internet dating safety tips previously described to protect your privacy. Avoid giving out your personal information too soon, and above all, do not have a guy pick you up at home until your GUT says it's okay. You can even try a Google search on his name, join a dating site that offers background checks, or go to the extreme of hiring a private investigator.

Once you start feeling comfortable with a Virtual Lover, avoid getting too busy for dates. In today's fast track world, we can too easily forget to take quality time offline. You will prolong finding out if he is "the one" by relying too much on wireless technologies. Go for a walk on the beach, share a picnic in the park, and make calls so you can hear their voice more often. Virtual Lovers are a great timesaver, but take time-outs from your career so you can quickly find out if he is your man.

Virtual Lover LIFE Questions

1. Are you seeking a long-term relationship or just dating?
2. How long have you been dating online?
3. Do you think that you can find love online?

WD | Wounded Divorcé

Wounded Divorcé Definition

Wounded Divorcés (WD) are typically men who have been so damaged by a previous marriage that they block out any possibility of a future partnership. There are usually two causes of this mindset: emotional trauma and/or financial loss. Emotional trauma can be caused by a sudden and unanticipated break-up. Alimony and settlement costs can create anger and resentment. In many WD cases, both causes are prevalent and lead divorced male candidates to build walls around themselves.

Wounded Divorcé Examples

I never met so many WDs before I moved to California, where community property laws tend to make divorce ugly. I dated two WDs who were charismatic, worldly, and dynamic individuals. However, they were damaged goods and not emotionally available.

WD #1 was a 41-year-old who made it clear from the beginning that he thought marriage was a hoax. He was married for six years and now shares custody of his daughter. This movie producer was a self-employed entrepreneur who had been in the business for years. I was completely blinded by his charisma and love for life, and was new to the WD game.

This WD told me he was financially damaged because his income was at its peak at the time of his divorce. While his new business was not as lucrative, he was required to maintain alimony payments based on his previously higher income. WD #1 also wanted our relationship kept quiet because he was not ready to go public or make a commitment. After three months of these antics, I got tired and believed him.

WD #2 was a 47-year-old actor who had been married for only four months—though this was long enough for him to lose all faith in that sacred institution. While there were no children, WD #2 had been emotionally wounded by his quick courtship (six months), marriage, and her sudden, unanticipated departure. However, his wallet was primarily unaffected because she had money. Instead, the emotional trauma prevented him from handling a relationship. He wanted to spend time with me almost every day, but made it clear that a long-term commitment was out of the question. I was smarter the second time and bowed out of this relationship after six weeks.

Even though both WDs told me about their hardships and inability to commit, I still tried to make the relationships happen. I told myself that our connection was strong enough to break their WD state of mind. In the end, I stopped kidding myself and today value their friendships with greater understanding. Both men continue to be determinedly single.

Wounded Divorcé Strategies

I recommend strongly that you listen to these warning messages early. Do not try to fix WDs. Give them time to recover at their own pace, while you move on to other opportunities. Avoid trying to convince yourself that you alone can fix what ails them. That miracle drug has yet to be invented.

Be careful not to misinterpret their desires to be physical for an emotional connection. They are wounded and want to be cuddled. However, they cannot mentally attach to you or any other female partner.

You need to take care of yourself first. Do not get hung up in a pattern of trying to fix WDs. While women tend to be nurturers, I recommend passing on these cases. His issues are not your responsibility, and the sooner you let go, the better chance you will have to meet someone who is mentally available.

Once you make a concrete decision to part ways, decide if you value the companionship enough to continue a friendship. Evaluate whether you can emotionally and physically detach. If you are open to a friendship, always give yourself a separation period first. You will need to build your ego back to a healthy state so spend time with available men to increase your confidence. You can later resume a friendship with the WD.

Wounded Divorcé LIFE Questions

1. Tell me about your relationship with your ex.
2. How did you part ways with your ex?
3. Do you ever want to get married again and why or why not?

XRE   X-Ray Eyes

X-Ray Eyes Definition

The X-Ray Eyes (XRE) male is primarily focused on peeling your clothes off and has sex tattooed across his forehead. His relationships are built upon sexual fantasies and physical satisfaction. He will blatantly share his needs with you. The X-Ray Eyes guy does not look beyond the sexual connection and may be disappointed in the long run with his partner selection. XREs openly expose their sexual desires from the beginning. Although men in general tend to be more physically motivated than their female counterparts, the XRE is the extreme.

X-Ray Eyes Examples

Because of the abundance of XREs, here are three examples:

A 35-year-old sales executive met XRE #1 at a political fundraiser in Washington, D.C. This guy made it clear that he was attracted to her from the start by complimenting her hair, jacket, and jewelry while staring down her shirt. The next week this XRE became more bold by telling her on the phone, "I can't wait to have sex with you in every position." This sexual fantasy was way too much information for her after only meeting the guy once. She listened to her GUT and hit the eject button immediately after this call.

My second example is one of my Internet candidates, whom I met for drinks. He was not as upfront in emails or on the phone about his X-Ray Eyes. During our visit, XRE #2 shared a red-alert story. After dating an Internet candidate for eight months, he suddenly discovered that she was, in his words, "an airhead." This revelation came to him during a trip to Paris where he learned she was not familiar with any Impressionist painters. I had to ask myself how he managed to date someone for that long without recognizing something so obvious. The answer could only be that he was an XRE blinded by sex. I never made contact with him again.

XRE #3 was another Internet contender. During our first ten-minute phone call, XRE #3 joined me online using Instant Messenger. He boldly asked me, "Do you own any super short skirts? I hope so. If so, meet me now!" He then decided to take a step further by describing our encounter. Here is what he envisioned with his X-Ray Eyes. He continued by writing this graphic description using Instant Messenger, "I wonder what it would look like while your hair is being slightly pulled from behind as your hands are on the wall. Me behind you kissing your back and neck." Men can be very bold when using IM. Yikes!

X-Ray Eyes Strategies

The minute you meet an extreme XRE, run like heck. These men are so physically oriented that even when they are with you, they are constantly looking around the room for other prospective bedmates. Regardless of how attractive you may be, the XRE will always have one eye on another. Unfortunately, these candidates have not evolved into well-rounded people and make horrible partners.

You are not a sex object. No one deserves to be viewed solely as a piece of meat. Don't take the XRE's priorities and comments personally. This mindset is not your problem. Don't be fooled by flattery, and see through the XRE's intentions.

All men will check out other women, but your job is to uncover the extremes of your man. Listen to your GUT in this case. If he is genuinely into you, then you may want to let a few glances slip by. Be true to yourself. Run, do not walk, and do not pass go, when you encounter the first signs of extreme XRE behavior.

X-Ray Eyes LIFE Questions

1. What is the first thing that you notice about a woman and why?
2. Can you describe the key characteristics of women in your past relationships?
3. What are the most important aspects of a relationship for you?

YE Young Explorer

Young Explorer Definition

The Young Explorer (YE) is a male who is more than 10 years younger than his female partner. These candidates are comfortable with the age gap and appreciate an older woman's companionship. The YE tends to be more mature than other men his age, and can be an excellent mate. Because they tend to have faced more life challenges, the Young Explorers will most likely enjoy your company over that of younger females. In addition, their youth can provide spontaneity and bring more energy to your daily routine.

Young Explorer Example

My 37-year-old girlfriend recently married a Young Explorer after less than a year of dating. This YE is a 25-year-old musician and my girlfriend is an actress. The couple met after he saw one of her theater performances. The YE was immediately intrigued and wanted to meet her.

While he was open about his desire to pursue a relationship, my friend was very apprehensive about getting involved with the Young Explorer. However, his persistence eventually persuaded her to go out on a date. She had the usual older woman insecurities about whether she could compete with the looks of candidates his age.

After six months of dating, the couple was totally committed and started making wedding plans. She recognized that this YE brought out her best qualities. He encouraged her to try new hobbies and enhance her outlook. For example, she started taking piano lessons and he convinced her to try snowboarding. In addition, this YE re-engineered her cynical perspective into a more positive and healthy outlook.

At the end of the courtship year, she married the Young Explorer. He addressed her age-difference concerns by making her feel beautiful inside and out. The happy couple bought a house, had a baby girl, and are now busy planning their second child.

While this first relationship is clearly built to last, another 40-something girlfriend dated a guy who was 12 years younger that I call the YE gold digger. This guy was a trust fund baby who had been cut off by his parents. When he showed up with a suitcase on a Saturday night, she thought he was just staying overnight. When he was still there on Tuesday, she started getting concerned that he was making himself a little too comfortable. She told me, "I could tell he was spoiled because he assumed that I would pay for everything and never bothered to say thank you." Okay, she admits the sex was great, but there was no real emotional connection. When this YE confessed that he was in a fight with his mother who thought he was "self-absorbed," the warning alarms blasted. She kicked him out within days, and I applaud her for listening to her GUT and firing him fast.

Young Explorer Strategies

Be cautious when considering a Young Explorer as a potential candidate. Consider his life experiences as a way to gauge his maturity compatibility. Evaluate whether his behavior matches your relationship expectations. Is there a balanced give-and-take or is he taking advantage of you?

If you decide that you want to get involved with a Young

Explorer, it is important to be very confident. You should be glowing with a positive attitude and personal satisfaction. Otherwise, your insecurities will be easy to spot and ultimately drive the YE away.

In addition, you need to give the Young Explorer room to experience life within his age range. Don't get worried or jealous if the YE wants to share time with his younger friends away from you. If you exhibit anger when he wants to run off to play, these emotional outbursts will cause unnecessary strain on the relationship.

Many people make these age-gap partnerships last for years. If a Young Explorer approaches you, don't let the difference in years automatically deter you. You may be pleasantly surprised to find a life partner below your age comfort zone. Observe his behaviors and listen to your gut when deciding whether to get serious with a YE.

Young Explorer LIFE Questions

1. What do you value in a relationship with an older woman?
2. What has been your past experience dating older women?
3. How do you feel about maybe being rushed to have children with an older female partner?

ZZ   Zodiac Zealot

Zodiac Zealot Definition

The Zodiac Zealot (ZZ) believes in planetary influences on relationships. ZZs look to astrologers and often psychics for guidance about partner selection, careers, and personal goals. They believe the zodiac has a major influence on their lives far beyond simply comparing astrological signs.

Zodiac Zealot Example

I went out with a 50-year-old acupuncturist who openly shared his beliefs in astrologers and psychics. His astrological bias was based on the fact that humans are 85 percent water, consisting of the same saline solution found in the ocean. This ZZ believed that humans are electromagnetic organisms greatly influenced by the planets in the same way that the moon impacts tides.

He asked for my astrological sign along with the time, date, and place of my birth. These facts were important for him to weigh before taking the relationship further. As we dug deeper into the astrological interpretation of our connection, I became more curious and even met with an astrologer. When he compared our signs, he shared that our planetary connection of Aries and Leo was a good basis for a successful relationship. His insights gave me a new perspective on dating dynamics.

In another extreme case, my astrologer moved from Los Angeles back to the United Kingdom to be with his soul mate. The couple met during an astrological conference in Oxford, England. He described their first encounter to me by saying, "Our opening conversation took place over her horoscope sitting having lunch one day. It was easy. Still is." He added, "Astrology is a language we share, a language that can describe everything under the sun."

This couple has the foundation for a perfect match. He has studied astrology for ten years, while she was just getting started. He explained, "Astrology is something we are both curious about, a shared interest." The couple is a great match because her astrological studies can help her appreciate his ZZ extremes. He is also open to learning about her expertise in architecture and finance. His final comment to me was, "Astrology was my path to a direct knowledge of the divine. That knowledge gives me the ability to accept all experiences that come my way, pleasurable and painful. That kind of acceptance makes all relationships joyous." This perfect match's mutual adoration of astrology makes this a passionate ZZ connection.

Zodiac Zealot Strategies

If you meet a Zodiac Zealot, recognize the importance of his perspective and don't immediately discount his astrological interests. Although you may not be familiar with this territory, you might learn something by keeping an open mind. The ZZ is more likely to commit to a relationship if he thinks there is an astrological connection.

Consider scheduling one visit with an astrologer to understand his beliefs better. You may find the information insightful or, at the very least, entertaining. While you may discover an astrological match, keep the feedback in perspective and evaluate other characteristics of this candidate and your relationship. If the ZZ exhibits the traits of other codes that can cause turbulence in a potential partnership, you probably need to part ways. However, if the stars are on your side, you might want to take a closer look before ruling out this contender.

You can even check out a zodiac calendar that will tell you more about the moon's patterns each month and how they impact your daily relationships. For example, did you know that the moon passes through each of the twelve zodiac signs every month? You might find patterns in the stars that help predict positive and negative impacts on certain days based on this star calendar. These patterns might give you clues for when it's time to lay low versus take more chances. With an open mind, I checked out a cosmic calendar with my ZZ astrologer. I found that when the moon was in my sign (Leo), I tend to have really good days. Okay, go ahead and laugh, but I can't count how many lucky things have happened to me with this book, and especially when the moon was in Leo (my book deal was delivered, *Cosmo* called for three different articles, the *LA Times* called, and more).

Test the waters with astrology, and then decide how much you want the stars to impact your life and relationships. Ask yourself whether a potential mate's ZZ extremes complement or clash with you.

Zodiac Zealot LIFE Questions

1. What value do you place on astrological matches?
2. Tell me about your experience with astrologers.
3. Are there zodiac signs that you steer away from dating and why?

Appendix I: ABC Codes Compatibility Quiz

How can you use the ABC Man Codes to check your compatibility with a potential Mr. Wonderful? Since guys can be more than one code, what does the combination mean? The codes include good guys, bad guys, and mostly maybe guys so you can quickly make Go/No-Go decisions.

What about your codes? These codes can easily swing both ways and apply to females. Your challenge is to find the right mix in a man that complements versus clashes with your codes. Use this quick reference guide as you complete the ABC Codes Compatibility Quiz. You want to identify the extremes of your potential Mr. Right before the wedding bells.

SMART ABC Man Codes— Quick Reference Guide

Good Guys	Maybe Guys	Bad Guys
Bachelor Available (BA)	All Sports Fanatic (ASF)	Hello Goodbye Guy (HGG)
Confident Metro Male (CMM)	Dysfunctional Guy with Issues (DGI)	Internet Psycho (IP)
Keeper of the Fire (KOF)	Executive Search Seeker (ESS)	Justifying Juggler (JJ)
Love Match (LM)	Fitness Extremist (FE)	Married but Available (MBA)
Nourishing Nester (NN)	Guy With Offspring (GWO)	Questionnaire Perfectionist (QP)

Good Guys	**Maybe Guys**	**Bad Guys**
Virtual Lover (VL)	Overachiever Obsessor (OO)	Wounded Divorcé (WD)
	Post-Traumatic Soul (PTS)	
	Relentless Renter (RR)	
	Social Guru (SG)	
	Tasmanian Traveler (TT)	
	Underestimated Ally (UA)	
	X-Ray Eyes (XRE)	
	Young Explorer (YE)	
	Zodiac Zealot (ZZ)	

You can ask your man to take this compatibility quiz to help you identify his codes or answer it for him. If you guess his personality extremes, show him your answers in a non-judgmental way to see if you guessed correctly. You also want to take the test to uncover the extremes of your characteristics and see how they compare.

Once you identify his codes, look at the combination of the characteristics objectively. If he is mostly the good and maybe codes, you should continue building a bond with your man. If you find him showing extremes for any of the bad codes, you probably want to run for the nearest exit sign. Even if the guy has a few good codes, the bad codes can spoil the relationship and minimize long-term potential. For example, you want to find the BA (Bachelor Available) and LM (Love Match), but if you find he is also a QP (Questionnaire Perfectionist), you should probably let him go even though it will be painful.

Gauge Your Compatibility by Rating Extremes 1–5

Using the questions and answers below for each code, you can quickly rate the results using a 1 (no signs of this code) to 5 (far extreme signs of this code) scale. Anyone who receives a 3 has the code characteristics. If you both have a 3, you are clearly a great match for that code. If you find your man falling into the extreme rating of a 4 or 5 on any question below, you have found his man code extremes.

Code Characteristics Scale

1. **No signs of this code**—You are definitely not this code.
2. **Not really this code**—You show slight signs of these characteristics.
3. **You are this code**—You meet the minimum requirements for this code.
4. **Extreme signs of this code**—You are on the extreme side of these characteristics.
5. **Far extreme signs of this code**—You are clearly the extreme version of this code.

Your next goal is to find out whether your codes mesh with his dominant characteristics. If either of you score 3, 4, or 5 on any question, add this code to the total package review. If your answers are more than two points away from your partner, the difference in extremes may create a clash. If he receives a 3, 4, or 5 for a bad code, you probably want to say "Next." Based on this ABC codes compatibility check, you can quickly determine whether there are any deal-breakers with a guy.

Have fun with this compatibility code check. Turn it into a sharing exchange game. You'll find it can be a great conversation piece. Even though this quiz is not based on science, it will help you gauge your GUT feelings and review the total package with a potential mate.

ABCs Codes Compatibility Check

	Man's Rating	Your Rating	Match?(Y/N)
Examples:			
BA	3	4	Yes
LM	1	5	No

Go/No Go Codes (one "No" = say, "Next!")

BA—Bachelor Available

What type of relationship are you seeking?

1. Seeking hot sex only.
2. Dating around.
3. Dating and open to a relationship.
4. Long-term serious relationship.
5. Seeking a life partner.

LM—Love Match

How would you describe your sexual compatibility?

1. Sex is not an important part of our relationship.
2. Sex is just fine with us.
3. I enjoy sex all the time with my partner.
4. Sex is an experience that I value every time with you.
5. Sex is often an out-of-body experience with you.

Good Guys (all "Yes" matches add value)

CMM—Confident Metro Male

What types of things do you like to share with a mate?

1. Sex is the main thing that we share.
2. Sunday afternoon football parties.

3. Planning dinner parties with my mate.

4. Going to dinner and the theater with other couples.

5. Shopping for clothes with my partner.

KOF—Keeper-of-the-Fire

Tell me how you like to romance a relationship.

1. I tend to make a big deal out of Valentine's Day.

2. I like to bring home flowers on her birthday.

3. It's fun to surprise her with dinner at a new restaurant once a month.

4. I enjoy planning weekend getaways for my sweetheart a few times a year.

5. I like to bring her little surprises often to spice up our relationship.

NN—Nourishing Nester

If I got really sick, what would you do?

1. I'd call your mother to see whether she could come over while I go to work.

2. I would call a doctor for you and pick up medicine on the way home.

3. If you needed me, I would rearrange my schedule to take you to the doctor.

4. I would make you my favorite chicken noodle soup and bring you hot tea.

5. I'd stay home from work and make sure you had whatever you needed.

VL—Virtual Lover

Do you believe that love can be found online?

1. No way, I would never try Internet dating.

2. I am willing to take a chance by searching for love online.

3. I've tried it and heard many success stories from friends.

4. Definitely, I think it is easier to flirt with someone online than in a bar.

5. Love can definitely be found online and I love using the features.

Maybe Guys (a "Yes" match can be an asset)

ASF—All Sports Fanatic

Which statement best describes your interest in sports?

1. I never watch sports.

2. I occasionally watch sports with friends and family.

3. I enjoy following my teams throughout the season.

4. I like to watch games on TV often and go to games monthly.

5. I prefer to plan a social schedule around my sports teams.

DGI—Dysfunctional Guy with Issues

How often do you have contact with your family?

1. My family is awesome and we talk almost daily.

2. I talk to my family once a week.

3. We see each other a few times a year.

4. I check in once in a while with my family.

5. I haven't seen my family in a few years.

ESS—Executive Search Seeker

What type of career match are you seeking?

1. No career match is needed.

2. I'd like to find someone that has a job.

3. I'd like to find someone with the same career and education.

4. My goal is find a mate with a great job and great income.

5. I want to find a peer partner with similar or higher income.

FE—Fitness Extremist

Which statement best describes your health and fitness style?

1. I never work out and really don't pay attention to diet.

2. I work out occasionally and avoid sweets.

3. I exercise several times a week and keep a balanced diet.

4. I need to go to the gym regularly and date someone who shares my workout schedule.

5. You'll find me at the gym five times a week and avoiding fatty foods.

GWO—Guy with Offspring

Do you have any children from a previous marriage?

1. No, I do not have any children that I know about.

2. I have never been married or had children.

3. I have 1 child and they sometimes live at home.

4. I have 2 children and they often live at home.

5. I have 3 children and they live at home.

OO—Overachiever Obsessor

How would you describe your career goals?

1. I've made my mark. I don't need to prove anything.

2. I have a few things left on my checklist to accomplish.

3. I enjoy meeting and setting new career goals often.

4. I like adding to the trophies on my wall every year.

5. My career is the most important driver in my life.

PTS—Post-Traumatic Soul

Have you ever dealt with a major tragedy that impacted your relationships?

1. I have unfortunately lost a few good friends and it shook me up.
2. I lost my job a few times and just had to take a break from people.
3. I was in a major earthquake and it took two years to get over it.
4. I have constant nightmares because I'm stressed about losing my job.
5. I lost a parent when I was young and have never really gotten over it.

RR—Relentless Renter

If you dated someone for a few years, would you be thinking about proposing marriage?

1. Yes, it would be time to make a decision whether to go the distance.
2. I would probably start looking at engagement rings with her.
3. I am not really interested in getting married.
4. I prefer to just live together forever over marriage.
5. I never want to get married so there would be no proposal.

SG—Social Guru

What best describes your social style?

1. I prefer to spend quality time with you over going out any night.
2. I like to go out with friends at least once a week.
3. My preference is for us to get together with friends most of the weekend.

4. I like organizing trips with friends and hanging out often with the crew.

5. I'm out most of the week for events and love seeing friends on weekends.

TT—Tasmanian Traveler

How often do you travel for work or pleasure?

1. I never travel for work, but like to take a nice vacation every year.

2. I travel once a month for business and then a few times a year for pleasure.

3. I'm on the road a few times a month for work and/or play.

4. You'll find me on the runway once a week for work.

5. It's hard to keep track of my schedule. Travel is a way of life for me.

UA—Underestimated Ally

Have you ever fallen for a girl who was a good friend first?

1. No, I've never dated a girl who was a friend first.

2. Dating friends is a fairytale that only happens in my dreams.

3. I've dated a few women that were friends at first.

4. I prefer being friends first before making romantic moves.

5. I have to be friends first before even thinking about dating someone.

XRE—X-Ray Eyes

What were you thinking when you first saw me?

1. I was thinking, wow, she's cute.

2. I thought you looked really fun and hot. I was really curious.

3. I was checking out your chest, sexy skirt, and long legs, to be honest.

4. You looked so sexy to me that I imagined taking your clothes off.

5. I wanted to go wild with you in the bedroom immediately.

YE—Young Explorer

Do you like to date older women?

1. No, I only want to date younger women.
2. I prefer to date someone who is the same age.
3. I like dating older versus younger women.
4. I prefer older women because they have experienced more in life.
5. I only date older women because I'm more comfortable with them.

ZZ—Zodiac Zealot

Do you think astrology plays a big role in relationships?

1. I don't pay any attention to astrology.
2. I read my daily horoscope for fun.
3. I only want to date certain astrological signs.
4. I check out a match potential using their birth date, place, and time.
5. I read about the daily lunar influences and plan dates around it.

Bad Guys (any 3, 4, or 5 rating is bad news)

HGG—Hello Goodbye Guy

Do you usually stay friends with someone after you date?

1. I always try to break up as friends.
2. I like to be able to call someone if I need to after a break-up.

3. It is really hard to be friends after a break-up.
4. After a break-up, I avoid the other person like the plague.
5. I cannot see myself as friends with an ex.

IP—Internet Psycho

What is the wildest thing that you have done to shock someone when dating online?

1. I sent someone a photo that was not me.
2. I wrote that I lived in Paris for two years when I have never left the country.
3. I asked someone if they wanted to be in my adult video online.
4. I sent someone a porno site link and invited them to come over for sex.
5. I stood someone up just for the thrill of making them mad.

JJ—Justifying Juggler

Have you ever slept with more than one woman in the same week?

1. I got stuck in between two lovers in college once.
2. Yes, it's happened a few times, but I quickly decided who I wanted to date.
3. Yes, I just love sex and can't resist women.
4. Yes, I prefer to date more than one woman at a time for variety.
5. Yes, I always date more than one woman because I can.

MBA—Married but Available

If you are married, why are you dating me?

1. I have never crossed the line and am committed to my wife.
2. I get tempted sometimes, but would not act on my desires.

3. I cannot resist being with you even though I'm married.

4. My wife understands that I can have sex with other partners.

5. I've been ready for divorce for years and love dating.

QP—Questionnaire Perfectionist

What are you seeking in your Ms. Right?

1. I'll know her when I see her.

2. There are a few things that I really want to find.

3. She must have a college degree, cook, and work out.

4. I have a list of my twenty requirements in a máte.

5. I have fifty must-haves in a mate that I need.

WD—Wounded Divorcé

If you are divorced, would you ever get married again?

1. Sure, it just wasn't the right match, but I want to get married again.

2. I would get married again if the right person came along.

3. I don't think so. It would have to be someone fantastic.

4. I'm not really interested in getting married again.

5. Absolutely not. Why would anyone ever want to get married?

Appendix II: Complete Your SMART Certification

Fast Track Dating Guide Review

Are you ready to be SMART Certified? Are you ready to get out there, get dates, and find your Mr. Right on a fast track? With these new SMART Man Hunting dating strategies, this certification test will be easy for you. Simply answer the following multiple-choice questions, and you will receive immediate feedback on your gained SMART Man Hunting knowledge.

SMART Certification Test

1. Before I broaden my Mr. Right Search, what needs to be in place for my Confidence Face Lift?
   a. Be happy with your life
   b. Go for your Passions
   c. Build your Support Network
   d. Pamper yourself
   e. All of the above

2. What are the success keys for the Winning Hunter's Strategy?
   a. Be patient and persistent, and don't take things too personally
   b. Bounce back from rejection
   c. Ask for help
   d. Use a give-and-take approach
   e. All of the above

3. What can make a Man Hunt and a Job Hunt successful?
   a. Boost your numbers
   b. Define your requirements
   c. Dress for success
   d. Evaluate the candidates closely
   e. All of the above

4. What New Era dating options can help me expand my Man Hunt?
   a. Check out casual chat rooms and singles events
   b. Step into Internet dating
   c. Try speed dating or silent dating
   d. Use professional matchmakers
   e. All of the above

5. How can I be SMART and safe when dating via the Internet?
   a. Search online using his name to find things he may be hiding
   b. Remain anonymous when emailing
   c. Never give out your home phone number prior to first meetings
   d. Use valet parking at public restaurants
   e. All of the above

6. How can I create an enticing Internet Dating Profile?
   a. Write a unique and friendly headline
   b. Post at least two current photos
   c. Write short essays versus a book
   d. Be positive and add a little humor
   e. All of the above

7. How can the SMART ABC Man Code definitions, tales, and strategies help me be smarter?
   a. Learn from true-story examples
   b. Laugh at mistakes and give myself a break
   c. Be more selective next time

    d. Run like heck from the bad ones
    e. All of the above

8. Who are some of the ABC good guys?
    a. Bachelor Available (BA)
    b. Confident Metro Male (CMM)
    c. Keeper of the Fire (KOF)
    d. Love Match (LM)
    e. All of the above

9. Who are some of the ABC bad guys?
    a. Hello Goodbye Guy (HGG)
    b. Internet Psycho (IP)
    c. Married but Available (MBA)
    d. Questionnaire Perfectionist (QP)
    e. All of the above

10. Who is a Red Flag Man?
    a. Sly Schemer
    b. Macho Mind
    c. Me-First Man
    d. All of the above

11. What are some red flag observations that I should notice on dates?
    a. Is he always late for dates?
    b. Does he take cell phone calls?
    c. Are his eyes wandering around the room?
    d. Does he only talk about himself?
    e. All of the above

12. What should I try to find out on a first date?
    a. Is there a Chemistry Connection?
    b. What do the non-verbal clues tell me?
    c. Do I want to kiss this candidate?
    d. Is he a Red Flag Man?
    e. All of the above

13. What are some good KISS questions for a first date?
    a. What do you like to do for fun?
    b. What is your favorite vacation getaway?
    c. Where did you grow up?
    d. What is your favorite ice cream flavor?
    e. All of the above

14. What are some First Date Discussion Bloopers to avoid?
    a. Leave the checkbook in the car
    b. Leave your exes in the scrapbook
    c. No need to broadcast your faults
    d. Avoid sharing too much information
    e. All of the above

15. What can you learn about a man by asking LIFE Questions before the wedding bells to help you avoid the "D" word?
    a. Lessons Learned—What has he learned out of life?
    b. Introspection—What deep thoughts are inside this guy?
    c. Flexibility—Can he compromise?
    d. Extremes—What are his extreme characteristics?
    e. All of the above

16. What should I try to discover on a second or third date?
    a. Ask for the Foundational Facts—age, family, marital history, and hobbies
    b. Quick Qualifiers—three things that each of you seek in a mate
    c. Showstoppers—things that will end a relationship's chance
    d. Is he Emotionally Ready?
    e. All of the above

17. What should my GUT tell me?
    a. Is he genuine?
    b. Does he care about my feelings?
    c. Does he have the right core characteristics?

    d. Is he trustworthy?

    e. All of the above

18. How can I ensure a lasting bond if I start getting serious with a Mr. Right candidate?

    a. Determine the ABC Man Code(s) for your male mate

    b. Analyze his flexibility using LIFE Questions

    c. Compare your personal priorities and qualities to his codes

    d. Review the Total Man, using Man Hunt Interview Practices

    e. All of the above

19. How can I complete my Final Man Analysis?

    a. Take the ABC Codes Compatibility Quiz

    b. Share answers to the LIFE Questions for his SMART ABC Man Code(s)

    c. Look at the dynamics of the Dating Assessment Dance

    d. Avoid rationalizing my way out of every opportunity

    e. All of the above

20. How can I identify my Mr. Wonderful?

    a. He is a Good GUT Man who is good in bed

    b. He has a great attitude and knows how to compromise

    c. His SMART ABC Man Codes complement versus clash with my codes

    d. He thinks I'm the hottest ticket in town!

    e. All of the above

If you answered "All of the above" for every question, give yourself a standing ovation. Congratulations, you are now on a fast track toward finding your Mr. Right using the SMART Man Hunting strategy and 21st-century technologies!

Thank You

MANY THANKS to my friends and active daters, whose insights and guidance helped me become a better person and Man Hunter. Their stories and advice can also help you find long-term happiness and Mr. Right:

Abigail, Alex, Anne, Alfred, Arthur, Angela, Alan, Anna, Adam, Alison, Andy, Amanda

Brigid, Betsey, Bob, Brent, Billy, Beth, Bethany, Brad, Bert, Brett

Caroline, Caroline, Cindy, Carl, Cloud, Cynthia, Chris, Christie, Chet

Dan, Dean, Dave, Debra, David, Doug, Dena, Diana, Dines, Donna

Emily, Elizabeth, Eleanor, Ellen, Eiko, Eric

Frances, Felice, Fady, Fred, Frank, Franco

Gail, Gayle, Gennifer, Genie, Greg, Gary, Gretchen, Gay

Hannah, Harry, Harris, Harriett

Irene, Ian, Ira, Ioana

Jane, Janet, Jim, Jeannette, Julia, Jon, John, Joan, Joe, Joshua, Jack, Jeff, Jan, Jeremie

Kate, Katie, Kristy, Ken, Karen, Kevin, Kellie, Karin, Katherine

Lenore, Londa, Laura, Lori, Larry, Lizi, LeighAnn, Lynn, Laurie

Mary, Marshall, Marc, Maura, Morte, Mary Helen, Margo, Mara, Michele, Mojoe, Ming, Mark

Nancy, Nette, Nikos

Ophelia

Paula, Peter, Pete, Patrick, Patti
Quentin
Riko, Roxana, Robin, Rachel, Richard, Rob, Ronda, Randi,
    Rod, Roland, Renee
Susie, Sue, Sandy, Stephanie, Sheila, Saeed, Stan, Scott,
    Sharon, Sarah, Stephen
Tacy, Tim, Tarver, Tom, Thomas
Vincent, Vic, Victoria, Venus, Vicki
Warren, Wallis, Will, Walker
Xana
Yolanda, Yvette
Zoe, Zack

About the Author

Liz H. Kelly is a Dating Coach, Author, Speaker and Contributing Writer for Yahoo! Personals, CupidJunction.com, Lookbetteronline.com, *MarsVenus.com* and *Smart Woman* magazine. Liz's passion for giving relationship advice led her to develop the SMART Man Hunting dating approach based on her twenty years of dating experience, including Internet Dating, Professional Matchmakers, Speed Dating, and Singles Events, along with interviews and coaching sessions with hundreds of active daters.

To create her SMART Man Hunting dating strategy, Liz drew heavily on her corporate experience in marketing communications, employee training, and sales presentation techniques to develop a Winning Hunter's Toolkit for finding "the one." With a MAS/Management degree from Johns Hopkins University and BA/Economics degree from the University of Maryland, Liz held management positions at T. Rowe Price, Sprint PCS, and Iridium. She most recently held positions as Vice President/Director, Customer Relationship Management for several Internet startups in Los Angeles.

Liz has shared her insights on such shows as *FOX News*, Dick Clark's *The Other Half*, Lifetime's *Speaking of Women's Health*, along with hundreds of radio shows such as *BBC WM Late Show* and WOR's *Joan Hamburg Show*. Her modern dating strategies have been featured in *Cosmopolitan, Glamour, USA Today, New York Post, Chicago Tribune*, and in hundreds of other print articles around the globe. Whether you are looking for a good catch or advising single girlfriends, Liz's book provides a balanced approach for keeping your sanity, humor, and heart available while seeking Mr. Right.

Visit www.smartmanhunting.com for more information about Liz Kelly's dating coaching services, seminars, and advice columns.